A. N Phillips

**Hindustani idioms, with vocabulary and explanatory notes, for the use of candidates for the higher standard**

A. N Phillips

**Hindustani idioms, with vocabulary and explanatory notes, for the use of candidates for the higher standard**

ISBN/EAN: 9783337157173

Printed in Europe, USA, Canada, Australia, Japan

Cover: Foto ©Paul-Georg Meister /pixelio.de

More available books at **www.hansebooks.com**

# HINDUSTANI IDIOMS

WITH

# VOCABULARY

AND

## EXPLANATORY NOTES

*For the use of Candidates for the Higher Standard*

BY

COLONEL A. N. PHILLIPS

LATE INDIAN ARMY

*(Certificate of High Proficiency, College of Fort William)*

LONDON:

KEGAN PAUL, TRENCH, TRÜBNER & CO., LTD.,

PATERNOSTER HOUSE, CHARING CROSS ROAD.

1892

# PREFACE.

In that amusing book, "Behind the Bungalow," the author, "Eha," remarks that the irate griff's, "*Ham roz roz hukm day, tum roz roz hukm nay, iswaste lakri,*" doubtless went home, but that it is given to few to be at once so forcible and explicit.

In the hope of rendering assistance to those who wish to learn Hindustani as they would a European language, *i.e.* idiomatically and as spoken by the Natives, instead of merely stringing together a number of words in slavish imitation of the English idiom, or forming such broken sentences as the above, I offer this little book to the public as the result of many years spent in India in active work amongst the natives of that country. It is intended to supplement, not to supplant any of the far too few books on the subject now in use, and may be read concurrently with such works as Kempson's *Exercises*, Holroyd's *Tashíl-ul-Kalám*, &c. This is the more necessary, as my book does not profess to teach the first principles of grammar, or, in fact, any of the more purely rudimentary parts of the language. My idea has been to give as many examples as possible of the more distinctly idiomatic differences between the two languages, and these in a really colloquial form, such as the student may expect to find in ordinary daily use ; and secondly, to give a number of words and phrases which, though in everyday use, are not to be found as a rule in the ordinary dictionaries and vocabularies. The very full vocabulary I have added, is intended to assist the student in the work of translation and in his studies generally, as well as in his daily intercourse with the natives, and for all ordinary purposes to supply, in fact, the place of a dictionary. I have endeavoured to give it as popular a character as possible by excluding, wherever practicable, all non-colloquial forms of expression. I have been guided to a great extent in the selection of sentences and choice of phrases in my book by the remembrance of my own difficulties, and I can only hope, therefore, that they may prove helpful to others similarly circumstanced, while one or two may perhaps thank me for introducing them to the *Ikhwán-us-safá*, the *Áráish-i-Mahfil*, and the *Taubat-un-Nasúh*, books which all should read who wish to acquire a real mastery of the language.

A. N. P.

*October*, 1892.

# INTRODUCTORY NOTE.

FULL particulars as to the pronunciation of Hindustani words when written in the Roman character will be found in Holroyd's "Hindustani Made Easy." The following note may prove helpful. 'A' without a mark over it is pronounced like 'a' in *woman*, *asleep*, &c., or like both 'a' and 'u' in *abundance*; with a mark over it, like 'a' in *father* or *mirage*. 'I' with the ordinary dot over it is pronounced like 'i' in *big ship*; with a long mark over it, like 'i' in *marine machine*. 'U' without a mark over it is pronounced like 'u' in *put*, *full*, *pull*, &c.; with a mark over it, like 'u' in *rúle*, *truth*, &c. 'E' and 'o' have no marks over them. The former has the sound of 'e' in *they*, *whey*, &c., and the latter the full sound of 'o' in *hole*, *pole*, &c. 'E,' however, is always short before 'h,' and the latter after all vowels, when it ends a word or a syllable (as in *bádsháh*, *mihtar*, &c.), must be sounded by a quick catching of the breath. In the Roman character 'h' must always be sounded, except in 'ch' and 'sh,' which represent respectively *che* and *shín*. The only occasion on which it is not sounded in the native character is at the end of words like *bachcha*, *darja*, *iráda*, &c. When it follows a consonant, except 'c' and 's' as above, and is followed by a vowel (as in *uṭháná*, *ghoṛá*, &c.), it must be aspirated as in words like *at home*, *uphill*, &c. 'R' also must always be sounded, even when there is no vowel between it and the next consonant, as in *sirf, shart,* &c. 'Ai' has the sound of 'i' in *file, mile,* &c., and 'au' the sound of 'ou' in *house.* Wherever in this book, or the vocabulary, vowels occur with a dot under them, it will be understood that the letter in Hindustani is *ain.* 'T's,' 'd's,' and 'r's' with dots under them are hard, and are pronounced by drawing the tongue well back: 'd' and 't' without dots are soft, and must be pronounced by putting the tongue to the teeth. 'N' with a mark under it is nasal, like 'n' in the French *main, pain,* &c. The Arabic *qáf* ق is represented by *q,* and is pronounced at the root of the tongue. *Khe* خ, which has the sound of 'ch' in *loch,* is represented by *kh,* and *ghain* غ by *gh.* The pronunciation of the latter more nearly resembles the sound made by gargling than anything else. I have not attempted to distinguish between the different 's's,' 'z's,' and 'h's,' as these can easily be found out if not known already. *Zhe* ژ, it should be noted, has the sound of 'z' in *azure.* It occurs very seldom, in a few words like *muzhda,* good news; *pazhmurda,* withered, &c. No other 'z' in the language has the same sound; the others are uniformly pronounced like 'z' in *zigzag, puzzle,* &c.

# CONTENTS.

Section I.—Examples of neglected idioms . . . . 1

Section II.—Apparent exceptions to the rule requiring *ne* before the past tenses of an active verb . . 12

Section III.—Sentences on general subjects . . 14

Section IV.—Family relationships . . . . 80

Section V.—Some legal and official phrases . . 83

Section VI.—Some Hindustani proverbs . . . 87

Section VII.—Extracts from the text-books, &c. . 91

Section VIII.—Rhymes . . . . . . . 103

# CORRIGENDA.

P. 46, sentence 297, for "more scattered and farther apart," read "scattered and far apart."

„ 65, note 431, for the Hindustani sentence at the end of this note substitute the following:—*pání chhichhlá hone se bhí*, or *go pání chhichhlá húá, taubhí*, &c.

„ 87, sentence 598, omit from this proverb the word "undried," which is superfluous.

„ 26, sentence 172, for *khair* read *khair*.

Vocabulary, p. 162, expunge note to "likelihood," and see revised note in *Addenda* at the end.

# HINDUSTANI IDIOMS.

## SECTION I.

### Examples of Neglected Idioms.

| English. | Hindustani. | Notes. |
|---|---|---|
| 1. As I was leaving the town I met this man on his way there. He was carrying a gun. Shortly afterwards I met his wife also on her way to the town, and after her I met his two brothers also coming to the town. | *Jiswaqt maiṉ shahr se rawána hotá thá, yih shak͟hs shahr ko áte húe mujhko milá. Bandúq háth meṉ liye játá thá. Thoṛí der ke bạ́d uskí jorú bhí shahr ko áte húe mujhko milí, aur bạ́d uske uske do bháí bhí shahr ko áte húe mujhko mile.* | There is a nice distinction in the Hindustani mind between *jab* and *jiswaqt*, which is very commonly overlooked. The rule to observe is, that whenever, "when" has the meaning of "as," or "while," *jiswaqt* should be used. Note that the idiom here is not "I met him," but "he met me." The *áte húe* is unaffected by gender or number, being in fact a participial adverb, with a preposition understood after *húe*. The difference between *liye jáná* and *lejáná* should be noted. The former means, to take, or lead, or carry *along*, and the latter, simply to take *away*. |

| English. | Hindustani. | Notes. |
|---|---|---|
| **2.** She is wearing the same dress to-day that she put on yesterday. | *Áj wuhí posháh pahne húe hai jo kal pahní thí.* | The above note on *áte húe* applies equally here. *Pahne húe* means, "in the act of wearing." If I said *pahntí hai*, the meaning would be, She is *putting on* a dress, not that she is *wearing* it. |
| **3.** He is holding me (or has hold of me) with both hands. | *Wuh mujhe donon̲ háth se pakṛe húe hai.* | Another instance of the same rule. If I said *mujhe pakaṛtá hai*, the meaning would be, not that he is *holding* me, but that he is *seizing* me. Wherever this form of the participle is used, it always implies a continuing act—"in the act of coming," "wearing," "holding," &c. I should add that the *húe* is very often omitted. |
| **4.** It is now ten years since I first came to this town. | *Mujhko is shahr men̲ áe húe ab muddat das baras kí húí.* | Here the sense is, "To me coming into this town a period of ten years attaches." No idiom in the language perhaps is more often transgressed than this. The common form |

| English. | Hindustani. | Notes. |
|---|---|---|
| | | of "*Jabse maiṉ is shahr ko áyá thá das baras húe,*" is simply Hindustani Anglicised. |
| 5. This was in the time of the mutiny, which is now 33 years ago. | *Yih to g͟hadr ke waqt meṉ thá, jisko* (not *jisse*) *ab ạrsa taintís baras ká húá.* | Here again the idea is that to the event in question a period of 33 years attaches. |
| 6. How many months is it since you sold him this bullock? | *Kaí mahíne húe jab tum ne yih bail uske háth beṉchá thá?* | Note that the idiom is *jab* and not *jabse.* The way in which the question |
| 7. How many years is it since your brother separated from you? | *Kaí baras húe jab tumhárá bhái tum se judá hogayá thá?* | frames itself in the Hindustani mind is, "How many months is it from *now* till the time *when,*" &c ? |
| 8. What is this box made of? | *Yih sandúq káhe ká hai?* (*Káhe ká baná hai?* is also correct, but less common). | This everyday idiom is not sufficiently known. *Káhá* is the form in the Braj dialect of the |
| 9. What did he beat you with? | *Tujhe káhe se márá?* | well-known interrogative *Kyá?* The latter, however, for want |
| 10. What shall we open this with? | *Isko káhe se kholeṉ?* | of an *h*, does not lend itself readily to inflection, hence the |
| 11. What shall I put it in? | *Káhe meṉ rakhúṉ?* | former has been substituted in cases such as those here given. |
| 12. What did you put it on? | *Tum ne káhe par rakhá thá?* | The only other form in which we have it |

| English. | Hindustani. | Notes. |
|---|---|---|
| | | is in the interrogative *Káhe ko?* What for? why? how? |
| 13. How many cuts did he give you with the cane? | *Tere kaí ben̲t mā-rīn̲?* | Lit. How many canes did he strike? how many riding switches did he strike? Understand *badan par* after *tere.* |
| 14. How many times did he strike you with his riding switch? | *Tere kaí gamchi-yán̲ márín̲?* | |
| 15. The horse was running away along the road. | *Ghoṛá saṛak se bhágá játá thá.* | *Bhágá játá,* not *bhág játá.* The latter would mean that the horse was making his escape *from* the road. |
| 16. Is there any house there at all? | *Wahán̲ ghar hai bhí?* | In these two sentences stress must be laid upon *hai* in order to give the sense. It is a form of interrogation very strongly suggestive of doubt. |
| 17. Is there any such order at all? | *Aisá koi hukm hai bhí?* | |
| 18. Speak out, my good fellow: nobody can hear you. | *Áwáz se bolo, jí: suná nahin játá.* | |
| 19. Speak, my good fellow: say, why did you go? | *Mun̲h se bolo, jí: tum kyún̲ ga, e?* | *Mun̲h se bolo* is the idiom, and not simply *bolo.* |
| 20. Go and see if he is at home. If he is, tell him to come to me. | *Jáo, dekho, ghar par hai, yá nahin̲. Agar hai, to use kahdo mere pás áná.* | *Ghar par,* not *ghar men̲.* Note that the use of *agar* in the first part of this |

| English. | Hindustani. | Notes. |
|---|---|---|
| | | sentence, viz. *agar ghar par hai yá nahin*, would be quite wrong, since the first "if" has the sense of "whether," which *agar* never has. |
| 21. Tell him to come without fail. | *Usse kahdo ki zarúr á jáná.* | There is no equivalent in Hindustani for "without fail" in the sense here given. The meaning is "he must be sure to come," and this *zarúr* expresses. *Bilá nághá* means, 'without intermission or break,' and its use here, therefore, would be obviously incorrect. *Ájáná* is simply an emphatic form of *áná*. |
| 22. One of them was lying on his back, another on his side, and the third face downwards. | *Ek to chit paṛá thá, ek to karwaṭ se paṛá thá, aur tísrá aundhá paṛá thá.* | |
| 23. He kept turning over from side to side all night. | *Wuh rát bhar karwaṭ badaltá rahá.* | |
| 24. First of all he got drowsy; then he fell asleep; and then he began to snore. | *Pahle únghne lagá; phir nínd á gaí; phir uske bád kharráṭe bharne lagá.* | The Hindustani for snoring seems so little known, that I have given it here. |
| 25. When I heard him snoring, then I knew he was asleep. | *Jab uske kharráṭon kí áwáz mere kán men paṛí, táb málúm húá ki usko nínd ága,í.* | |

| English. | Hindustani. | Notes. |
|---|---|---|
| 26. Bring it into the light: how can you read it in the dark? | *Chándne men láo: andhere men kyá paṛhá jáegá?* | This word *chándná* seems but little known. It is however the right word to use here, especially if the light spoken of be daylight. |
| 27. This work is beyond me. | *Yih kám mujhse nahin ho saktá.* | This is a much more emphatic form of expression than *yih kám main nahin kar saktá.* It is also more idiomatic. |
| 28. I cannot read this letter at all. | *Yih khatt mujhse paṛhá nahin játá.* | |
| 29. I cannot bear this pain. | *Is dard kí mujh se bardásht nahin ho saktí.* | |
| 30. There is no fighting against destiny. | *Taqdír se laṛá nahin játá (Bágh-o-Bahár.)* | |
| 31. The stain will never now come out of this cloth. | *Is kapṛe men jo dhabbá paṛ gayá hai, ab nikalne ká nahin.* | This is the usual word for a stain on cloth. |
| 32. He has gone to Delhi to see his brother. | *Wuh Dillí gayá hai apne bháí se milne ke wáste.* | If I said here, *apne bháí ko dekhne ke wáste*, the idea conveyed would be that he had gone to inspect his brother rather than to enjoy his society. |
| 33. This road is very steep. | *Yih rásta bahut ḍháldár hai.* (Lit. sloping.) | *Ḍhálú* is also used. *Ḍhál* means a slope, an incline. |

| English. | Hindustani. | Notes. |
| --- | --- | --- |
| **34.** Who came first of all (or in the first place)? | *Pahle pahal kaun áyá thá?* | |
| **35.** Speak quietly (or calmly), think what you are saying. | *Sambhalke kahiyo, soch samajhkar kahiyo.* | |
| **36.** After their parents' death there was no one left to look after the house. | *Unke má báp ke mar jáne ke bád, ghar ká sambhálnewálá koí nahiṉ rahá.* | *Sambhálná* means to manage, to control, to look after—*sambhalná* to be self-restrained, calm, &c. |
| **37.** Do you look after (or take in hand) the smaller children. | *Chhoṭe bachchoṉ ko tum hí sambhálo.* | |
| **38.** He threw it out of the window when no one was looking. | *Logoṉ kí nazar bacháke* (or *ánkh bacháke*) *khiṛkí kí ráh se phenk diyá.* | If I said here, *jab koí nahin dekhtá thá,* it would not be Hindustani. *Nazar bacháke* means, avoiding observation. |
| **39.** I have never had occasion to go there; when opportunity offers I shall certainly go. | *Abtak wahán jáne ká ittifáq nahiṉ húá; jab mauqa milegá maiṉ zarúr já,úngá.* | Note *mauqa* for opportunity. |
| **40.** How should I go there when the Saheb has forbidden me? | *Jab Sáheb ne mujhko mana kiyá, to maiṉ wahán kyúṉ játá?* | Note the use of the indicative in these sentences. It is more emphatic than the subjunctive, and implies a distinct denial of the thing |
| **41.** How can one possibly see so far? | *Itní dúr tak nazar kyúṉ paṛtí?* | |

| English. | Hindustani. | Notes. |
|---|---|---|
| 42. Seeing it is a three months' voyage how could he arrive in one month ? | *Jab ki tín mahíne ká safar húá, to ek mahíne men wuh kyun pahúnchtá ?* | asked. This form is always used when the question asked demands a negative answer. |
| 43. After building this house at my own expense for my own residence, why should I now sell it ? | *Jabki yih makán main ne apní hí lágat se apne hí rahne ke líye banwáyá hai, to ab main kyún bechtá ?* | Note *lágat* for cost or expense. |
| 44. The gun was resting against the wall. | *Bandúq díwár ke saháre kharí thí.* | Lit. "With the help of the wall was standing up." Understand *se* after *saháre.* |
| 45. The Saheb laid down his gun against the wall. | *Sáheb ne apní bandúq díwár ke saháre kharí kar rakh dí.* | |
| 46. The moment the fire touched the powder it exploded. | *Bárút ág ke lagtí hí bhak se uṛ ga,i.* | Note *bhak se uṛjáná* for ' to explode." |
| 47. That was a very long shot, Saheb. | *Yih to baṛí dúr ká nishána thá, Sáheb.* | Lit. "distant mark.' ' |
| 48. He missed the mark twice. | *Do dafẹ* (or *martabe*) *uski goli khatá kar ga,i.* | The idiom is not usually that the marksman misses, but that his shot |
| 49. The third time he hit the bull's-eye in the centre. | *Tísrí dafẹ golí quljhaṛí ke bíchon bích lag ga,í.* | misses. Note that to miss is *khatá kar jáná* and *chúkná.* |
| 50. How do you know that he missed the mark ? | *Tumhen kaise málúm ki nishána chúká hai ?* | |

| English. | Hindustani. | Notes. |
|---|---|---|
| 51. Why if it had hit, shouldn't we have heard it? | *Bhalá, golí lagne se, kyá, uskí áwáz na átí?* | |
| 52. He has good tools, but he does not know how to use them. | *Uske auzár to achchhe hain, magar wuh nahin jántá ki unko kaisá baratná cháhiye.* | Note *baratná* and *bartáo.* |
| 53. He must learn the use of them. | *Unká bartáo to síkhná cháhiye.* | |
| 54. Bring your witnesses with you. | *Apne gawáhon ko apne sáth liwá láo.* | Note that to bring another person with you is *liwá láná*, but that to bring an article with you is *lete áná* or *letá*, or *letí, áná*, according to the gender, or position in life, of the person addressed. |
| 55. Bring my book also along with you, will you? | *Merí kitáb bhí apne sáth lete áiyo; bhalá?* | The interrogative *bhalá?* or *achchhá?* so usual at the end of sentences of this description, seems to mean, "You will, won't you?" or something similar. |
| 56. This is mere hearsay. | *Yih sirf suní sunáí kí bát hai.* | |
| 57. Take out the whole fifteen. | *Pandrah ká pandrah nikál do.* | |
| 58. Give me the whole thousand. | *Hazár ká hazár mujhe de do.* | |
| 59. The whole flock rose as one bird. | *Jhillaṛ ká jhillaṛ uṭh gayá.* | |
| 60. The whole village was in an uproar. | *Gánw hí gánw ká rúká raulá ho rahá thá.* | This expressive doubling of a word to express "the whole of it," is very common and should be noted. |

| English. | Hindustani. | Notes. |
|---|---|---|
| 61. The horse shied on seeing the elephant. | Ghoṛá háthí ko dekhke bidak gayá. | |
| 62. The people about me are very quarrelsome. | Mere pás-paros ke log baṛe jhagṛálú haiṉ. | Bakheriyá and takrárí also mean quarrelsome. |
| 63. The elephant's feet kept slipping while crossing the river. | Daryáo ke pár jáne meṉ háthí ke pair rapṭe rapṭe játe the. | Rapaṭ jáná and phisal jáná both mean to slip, but the former has, I think, a more general application than the latter. |
| 64. Every stroke of the cane raised a weal. | Har ek beṉt ke lagne par ḍaulí uṭh kharí húí. | |
| 65. I have lost my bunch of keys. | Merí chábiyoṉ ká lachchhá khoá gayá hai (or 'kho gayá hai.) | Another word for "bunch" is guchchha. |
| 66. This man chased the thief, and after an hour overtook him. | Yih chor ke píchhe bhágá, aur ek ghanṭe ke bád usko já liyá. | Já lená is the proper Hindustani for "to overtake." The dictionaries do not give the proper word. |
| 67. Guns and gunpowder need to be handled carefully, as they are both dangerous things. | Bandúq bárút se jo kám chaláwe, cháhiye ki hoshiyárí se chaláwe, iswáste ki yih donoṉ khatarnák chízeṉ haiṉ. | |
| 68. A stick is solid, but a bamboo is hollow. | Lakṛí hai ṭhos, magar báṉs hai polá. | Ṭhos means solid, compact, and polá, hollow. Another word for hollow is khokhlá. |

| English. | Hindustani. | Notes. |
|---|---|---|
| 69. This bridge has got broken through the force of the current. | *Yih pul dhár ke toṛ se ṭúṭ gayá hai.* | |
| 70. My feet are sinking in the mud. | *Mere páoṉ kíchaṛ meṉ dhas játe haiṉ.* | |

# SECTION II.

## Apparent Exceptions to the Rule requiring the use of *ne* before the Past Tenses of an Active Verb.

| English. | Hindustani. | Notes. |
| --- | --- | --- |
| **71.** When it has been settled what day the marriage is to be, let me know. | *Jab yih bát qarár páí ki shádí kaun táríkh hogí, to mujhe khabar kardená.* | The seven most prominent apparent exceptions to the above rule are the following: *qarár páná*, to be fixed or settled; *dikhái dená*, to appear or be visible; *sunái dená*, to be heard; *chhulái dená* to be felt; *dekhá karná*, to look on; *suná karná*, to listen; and *chal dená*, to decamp. Despite their active form, these are all really neuter verbs, and as such are treated. *Dekhá karná* and *suná karná* are really nothing more than alternative forms of *dekh rahná* and *sun rahná*. *Dikhái dená* and *nazar áná* are interchangeable terms. |
| **72.** It was at length decided that it would be best to burn them. | *Ákhir-kár yihí ráe qarár páí, ki inká jalá dená hí bihtar hai.* (*Taubatu-n. Nasúh.*) | |
| **73.** The hills were visible this morning from a great distance. | *Subh ko pahár baṛí dúr se dikhái díye the.* | |
| **74.** Just then the carriage came in sight at a turn in the road. | *Usí waqt saṛak ke ek moṛ par gáṛí dikhái dí thí.* | |
| **75.** While the riot was going on in the bazar, this woman stood looking on. | *Bázár men jiswaqt balwá ho rahá thá, yih ąurat khaṛí hokar dekhá kí.* | |
| **76.** While the robber was beating his father, this man stood looking on. | *Jiswaqt ḍákú iske báp ko már rahá thá, yih ádmí khaṛá hoke dekhá kiyá.* | |

| English. | Hindustani. | Notes. |
| --- | --- | --- |
| 77. The three brothers also stood looking on. | *Tínon bhái bhí khaṛe hoke dekhá kiye.* | The rule as shown in these sentences applies equally to *suná ḳarná*, and to all other compound verbs of this class. |
| 78. The thief snatched the ornament out of his hand and decamped. | *Chor uske háth se zewar chhín karke, chal diyá.* | |
| 79. His wife also took up a shawl and made off with it. | *Uskí jorú bhí ek shál uṭháke chal dí.* | |
| 80. In like manner two of his companions took certain property and went off with it. | *Isí tarah* uske do sáthí bhí kuchh mál uṭháke chal diye.* | Note *sáthí* for companion. * Pron. *tareh.* |
| 81. When I put my hand on him, I could feel something like a swelling underneath his clothes. | *Main ne jo háth lagáyá, to uske kapṛe ke níche se ek waram sá chhuláí diyá thá.** | Note *waram* for swelling. Another word is *sújan.* **Málúm húá thá* would be the more usual way of expressing this. |
| 82. A sound like singing came from inside the house. | *Ghar ke andar se ek gáne kí sí áwáz sunáí dí.*† | † *Kán men paṛí* would be the more usual form of expression. |

# SECTION III.

## Sentences on General Subjects.

| English. | Hindustani. | Notes. |
|---|---|---|
| **83.** Can you read and write? | 1. *Kuchh paṛhe ho?* 2. *Kuchh likhá paṛhá jánte ho?* | The first of these is the more usual way of asking this question. *Paṛhná* has three meanings, to read, to recite, and to receive instruction, just as *paṛháná* means to impart instruction, to teach. To teach a parrot to speak, for instance, is *tote ko paṛháná.* The question here asked simply means, therefore, "Have you received any instruction?" |
| **84.** Unless these children are educated, they will go to the bad. | *Agar in bachchoṉ kí tálím na ho, to bigaṛ jáenge.* | |
| **85.** Evil companionship has quite demoralized this young man. | *Bad-atwár logoṉ ki burí suhbat ne is jawán kí miṭṭí bilkull kharáb kardí hai.* | |
| **86.** He has gone quite to the bad of late. | *Áj kal uskí miṭṭí bilkull kharáb hoga,í.* | |
| **87.** To be on the safe side (or, 'for safety's sake') I wrote to him this morning to come at once. | *Ihtiyátan maiṉ ne fajr ko usko likhá thá ki fauran áјáe.* | *Ihtiyát* means care, precaution. |
| **88.** I also took the precaution of sending information to the Saheb. | *Ba nazar ihtiyát ke maiṉ ne Sáheb ke pás bhí ittilá bhejí.* | *Ba nazar,* followed by *ke,* means, with a view to. |

| English. | Hindustani. | Notes. |
|---|---|---|
| 89. I feel certain he will be here by to-morrow evening, if not before. | *Yaqín hai ki, subh nahin,* to kal shám tak zarúr á jáegá.* | * Lit. "If not in the morning." Natives dispense with *agar* as much as possible. |
| 90. Things that were not to be had there, are procurable here. | *Aisí chízen̲ ki jo wáhán̲ baham nahin̲ pahúnchtí thín̲, yahán̲ mil saktí hain̲.* | The three verbs are, *milná, baham pahúnchná,* and *muyassar honá.* Good writers always write *pahúnchná* with a *wáo,* as it is pronounced. |
| 91. If it can be got, I will send it you. | *Agar baham pahúnche, to pahúnchá dúngá.* | |
| 92. He procured a little of all of them. | *Thoṛí thoṛí sab baham pahúnchá lín̲.* (*Taubatu-n. Nasúh.*) | |
| 93. Such things are not to be had here. | *Aisí chízen yahán̲ muyassar nahin̲ hain̲.* | |
| 94. His house is beyond the town, and his shop on this side of it. | *Uská makán hai shahr se pare, aur uskí dukán shahr se ware.* | |
| 95. Was he lying on the inner side of the wall, or on the outer side? | *Díwár kí andarlí taraf paṛá thá, yá báharlí taraf?* | |
| 96. Now, settle this matter to-day. | *Ab is bát ko tai kardo áj.* | *Tai karná* has two meanings, to travel and to settle. |
| 97. Until this matter has been cleared up, nothing can be done. | *Jab tak is bát ká tasfíya na ho, kuchh ho nakin̲ saktá.* | |

| English. | Hindustani. | Notes. |
| --- | --- | --- |
| 98. This bungalow was built for the accommodation of travellers. | *Yih banglá musáfiron kí rafáhiyat ke liye támír húá thá.* | Note *rafáhiyat.* |
| 99. The house that I built with my own money has been blown down in the storm, and the debris is still lying there. | *Wuh makán jo main ne apní lágat se chunwáyá thá túfán men gir gayá hai, aur malbá abtak wunhín pará hai.* | *Chunná* is common Hindustani for 'to build,' and *chunwáná* for 'to cause to be built.' *Ándhíse* would be quite as correct as *túfán men.* |
| 100. If any one has been injured through me, I am prepared to make amends. | *Agar mere sabab kisí ko zarar pahúnchá ho, to main taláfi dún.* | *Zarar* means injury of any kind; *nuqsán,* generally loss. A less common word for injury is *gazand.* |
| 101. The Saheb's arrangements were so excellent that no one was injured. | *Sáheb kí khushtadbírí kí wajh* se zarar kisíko nahin pahúnchá.* | * Pron. *wajeh.* |
| 102. Through this merchant's becoming bankrupt, my friend has sustained great loss. | *Is saudágar ke diwálá nikal jáne se mere dost ká bhárí nuqsán húá.* | |
| 103. When did he go bankrupt? | *Diwála kab nikál díyá?* | |
| 104. How will this inconvenience you? | *Isse tumhárá kyá harj hogá?* | Note *harj,* it is a very common word and generally means hindrance or inconvenience |

| English. | Hindustani. | Notes. |
|---|---|---|
| 105. Does this shopkeeper require cash payment, or does he give credit? | *Yih dukándár naqd bechtá hai, yá udhár bechtá?* | |
| 106. Which is the item in this account which you consider doubtful (or suspicious)? | *Is hisáb men̲ wuh kaun sí raqam hai jo tum mushtabeh samajhte ho?* | |
| 107. Please give me some small coin with the rupees. | *Rúpaiyon̲ ke sáth kuchh rezgárí bhí díjiyo.* | |
| 108. Have you any small change about you? If you have, give me some, like a good fellow. | *Áp ke pás kuchh kherja hai? Hai, to mihrbání karke thoṛá sá mujhe díjiyo, mard-i-ádmí.* | *Kherja* is a common word in the N.W. Provinces for small change. |
| 109. Are you responsible for this man's pay, or am I? | *Is shakhs kí tankhwáh áp ke zimme hai, yá mere zimme?* | The real meaning of *zimma* is responsibility arising out of an assumed or accepted charge. |
| 110. The canal on the other side of the town has only lately been made; the college on this side is of long standing. | *Shahr kí parlí taraf jo nahr hai, wuh áj kal kí baní húí hai; uskí warlí taraf jo madrasa hai, wuh bahut din ká hai.* | |
| 111. Taking advantage of his youth, the cunning rogue wheedled him out of all his money. | *Usko laṛká samajhkar, is ạiyár ne phuslá phuslákar, uská ṭamám rúpiya le liyá.* | This use of *samajhná* is most common and should be noted. Natives of India never use many |

| English. | Hindustani. | Notes. |
|---|---|---|
| **112**. Out of deference to her age, I made her a respectful salutation. | *Main̲ use derína samajhkar, dast ba sar huá.* (*Bág̲h̲-o-Bahár.*) | words where one will do. "Recognising the fact" is what it really means here. |
| **113**. Taking advantage of her being a woman, he dispossessed her of the jewel by force. | *Usko ạurat samajhkar, uske háth se zabardastí se zewar chhín liyá.* | |
| **114**. When I accosted him on the road, he behaved with the greatest rudeness. | *Ráste men̲ jab main̲ ne use ṭoká, wuh bahut be-adabí se pesh áyá.* | *Ṭokná* means to accost, and also to take to task. |
| **115**. On my taking him to task for saying this, he denied having said it. | *Is bát ke kahne par jo main̲ ne use ṭoká, to inkár kiyá, ki main̲ ne nahín̲ kahá.* | The use of *jo* for 'when' is very common. |
| **116**. He treated me with the greatest kindness. | *Wuh mere sáth bahut mihrbání aur k̲h̲átirdárí se pesh áyá.* | *Pesh áná* means to treat, to behave, to demean oneself. |
| **117**. He has lots of plans, but none of them succeed. | *Uskí tadbíren̲ bahut hain̲, magar ek bhí pesh-raft na hotí.* | |
| **118**. The affair is the talk of the town. | *Is bát ká charchá tamám shahr phailá húá hai.* | *Charchá* also means fashion, vogue, &c. |

| English. | Hindustani. | Notes. |
|---|---|---|
| 119. Last year, go where you would, look where you would, this was all the rage; this year, on the contrary, you never hear it mentioned. | *Parke sál* (*or pár sál, or sál guzashte*) *jahán̲ jáo, jahán̲ dekho, bas, isíkí garm-bázári; phir ab ke sál kahín̲ uská zikr hí nahín̲.* | It is more idiomatic to omit the verb here after *garm-bázárí*. This word means "a brisk market." |
| 120. The raging of the plague. | *Wabá kí garm-bázárí.* | This grimly expressive phrase is from the *Taubatu-n-Nasúh.* |
| 121. The baniya's things were lying all strewn about upon the ground. | *Baniye kí jins zamín par sab idhar udhar khinḍí paṛí thín̲.* | |
| 122. I am aching all over from the motion and jolting of the carriage. | *Gáṛí ke takán aur hachkolon̲ se merá tamám badan dard kartá.* | *Takán* means mental agitation as well as bodily. |
| 123. Listen to what I say, and lay it to heart, and act upon it. | *Merá kahná suno, aur k͟hátir men̲ láo, aur uspar ạmal karo.* | |
| 124. In whose possession is this land? | *Yih zamín kiske qabze men̲ hai?* | |
| 125. I am in possession of this land. | *Is zamín par main̲ qábiz hún̲.* | Note these three forms, of *qabza, qábiz,* and *maqbúza.* |
| 126. How long has it been in your possession? | *Tumhárí maqbúza kab se húí?* | |

| English. | Hindustani. | Notes. |
|---|---|---|
| 127. People complain of this man, that he does his work in a very perfunctory manner. | *Log shikáyat karte hain ki yih ádmí apná kám sahl-angárí se kartá hai.* | *Sahl-angárí se* means "with an utter lack of interest." Apathy perhaps expresses the word as well as any other. |
| 128. He gets through his work somehow, but in a very half-hearted way. | *Wuh apná kám jon ton kartá hai, magar be-dilí se kartá hai.* | |
| 129. He says he is well able to perform the work. | *Wuh kahtá ki is kám ko main ba-khúbí anjám de saktá hún.* | |
| 130. Wait a bit; let me finish what I am doing, and then I'll attend to you. | *Thame raho; mujhko is kám se fursat hone do, to mai tumhárí taraf mutawajjih hún.* | *Thame rahná*, and *ṭhahar jáná* both mean "to wait." |
| 131. The Saheb's attention must be called to this, as it is a most important matter. | *Is bát kí taraf Sáheb ko zarúr tawajjuh diláná cháhiye, kyúnki niháyat zarúr bát hai.* | |
| 132. If no steps are taken to put a stop to this, such illnesses must be looked for. | *Agar iske insidád ke liye koí tadbír na kí jáwe, to aisí bímárián mutasawwir hain.* | *Mutasawwir honá* is the correct Hindustani wherewith to express these phrases. See Note to 224. |
| 133. If no rain comes, we may expect a failure of the crops. | *Agar bárish na áwe, to khetiyon kí kharábí mutasawwir hai.* | |

| English. | Hindustani. | Notes. |
|---|---|---|
| 134. Prevention is better than cure. | *Peshtar ká insidád píchhe ke mu,ạlaje se bihtar hai.* | *Mu,ạlaja* from *ịláj.* |
| 135. This is a matter of daily occurrence. | *Yih bát roz húá kartí hai.* | These three verbs, *húá karná,* to occur constantly, *jáyá karná,* to go constantly, and *kiyá karná* to do constantly, may serve as examples of a class which is common. The *húá, jáyá, kiyá,* &c., never change their forms, the *karná* alone agreeing with the gender and number of the agent. |
| 136. He goes to his friend's house every day. | *Wuh apne dost ke ghar par roz jáyá kartá hai.* | |
| 137. He works with his brother regularly. | *Wuh apne bhái ke sáth barábar kám kiyá kartá hai.* | |
| 138. Who first introduced this custom? | *Ibtidá meṉ is riwáj ko kisne barpá kar diyá?* | |
| 139. This custom, Saheb, has come down to us from the days of Akbar. | *Yih riwáj, Sáheb, Akbar bádsháh ke dinoṉ se barábar chalá áyá hai.* | |
| 140. Who are the promoters of this scheme? | *Is mansúbe ke barpá karne-wále kaun haiṉ?* | *Bar pá karná,* as the word implies, means literally "to set on foot." |
| 141. What in your honour's opinion is the actual value of this house? | *Áp ke nazdík is makán kí máliyat kitne rúpai kí hai?* | *Qímat* is the price of a thing, *máliyat* its actual value. |
| 142. We may learn from knowledge and experience what is the use of everything. | *Ịlm aur tajriba se har ek chíz kí manfaạt mạlúm ho saktí hai.* | *Manfa,ạt* answers to our word "good" in the sentence, "What is the good of this thing?" and to our word "use" in the same sense. |

| English. | Hindustani. | Notes. |
|---|---|---|
| **143.** Well then, we can also find out what is the good of toads, frogs, snakes, &c. | *Khair, to yih bhí málúm ho jáe, ki beng, mendak, sámp, waghaire kí kyá manfaut hotí hai.* | |
| **144.** This kind of gun is but little used now-a-days. | *Is qism kí bandúq ká istimál áj kal kam hotá hai.* | |
| **145.** If any one stands just here and shouts, the echo of his shout will come back from the hill. | *Agar koí is jagah khará hoke hánk máre, to uskí hánk kí sadá pahár kí taraf se wápas áwe.* | Note *sadá* for echo. |
| **146.** The shopkeeper flicked up the rupee, and on its giving out a ringing sound he knew that it was a good one. | *Dukándár ne rúpiye ko chutkí lagáí; jab uskí jhan kí sí áwáz áí, to málúm húá ki achchhá rúpiya hai.* | |
| **147.** As good luck would have it, he hadn't left the house when I arrived. | *Husn-i-ittifáq se wuh abhí ghar se nahín chalá thá, ki ismen main já pahúnchá.* | In these phrases from the Persian the *izáfat* "i" is almost always omitted in conversation, so that *husn-i-ittifáq* becomes *husn ittifáq*; *tálib-i-ilm*, a student, *tálib ilm*; *málik-i-makán*, the master of the house, *málik makán*, &c. |
| **148.** By a lucky accident the Saheb was going by with his gun just as the tiger emerged from the jungle. | *Husn-i-ittifáq se sher jiswaqt jangal se niklá thá, usí waqt Sáheb bandúq liye húe ustaraf se guzrá thá.* | |

| English. | Hindustani. | Notes. |
|---|---|---|
| **149.** It was his good fortune to come under the Saheb's notice just when he most needed a helping hand. | Yih uski <u>kh</u>ush-nasíbí thí, ki jiswaqt usko madad aur dastgírí ki <u>kh</u>áss hájat aur zarúrat thí, usiwaqt Sáheb kí nazar uspar paṛí. | |
| **150.** The door kept banging all night, either against the doorpost or something else, and entirely prevented my sleeping. | Kiwáṛ kí, yá to chauk<u>h</u>aṭ se yá aur kisí chíz se, rát bhar ṭakkar ho rahí thí, jiske sabab merí nínd bilkull uchát hogaí, (or játí rahí.) | |
| **151.** He didn't at all like my saying this. | Merá yih bát kahná usko sa<u>kh</u>t nágawár málúm húá. | Lit. "it was most distasteful to him." |
| **152.** It was most painful (or distressing, or trying) to him to see his father in such a plight. | Apne báp ko aisí hálat men dekhná usko bahut shaqq guzrá thá. | |
| **153.** He replied, we put up with all this oppression, and when driven to extremities, we leave their country. | Usne kahá, ham yih zulm sab apne úpar gawárá karte hain, aur kabhí ájiz hokar, unke mulk se nikal játe hain. (I<u>kh</u>wánu-s-Safá.) | |
| **154.** The beauty of it is, that when I gave him the gun, he didn't in the least know how to use it. | Lutf yih hai, ki jab main ne uske háth men bandúq dí thí, wuh uske bartáo se bilkull ná-wáqif thá. | |

| English. | Hindustani. | Notes. |
|---|---|---|
| 155. The mischief of it is, that the Saheb is sure now to cancel his permission (or "to withdraw his sanction"). | G͟hazab yih hai, ki ab Sáheb apní ijázat ko mansúk͟h kar legá zarúr. | Might also be translated, "the worst of it is." |
| 156. There is no outlet for this water, otherwise how would it collect like this? | Is pání ká koí nikás nahin̲ hai, nahín̲ to istarah*kyún̲ jama͟ hojátá? | * Pron. istareh. |
| 157. You don't think there would be any harm, do you, in my spending some of the money in my hands on this work? | Agar main̲ us rúpai men̲ se ki jo mere háth men̲ hai kuchh thoṛá sá is kám men̲ sarf karún̲, to áp ke nazdík kuchh qabáhat to nahín̲ hai? | Anything morally wrong is qabáhat. The word is in common use, and answers to our words "harm" and "impropriety." |
| 158. In this matter we should look at the motive. The question is, did he do it from a good motive or from a bad one? | Is bát men̲ niyat par liház honá cháhiye. Bát yih hai, ki nek-niyati se isne yih kám kiyá, yá bad-niyatí se? | |
| 159. Does the evidence tell for or against him? | Yih gawáhí uske mufíd hai yá uske muzirr? | Lit. "profitable or damaging;" mufid from fá,ida, and muzirr from zarar. |
| 60. There is no connection between the two things. | In do báton̲ ká ta'al-luq hí nahín̲. | |

| English. | Hindustani. | Notes. |
|---|---|---|
| **161.** There is nothing to be gained by asking irrelevant questions. | *Ghair - muta,alliq suwál karne se kuchh fá,ida nahín.* | |
| **162.** If this man is innocent, he ought to be acquitted; if he really perpetrated (or "was the perpetrator of") this crime, he ought to be severely punished. | *Agar yih ádmí be-qusúr hai, to barí honá cháhiye; agar wáqaí is jurm ká murtakib húá, to uskí sakht sazá honí cháhiye.* | *Barí honá* means to be acquitted, *rihá honá* or *rihái páná*, to be released. |
| **163.** The two were talking together on the road. | *Yih donon ráste men ham-kalám ho rahe the.* | Educated Natives always use *yih* and *wuh* with the plural in preference to *ye* and *we*. |
| **164.** This created a kind of suspicion against him in the Saheb's mind. | *Is bát se Sáheb ke dil men uskí taraf ek bad-gumání sí paidá hogaí.* | |
| **165.** He has been in hiding for the last four days. | *Chár roz se wuh rúposh hai.* | |
| **166.** It seems highly probable that he has absconded. | *Gumán ghálib hai ki farár hogayá hogá.* | *Farár honá* and *mafrúr honá* both mean "to abscond." |
| **167.** I learn from the police that his two companions absconded yesterday. | *Pulís kí zabání málúm hotá ki uske do sáthí kal mafrúr húe the.* | Understand *se* after *zabání.* |

| English. | Hindustani. | Notes. |
|---|---|---|
| 168. People were greatly surprised to hear of his arrest. | Uskí mák͟húzí kí k͟habar sunkar, logon ne bahut taąjjub kiyá. | Mák͟húzí has a more extended meaning than giriftárí, and answers more to our expression of "being run in." |
| 169. The hearing of the case will come on after a week. | Muqaddame kí samáąt ek hafte ke báḍ hogí. | |
| 170. Grant for the sake of argument that he did not know of it at the time; still was it not his duty when he came to know of it, to inform the Saheb? | Farz karo ki uswaqt ná-wáqif thá, sahí; phir jab usko k͟habar hogaí, kyá, usko lázim na thá ki Sáheb ke pás jáke ittilą́ kar detá? | Farz karná means to grant for the sake of argument, taslím karná, to admit unconditionally. Sahí is a word used at the end of a clause, as here (never in the beginning or middle), to emphasize concession, and seems generally to have the meaning of "really" or "truly." Note the peculiar idiom, mujhko taslím. It is equivalent to main taslím kartá. |
| 171. Yes it was— I admit it; but even then, his offence is not such a heinous one that it can't be forgiven. | Háṉ, Sáheb, thá, mujhko taslím; magar phir bhí, qusúr uská aisá sangín nahíṉ hai ki mu,ąf na ho sake. | |
| 172. All right, he is ill then (conceding the point in order to end the discussion), but what has his being ill or well got to do with you? | K͟hair, bímár, sahí; lekin uskí bímári yá tandurustí se tumko kyá wásta? | |
| 173. He is hard of hearing, and his brother has failing sight. | Wuh kam suntá hai, aur uská bháí kam dek͟htá hai. | |

| English. | Hindustani. | Notes. |
|---|---|---|
| 174. I give according to my means. | *Main apní haisiyat aur gunjá,ish ke mutábiq diyá kartá hún.* | *Gunjá,ish* means room, space, capacity; *haisiyat* means capacity in the sense of ability, function, &c. and it also means condition. |
| 175. I cannot afford to give more than this. | *Isse ziyáda dene ki merí gunjáish nahín.* | |
| 176. If there is space enough, put it in the north room. | *Agar gunjá,ish* ho, to uttarwále kamare men rakho.* | Also *jagah.** |
| 177. His condition in life appears to be that of a poor man. | *Uskí haisiyat záhirí gharíb ádmí ki sí málúm hotí hai.* | |
| 178. This man is able to tame every kind of animal. | *Yih ádmí har ek qism ke jánwar ko hilá saktá hai.* | *Hiláná*, and *rám karná* both mean to tame; *hilná* and *pos mánná*, to be tamed. |
| 179. This leopard is already tamed. | *Yih tendúá hil chuká hai.* | |
| 180. It is sometimes very difficult to tame tigers. | *Sher ká rám karná kabhí kabhí bahut dushwár hotá hai.* | |
| 181. Small birds become tame in a very short time. | *Chhoṭí chiṛiyán thoṛe dinon men pos mántí hain.* | |
| 182. This science teaches the properties of things, both animate and inanimate. | *Ján-dár chízon aur be-ján chízon in donon kí sifaten is ịlm se málúm hotí hain.* | |

| English. | Hindustani. | Notes. |
|---|---|---|
| **183.** If an incision be made in the bark of this tree, a milk-like sap will exude, but take care it does not touch your hand or your body, for if it does it will raise a blister. | *Is darak̲h̲t ke bakkal men̲ agar chheh díyá jáe, to ek ras misl dúdh ke niklegá, lekin k̲h̲abardár ki háth par yá badan par na lag jáe, nahín̲ to ábila paṛ jáegá.* | *Chheh dená* (not *karná*) is to make an incision. *Ábila* and *phapholá* both mean "blister." |
| **184.** Gesticulation is the work of the actor and the buffoon; evasion is the work of the unprincipled and of knaves. | *Bháo batáná bhánḍon̲ khilonon̲ ká kám hai; bálá batáná beímánon̲ aur dag̲h̲ábázon̲ ká kám hai.* | *Bhánḍ* and *khiloná* both mean a comic actor. |
| **185.** Are your own and your father's lands some distance apart, or are they close together? | *Tumhárí zamín aur tumháre báp kí zamín alag alag hai, yá pás hí pás hai?* | |
| **186.** No, Saheb, they are divided by a river. | *Nahín̲, Sáheb, bích men̲ ek to daryáo paṛtá hai.* | |
| **187.** My house is shut off from his by a wall. | *Mere ghar aur uske ghar ke bích men̲ ek to díwár há,il hai.* | *Há,il* intervening, obstructing, is a useful word to remember. The *common* Hindustani, however, here would be, *díwár áí hai.* Anything that acts as a barrier is *há,il.* |
| **188.** Through the river's intervening between their village and the jungle, the villagers are protected from the wolves. | *Gánw̲ aur jangal ke bích men̲ daryáo há,il hone kí wajh se, gánw̲-wále bheṛiyon̲ se mahfúz rahte hai.* | |

| English. | Hindustani. | Notes. |
|---|---|---|
| **189.** In this part of the country agriculture is mainly dependent on irrigation. | *Is atráf men̲ kásht-kárí beshtar síchne par* (or *áb-páshí par*) *mauqúf hai.* | A more pedantic form would be, *kásht-kárí ká madár beshtar síchne par hai*, and *madár saudágar logon̲ ke kár-o-bár ká beshtar kishtiyon̲ par hai; madár* meaning dependence, or lit. a centre or pivot on which anything rests or turns. Compare our "Everything hinges on this." |
| **190.** In Assam the local trade has to be carried on for the most part by means of boats. | *Áshám ke mulk men̲ saudágar logon̲ ká kár-o-bár beshtar kishtiyon̲ par mauqúf hai.* | |
| **191.** When others are allowed to go there and to take part in this, why should *I* be debarred? | *Jab aur logon̲ ko wahán̲ jáne aur is bát men̲ sharík hone kí ijázat húí, to main̲ kyún̲ mahrúm rahún̲?* | |
| **192.** I only play for amusement, I do not gamble. | *Main̲ dil-lagí ke wáste kheltá hún̲, júá nahín̲ kheltá.* | |
| **193.** The man has now come out in his true colours. | *Ab is shakhs kí qala,í khul ga,í.* | Lit. "his tinning has come off." |
| **194.** This man's one wish is, that something should go wrong with your honour's administration; he will then have gained his object. | *Harwaqt is shakhs kí yih tamanná hai, ki huzúr kí amaldárí men̲ kuchh futúr á jáe, to uská matlab bar áwe.* | *Futúr* means "something wrong;" "a screw loose somewhere," as we say. |
| **195.** I can't imagine what has gone wrong with his temper of late. | *Nahín̲ málúm áj-kal iske mizáj men̲ kyá futúr á gayá hai.* | |

| English. | Hindustani. | Notes. |
|---|---|---|
| **196.** Should there be any flaw in this document, the pleader is such a sharp fellow that he is sure to detect it. | *Is dastáwez men̲ agar koí suqm ho, to vakíl aisá tez-fahm shak̲h̲s hai ki zarúr pakṛegá.* | *Suqm* means a flaw or a weak point. Its primary meaning is sickness or infirmity. |
| **197.** So long as I am to the fore, what right (lit. "power") has any one else to interfere in my household affairs ? | *Mere hote, aur kiskí majál hai ki mere ghar ke kám káj men̲ dak̲h̲l de?* (or *mudák̲h̲alat kare*). | Understand *men̲* after *hote* : we shall then see that the phrase means "during my being." |
| **198.** His family contains an ignoramus, a fool, and a "ne'er-do-weel." | *Uske k̲h̲ándán men̲ ek to hech-ma-dán hai, ek to ahmaq hai, aur ek to ná-ba-kár hai.* | |
| **199.** Such a procrastinating, evasive, tricky fellow I never saw in all my life. | *Aisá imroz-fardá, ṭál-maṭol, híla-hawála karne-wálá main̲ ne ụmr-bhar* nahín̲ dekhá hai.* | * Pron. *ụmar-bhar.* |
| **200.** One day an illiterate man was going somewhere or other along an unknown road. When he had got half-way, he met a friend of his, but he pretended not to know him and kept on his way. | *Ek roz ek anpaṛhá ádmí ek andekhe ráste se kahín̲ ko játá thá. Ádhí ráh men̲ uská ek dost usko á milá, par yih anján ban-kar áge hí chalá.* | This Hindi prefix *an-* answers to our *un-*, &c., and to the Persian *ná*. *Anján banná* means to pretend not to see, or perceive, or be aware of a thing. |

| English. | Hindustani. | Notes. |
|---|---|---|
| 201. Does not this little incident teach us, that the illiterate are sometimes deficient in good manners? | *Is chhoṭí sí wáridát se hamen̲ yih táʻlím hotí na, ki anpaṛhe logon̲ kí chál-ḍhál men̲ kabhí nuqs bhí hotá hai?* | *Wáridát* is really a plural noun, but it is always used in the singular, as here. |
| 202. The master of the house was stretching, his wife yawning, and a handsome Kabuli cat was sitting purring before the fire. | *Makán ká málik angṛáí letá thá, uskí bíbí jamháí letí thí, aur ek to k͟húbsúrat Kábulí billí ág ke sámne baiṭhí k͟hur-k͟hur kar rahí thí.* | |
| 203. Perceiving from the Saheb's face and manner that his visit was unwelcome, he made his salaam and came away. | *Jab Sáheb ke bashare aur tarz-i-guftgú se táṛ gayá ki merá yahán̲ áná Sáheb ko nágawár hai, to salám karke báhar nikal áyá.* | *Táṛ jáná* is to perceive a thing from indications or signs. |
| 204. There is no knowing how Kalim came to guess what was in Nasuh's mind. | *Kalím nahín̲ mạlúm kyún̲kar Nasúḥ ke batún ko táṛ gayá.* (*Taubatu-n-Nasúḥ.*) | |
| 205. On the thief's being caught and his person searched, a lady's watch and a pair of child's shoes were found in his clothes. | *Jab chor pakṛá gayá aur uske badan kí taláshí lí ga,í, to ek bibiyána ghaṛí aur ek joṛí bachkaní jútiyán̲ uske kapṛe men̲ se barámad húín̲* (or *niklín̲*). | The words "lady's" and "child's" here are adjectives, being expressive not of ownership but of quality, and accordingly this is the form that they take in Hindustani. *Bachkaná* is subject to inflection, *bibiyána* is not. |

| English. | Hindustani. | Notes. |
|---|---|---|
| **206.** On his house being searched, a quantity of stolen property came to light. | *Jab uske ghar kí taláshí lí ga,í, to bahut sá chorí ká mál barámad húá.* | |
| **207.** The murderer fired off the gun through a chink in the door. | *Khúní ne kiwáṛ ke ek darz men se bandúq márí.* | Note *darz* for chink. |
| **208.** If the thief's clothes had been thoroughly searched, a valuable jewel would also have been found on him. | *Agar chor ke kapṛe achchhí tarah* jháṛe liye játe, to ek qímatí zewar bhí niklá húá hotá.* | *Jháṛ lená* means to search thoroughly, to rummage. * Pron. *tareh.* |
| **209.** No clue to the murderer has yet been discovered. | *Abtak khúní ká koí patá nahín lagá.* | *Patá lagná* and *patá milná* are used indifferently. Both these and *patá lagáná* are idioms to be noted. |
| **210.** Go and find out where he is; when you have found out this, then come again and let me know. | *Jáo, uská patá lagáo; jab patá lagáyá, to phir áo, mujhe khabar kar dená.* | |
| **211.** I don't know the Saheb's address; if I knew it, I should send a letter to that address. | *Sáheb ká patá mujh ko málúm nahín; agar málúm hotá, to khatt us pate par bhej detá.* | |
| **212.** The poor fellow's hand was simply hanging on by a strip of skin. | *Bechára ká háth faqat ek ṭukṛe chamṛe se hilgá rahá thá.* | We speak of a thing hanging on by, or hanging on to, another thing; this is |

| English. | Hindustani. | Notes. |
|---|---|---|
| **213.** The padlock is still hanging from the hasp where I put it. | *Tálá usí kundí se hilgá rahá hai jahán main ne hilgáyá thá.* | represented in Hindustani by *hilgá rahná.* An earring from a lady's ear and a padlock from a hasp are good examples. |
| **214.** If a man have no occupation, he can neither be well nor happy. | *Agar ádmí ká koí mashghala na ho, na badan durust rahtá, na tabíạt khush hotí.* | |
| **215.** Why speak of a year? he has squandered his whole life: why speak of a thousand rupees? he has cast to the winds his whole capital. | *Usne, ek baras kyá? sárí ụmr ganwáí; hazár rúpiya kyá? apná tamám sar-máya barbád kar diyá.* | Note *ganwáná* and *sar-máya.* The latter means stock-in-trade capital, &c. |
| **216.** This man has already undergone his punishment; how can he be punished twice over? | *Yih ádmí apní sazá bhugat kar chuká hai, to phir dobára uskí sazá kyúnkar ho saktí.* | *Bhugatná* means to undergo, to suffer. |
| **217.** I was present while the bargaining was going on, but I was not present when it was concluded (when the price was fixed). | *Saudá ke waqt maujúd to thá, lekin bháo chukne ke waqt main maujúd nahín thá.* | This meaning of *saudá* should be noted. |
| **218.** Make much of this opportunity; it may be that you won't get such another opportunity the whole of your life. | *Is mauqa ko ghanímat jáno; sháyad aisá koí mauqa phir ụmr bhar na mile.* | *Ghanímat jánná* means to make much of a thing, to realise its full value. |

| English. | Hindustani. | Notes. |
| --- | --- | --- |
| 219. At last things came to such a pass, that he could not go outside his house without his life being in danger. | *Ákhir-kár yih naubat pahúnchí, ki agar ghar se kahín kisi waqt báhar nikal jáe, to ján ká khauf hotá.* | Perhaps the best explanation to give of *naubat* is, that when things have been going from bad to worse, *naubat* is the word that we always find used to express their latest and worst stage. |
| 220. This then is the state of things with your brothers, and you are quite unconcerned. | *Pas, tumháre bháíyon kí yih naubat, aur tum be-fikr ho.* (*Bágh-o-Bahár.*) | |
| 221. From opposition we shall next pass to the fighting stage. | *Mukhálafat se phir laṛáí kí naubat pahúnchegí.* (*Ikhwánu-s-Safá.*) | *Muzáhamat* is also opposition. |
| 222. He is so touchy that he takes offence at the least thing. | *Wuh aisá názuk-mizáj ádmí hai, ki zarrá sí bát par barham hojátá hai.* | *Tunuk-mizáj* is another word that expresses this. |
| 223. In chess it is natural ability that is called into play (or "that has to bear the strain"), in cards, memory. | *Shatranj men tabíạt par zor paṛtá hai, ganjífe men, háfize par.* (*Taubatu-n-Nasúh.*) | |
| 224. If he will always eat indigestible things, he must expect to suffer from indigestion; if he ate wholesome things, his digestion would be right enough. | *Agar wuh saqíl chízen hamesha khátá, to bad-hazmí mutasawwir hí hai; agar khush-gawár chízen khátá hotá, to uská házima durust rahtá.* | See note to sentence 132. *Mutasawwir* expresses in one word all that the English does. The phrase "calculated to produce" should be similarly translated, |

| English. | Hindustani. | Notes. |
|---|---|---|
| **225.** How many bars has this cage, and what are they made of? | *Is pinjre kí ka,í kámpen hain, aur káhe kí hain?* | as the Hindustani form for this would be "likely to result from." |
| **226.** A hole large enough for the passage of a man's body. | *Ek súrákh ádmí ke guzar ke qábil.* | |
| **227.** I bade adieu that same day both to the school and to the Bahár-dánish. | *Maktab aur Bahár-dánish ko to main ne usí din salám kiyá thá.* (*Taubatu-n-Nasúh.*) | |
| **228.** The Rajah has entirely abolished the custom within his own jurisdiction. | *Rájá saheb ne apne qalam-rau men is ráh wa rasm ko bilkull uṭhá diyá hai.* | *Uṭhá dená* is the usual Hindustani for "to abolish." |
| **229.** One's reason refuses to believe that anyone in the possession of his senses would have done such a thing. | *Ạql qabúl nahín kartí ki koí ádmí apne hosh-hawáss kí durustí men aisá fẹl kare.* | "*E*" with a dot under it means that the letter is an *ain.* |
| **230.** As the place where the bag was found is four miles from the village, it is unreasonable to suppose that any one of the villagers threw it there. | *Chúnki wuh mauqa jahán thailí pái ga,í gánw se do kos ká fásila rakhtá hai, to qaiyás nahín cháhtá ki kisí gánw-wále ne wahán phenk dí ho.* | Both *qaiyás cháhná* and *fásila rakhná* are important idioms. *Fásila* means "distance" or "interval." I have written *qaiyás* as it is always pronounced. |

| English. | Hindustani. | Notes. |
|---|---|---|
| **231.** As this box which he left in my charge contains all his necessaries, it is reasonable to suppose that he will come back again to take it away. | *Chúnki is sandúq men jo wuh mere supurd rakh gayá thá uskí sab zarúriyát hain, to qaiyás cháhtá ki phir zarúr wápas áwegá usko lejáne ke wáste.* | *Joki* can be substituted for *chúnki* in both these sentences, if desired, as they both mean the same. |
| **232.** The bay horse is in his stall, the chestnut mare has gone to the nalbund, the dun horse is grazing in the field, the dark brown horse has gone out in the buggy, and the roan is pawing the ground in the stable as he sees his food being got ready. | *Kumait ghorá apne thán men hai, surang ghorí nálband ke yahán ga,í, samand ghorá khet men chartá hai, mushkí ghorá báhar baghí men gayá, aur chíná ghorá apne dána kí taiyárí dekhkar, istabal men táp mártá hai.* | Bay, *kumait ;* chestnut, *surang ;* dun, *samand ;* dark-brown, *mushkí ;* roan, *chíná ;* grey, *sabzí.* |
| **233.** The grey mare has a dash of red in her. | *Sabzí ghorí kí rangat men kuchh surkhí kí damak hai.* | |
| **234.** When the horse shied, the saddle shifted a little, but the Saheb had such a firm seat that he was not in the least shaken. | *Jab ghorá bidak gayá, zín thorá sá khaská, magar Sáheb aisá jamke baithá thá, ki zarrá bhí nahín hilá.* | *Khasakná* means to shift, to become displaced. |
| **235.** Let his anger cool down a bit ; it is useless speaking to him in his present state. | *Uská ghussa faro hojáne do ; ab kí hálat men usko kahná lá-hásil hai.* | *Faro hojáná* means to subside. The Hindi equivalent is *tham jáná.* |

| English. | Hindustani. | Notes. |
|---|---|---|
| **236.** Take care that no one's name is omitted from this list. | *Khabardár ki is fihrist se kisí ká nám faro-guzásht na ho.* | The other words for "omitted" are *chhúṭ gayá* and *matrúk.* |
| **237.** Humility is becoming to those who are full of faults. | *Farotaní aison ke liye munásib hai, ki jo ʻaib se bhare hain.* | |
| **238.** Are you speaking in jest, or in earnest? | *Tum ṭhaṭhe se kahte ho, ki satbháo se kahte ho?* | |
| **239.** This is not a superficial stain (or spot), it is a deep-seated one, that is why it won't come out. | *Yih dágh úparí dágh nahín hai, jigarí hai, is wáste nikaltá nahín.* | Note *jigarí* for deep-seated. It comes from *jigar,* the heart, or liver. |
| **240.** In the middle of the night I heard a noise inside the house, which made my heart stand still, for I thought a thief must somehow or other have got in. | *Ádhí rát ko ghar ke andar ek biṛak sá mujhe málúm húá, jisse merá kalejá dhak se rahgayá, aur yih khiyál men áyá, ki kahín chor na ghusá ho?* | *Biṛak* means a vague, indefinite sound, which *áwáz* does not adequately express. *Kalejá* is often used for heart. *Kahín,* as used here, corresponds to our "possibly," "by any chance." |
| **241.** May he not possibly be asking for the fop, Mirzá? | *Yih kahín Mirzá bánke ko na púchhte hon?* (*Taubatu-n-Nasúh*). | |
| **242.** The bystanders (people) were so taken with the smartness of his replies that they began to applaud him. | *Uske jawábon kí barjastagí ne logon par aisá asar kiyá, ki uskí shábáshí karne lage.* | *Barjasta* means prompt, smart, apt; and *barjastagí,* of course, the corresponding nouns. |

| English. | Hindustani. | Notes. |
| --- | --- | --- |
| **243**. How long have you known this person? | *Tumko kab se is shakhs kí ján-pahchán hai?* | |
| **244**. As long as I can remember anything. | *Jab se main ne hosh sambhálá.* | *Lit.* "Since I got control of my intelligence." I know of nothing in Hindustani that comes nearer to the English than this. |
| **245**. I prefer living in England to living in India. | *Inglistán men muqím honá Hindústán men qayám rakhne se mujhko ziyáda pasand hai.* | |
| **246**. He wanted to get on board ship and make his escape from India, but at the last moment he was so beset with creditors that he was unable to get away. | *Usne cháhá ki jaház par charhke Hindústán se bhág jáe, lekin rawánagí ká waqt jab áyá, to itne qarz-khwáh uske dámangír hoga,e, ki jáne nahín páyá.* | Note this expressive word *dámangír*, "holding on to the skirt." |
| **247**. The labour and effort of years through one day's folly have gone for nothing. | *Barson kí mihnat aur koshish ek hí din kí himáqat se akárat ga,í.* | Note *akárat jáná*, to go for nothing, and *akárat karná*, to undo, to nullify. |
| **248**. If at any time he did anything good, he afterwards undid it all by some improper act or other. | *Agar kabhí kuchh nekí bhí kí ho, to píchhe koí harakat be-já karke, usko bhí akárat kar diyá.* | |
| **249**. I can reach the ceiling when I stand on tip-toe. | *Panjon ke bal jab khará hotá, to háth chhat talak pahúnchtá hai.* | *Panjon ke bal*, on tiptoe. |

| English. | Hindustani. | Notes. |
| --- | --- | --- |
| 250. The unfortunate fellow fell headlong to the ground from an upper window of a two-storeyed house. | *Kambakht ek domanzile makán kí úpar wálí khiṛkí se zamín par sir ke bhal gir paṛá.* | *Sir ke bhal*, headlong. |
| 251. Walk quietly and speak in whispers, so as not to disturb the patient. | *Dabe páon se chaliyo, aur bolne ke waqt phusphusáke boliyo, na ho ki áwáz bímár ke kán tak pahúnchke usko diqq kare.* | *Dabe páon se chalná*, to walk quietly or softly. |
| 252. This young man is so refractory that he won't obey even his own father. | *Yih jawán aisá mutamarrid hai, ki báp tak ko bhí nahín mántá.* | This interposition of *tak* between the noun and the ordinary preposition, to increase the emphasis, is common, and should be noted. The two next sentences are similar instances. |
| 253. They had not even time to make their wills. | *Wasíyat karne tak kí muhlat na thí.* | From the Taubatu-n-Nasúh. |
| 254. Before I had time to say Yes (or "I had not time to say Yes before,") he lifted me up into the carriage. | *Hámí bharne tak kí muhlat na milí, ki itne men usne mujhko uṭhákar gáṛí men baiṭhá díyá.* | The real meaning of *hámí bharná* (small "h") is "to say yes," hence to consent, to agree. |

| English. | Hindustani. | Notes. |
|---|---|---|
| **255.** A turning of the tables indeed, for the thief to give the police officer a dressing! | *Ulṭá chor kotwál ko ḍánḍe!* | This one word *ulṭá* corresponds to, and fully expresses, our phrases "turning the tables," "reversing the order of things," &c., and where so used, it always agrees in form with the agent. 255 and 256 are Hindustani proverbs. |
| **256.** It is a case of opportunity entirely, when the heron pounces on the falcon. | *Samai paṛe kí bát, báz par jhapṭe bagulá.* | |
| **257.** When harsh things were said to him, he turned them off with a smile. | *Sakht bát sunkar, ulṭe muskurá dete the.* (*Taubatu-n-Nasúh.*) | |
| **258.** I took their part against you. | *Main ulṭí unkí himáyat letí thí.* (*Taubatu-n-Nasúh.*) | |
| **259.** He wouldn't stop for me. | *Mere rokne se nahín ruká.* | |
| **260.** This conjurer turns sticks into snakes. | *Yih jádúgar lakṛiyon ko sámp kar dikhátá hai.* | *Kar dikháná* is a somewhat puzzling phrase: it means to change one thing into another; it also means, in a more general sense, to carry out, to perform. |
| **261.** Two men were fighting in the bazaar, and on my going to separate them (or "to mediate between them,") one of them hit me on the head with his lathi. | *Do shakhs bázár men laṛ rahe the, main jo bích-bicháo karne gayá, to ek ne mere sir par láṭhí márí.* | |

| English. | Hindustani. | Notes. |
|---|---|---|
| 262. Formerly this man was a very bad character, but he is now quite reformed. | Pahle yih sha<u>kh</u>s bahut hí bad-chalan thá, par ab to isláh-pazír hogayá hai. | The affix *pazír* means "receiving," "partaking of," "subject to," &c. |
| 263. This is a man of good character, and he always has been so. | Yih to nek-chalan ádmí hai, aur hamesha se uskí yih kaifiyat hai. | |
| 264. As regards honesty, the two are much of a muchness. | Diyánat-dárí ke e'tibár se in dono<u>n</u> kí kuchh ek hí sí kaifiyat hai. | *Ke e'tibár se* here means "from the point of view of." See sentences 300 and 301. |
| 265. What hardships I had to undergo on this journey, your honour yourself knows. | Is safar me<u>n</u> main ne jaisí kuchh sa<u>kh</u>tiyá<u>n</u> khainchí<u>n</u> thí<u>n</u>, áp ko bhí málúm hai. | This *jaisá kuchh* idiom should be noted. |
| 266. His complaint is that your cattle go into his sugar-cane every day. | Uskí yih shikáyat hai ki tumháre dangar roz uskí íkh me<u>n</u> ba<u>r</u> játe hai<u>n</u>. | In the N.W. Provinces *dangar* is the common word for "cattle," and *ba<u>r</u>ná* for "to enter, go into." The bookword for cattle is *maweshí*. |
| 267. I have lost a cow and two horses from the jungle. | Merí ek gá,e aur do gho<u>r</u>e jangal se ral ga,e. | *Ral jáná* is in common use in the N.W.P. for "to be lost, to stray." |

| English. | Hindustani. | Notes. |
|---|---|---|
| **268.** This horse's shoes are a good deal worn; have him re-shod. | *Is ghoṛe ke nál khiyá ga,e hain; unko khulwádo aur na,e nál bandhwádo.* | The verb is *khiyáná*; it would not be right therefore to say *khiye ga,e*, as this would be altering the form of the verb. |
| **269.** Cattle and camels both chew the cud. | *Bail kí zát aur únṭ kí zát donon jugálí kartí hain.* | |
| **270.** Intellect is not confined to any one sex; there are intellectual men and there are intellectual women. | *Ạqlmandí kisí ek jins par munhasir nahín hai; ạqlmand mard bhí hain, ạurat bhí hain.* | *Jins* is the word for "sex." *Munhasir* means "confined, or restricted to," and the preposition used with it is *par*, not *ko*. |
| **271.** This man is a most perfect mimic. | *Taqlíd is shakhs par khatm hai.* | Lit. Mimicry reaches completion in this person. |
| **272.** I greatly dislike having the soles of my feet tickled. | *Páon ke talwon ká dúsre se gudgudáyá jáná mujhko bahut burá lagtá hai.* | |
| **273.** This man is easily put out; his brother is a man of a robust temperament, but his uncle is capricious (or changeable), one thing to-day and another to-morrow. | *Yih ádmí hai tunukmizáj; uská bhái pukhta mizáj ádmí hai, magar uská chachá mizáj ká mutalauwin hai, áj ko achchhá, kal ko burá.* | |
| **274.** In this dispute, without a doubt he was in the right and his brother in the wrong. | *Is takrár men beshakk yih haqq par thá, aur uská bhái náhaqq par.* | |

| English. | Hindustani. | Notes. |
|---|---|---|
| 275. I did not know in what way I ought to send it. | *Yih mujhko málúm nahín thá ki kis sabíl se usko bhej dená cháhiye.* | |
| 276. No doubt this was the Nemesis on his evil deeds. | *Be-shakk yih uskí bad-káriyon kí shámat se húá thá.* | *Shámat* corresponds in meaning to our word Nemesis. |
| 277. But for this a knowledge of the language is a *sine quâ non.* | *Magar is men zabán-dání shart hai.* | *Shart* corresponds to our *sine quâ non.* |
| 278. It is the way of the ungrateful to forget favours bestowed. | *Ne'amaton ká bhulá dená nimak-harámon ká taríqa hai.* | *Bhulá dená* is the causal of *bhúl jáná*, and implies a deliberate act, to banish from the mind. |
| 279. I was prevented yesterday from waiting on your honour by sickness in my family. | *Kal ghar men bímárí hone kí wajh* se main áp ke pás házir hone se mázúr húá thá.* | *Mázúr honá* is to be prevented, in the sense of having a *valid excuse* (uzr) for not doing a thing. The idiom is a common one. * Pron. *wajeh.* |
| 280. This person loses no opportunity of running me down, or of singing the praises of his friend. | *Har waqt aur har mauqa yih shakhs merí mazammat kartá hai, aur apne dost kí tahsín-o-tárif.* | |
| 281. These people plague the very life out of me. | *Yih log merí ján khá játe hain.* | |

| English. | Hindustani. | Notes. |
|---|---|---|
| **282**. You cannot praise this thing too highly. | *Is chíz ko jitná saráhiye ba-já hai.* | *Saráhná* is Hindí for "to praise." |
| **283**. Well, and what do people put this down to? (or "what do they assign as the cause of this?") | *Ák͟hir, log iská sabab kyá qarár dete haiṉ?* (*Taubatu-n-Nasúh.*) | *Qarár dená* means to constitute, to set up, to establish. |
| **284**. This self-constituted (or "this would-be") hero! | *Yih jo apne tà,íṉ bahádur qarár detá hai!* | |
| **285**. In point of fact he is a perfect coward. | *Haqíqat meṉ wuh to buz-dil hai pakká.* | *Buz-dil* means "goat-hearted," and answers to our "chicken-hearted." |
| **286**. These soldiers displayed great cowardice during the action. | *Laṛáí ke waqt in sipáhiyoṉ ne bahut buz-dilí dikhái.* | |
| **287**. If this man is not punished, others will probably be emboldened to do the like acts. | *Agar is ádmí ko sazá na mile, to auroṉ ko bhí sháyad aisí harakatoṉ ká hausila ho.* | Sentences 287 to 290 will show in what sense this word *hausila* is generally used. Perhaps "a spirit to do and dare" would be as good a general meaning to give of the word as any other. |
| **288**. If these people get no reward from Government for this service, their aspirations will be repressed. | *Agar in logoṉ ko is kár-guzárí ke liye sarkár se kuchh inám na mile, to unká hausila past hojáegá.* | Note *kár-guzárí.* |

| English. | Hindustani. | Notes. |
|---|---|---|
| 289. Repeated failures have disheartened (or "discouraged") him. | *Mutawátir ná-kámyábiyon ke sabab ab yih bad-hausila hogayá hai.* | *Mutawátir* means often repeated, constant. |
| 290. He is a very ambitious man. | *Wuh bahut hausilamand ádmí hai.* | |
| 291. The soldiers are tired out through constant marching. | *Mutawátir kúchon ke sabab sipáhí log bahut thake mánde hain.* | |
| 292. The colour of this cloth has become faded through age. | *Yih kaprá bahut din ká puráná hai, is wáste uská rang mánd hogayá hai.* | Note *mánd* for "faded." |
| 293. The light of the moon pales before that of the sun. | *Súraj ke jalwa ke áge chánd kí roshní phíkí* (or "*zard*") *hojátí hai.* | *Phíká* means faint, pale, "washed out." As applied to food, it means insipid. |
| 294. There is a dry well outside the town, the mouth of which is flush with the ground. | *Gánw ke báhar ek to andhá kúá hai, jiská munh zamín-doz hai.* | A dry well is called *andhá* because of the absence of brightness and sparkle which water gives. Note *zamín-doz* for "flush with the ground." |
| 295. As she was all alone in the house, the old woman placed a bedstead against (lit. "across") the door, and then went to sleep. | *Ba nazar iske ki ghar men akelí thí, burhiyá ne ek to chárpáí kiwáron men* (not "*par*") *ará dí thí, aur so ga,í.* | *Ará dená* means to place one thing across another. |

| English. | Hindustani. | Notes. |
|---|---|---|
| 296. The jungle here is very dense; it is utterly impossible for a man to go through it. | *Yahán ká jangal bahut gunján hai; usmen ádmí ká guzar ho hí nahín saktá.* | Note *gunján* for "dense." |
| 297. In my brother's garden the trees stand close together; in my garden they are scattered and far apart. | *Mere bhái ke bágh men darakht hain ghane ghane; mere bágh men hain chhíde chhíde.* | It is common, for the sake of expressiveness to place the adjective, as here, at the end of the clause, and after the verb. *Ghaná* and *chhídá* are opposites. |
| 298. By this will you come in for five thousand rupees. | *Is wasiyat-náma kí rú se tum pánch hazár rúpai ke wáris húe ho.* | "By," in the sense here given, is always rendered *kí rú se.* |
| 299. According to this man the Saheb arrived yesterday. | *Ba qaul is shakhs ke Sáheb kal pahúncha thá.* | *Qaul* here means "word" or "assertion." |
| 300. A horse's colour has to be decided more or less with reference to his mane and tail; a bay horse's tail and mane, for instance, are always black. | *Ghoṛe kí rangat kam-ziyáda yál aur dum ke e'tibár se tajwíz honí cháhiye; maslan, kumait ghoṛe kí dum aur yál hamesha kálí hotí hai.* | This use of *e'tibár* occurs in sentence 264. *E'tibár se* means literally "on the credit of," but in these and similar sentences it means practically "from the point of view of," or "with reference to." |
| 301. From the religious point of view hatred is a great sin. | *Adáwat to díndárí ke etibár se baṛá gunáh hai.* (*Taubatu-n-Nasúh.*) | |

| English. | Hindustani. | Notes. |
|---|---|---|
| 302. This man is not to be trusted. | *Is ádmí ká kuchh e'tibár nahíṉ hai.* | |
| 303. Trot the horse. That will do. Now canter him, and let me see how he goes. | *Ghoṛe ko dulkí chaláo. Bas, ab sarpaṭ dauṛáo, maíṉ dekhúṉ kaisá játá.* | |
| 304. The roan reared with me to-day out riding and fell backwards. | *Chíná ghoṛá áj hamárí sawárí meṉ síkh-pá hogayá thá, aur dum kí taraf se gir paṛá.* | Note *síkh-pá* for "rearing." |
| 305. This morning, at the first glimmer of dawn, he started for Delhi in an ekka, and he will return in the evening on a pony. | *Áj baṛí fajr ko, pau phaṭne ke waqt, wuh ba-sawárí ikke ke Dillí gayá thá, phir shám ko ba-sawárí ṭaṭṭú ke wápas áwegá.* | There is no distinction in Hindustani between riding and driving; both are *sawárí*. It would of course be quite correct to say *ikke meṉ gayá*, or *ṭaṭṭú par áwegá*, instead of the form here given. |
| 306. All my horses have bushy tails. | *Mere sab ghoṛoṉ kí dumeṉ guchchhedár haiṉ* (or "*lachchhedár*.") | |
| 307. O King! forego the blood (spare the life) of me the unfortunate one, and take (confiscate) the whole of my property, which is beyond reckoning and computation. | *Ai bádsháh! mujh kambakht ke khún se darguzar kar, aur jitná mál merá hai (ki gintí aur shumár se báhar hai) sabko zabt kar le.* (*Bágh-o-Bahár.*) | Note the substitution of *ki* in this sentence for our "which." *Jo* should never be used in such cases. This is one of the peculiar idioms of the language. |
| 308. You want to talk me over. | *Mujhe tú bátoṉ meṉ phuslátá hai.* (*Bágh-o-Bahár.*) | |

| English. | Hindustani. | Notes. |
|---|---|---|
| **309.** Mortality is such a self-evident thing, that no one in the world thinks of denying it. | *Faná ek aisí badíhí bát hai, ki dunyá men koí uská munkir nahín hai.* (*Taubatu-n-Nasúh.*) | Note *badíhí* for "self-evident." *Munkir=inkár karnewálá.* |
| **310.** All living things in the world are subject to mortality (or "mortal"). | *Dunyá kí kull jándár chízen faná-pazír hain* (or "*fání*"). | This affix *pazír* occurs in sentence 262. |
| **311.** Not long ago these people were cannibals; they have now become more or less civilized. | *Kuchh din pahle yih log mardum-khor the; ab to kisí qadar ádmiyat pakrí hai.* | Note *ádmiyat pakarná* and *ádmiyat men áná*, to become civilized. |
| **312.** Since these people became civilized, they have given up their evil habits. | *In logon ne jab se ádmiyat men á,e, apní burí ádaton ko chhor diyá hai.* | |
| **313.** When a man's habits have become fixed, it is no easy thing to change his manner of life. | *Jab ádmí kí ádaten rásikh hogaí hain, to apní tarz-i-zindagí ko badalná ásán amr nahín hai.* | Note *rásikh* for "fixed, established." *Tarz*, manner, occurs once before in sentence 203. |
| **314.** These people haven't a spark of humanity in them. | *In logon men insániyat kí bú tak nahín hai.* | Note this substitution of *bú* (smell) for our "spark" or "vestige." Also of *tak* for *bhí*. Not only is the former (meaning "so much as") more emphatic, but *bú bhí* would be a particularly awkward combination. |
| **315.** Women are more soft-hearted and sympathetic than men. (Lit. "As compared with men, in the hearts of women there is," &c.) | *Mardon kí nisbat auraton ke dilon men narmí aur riqqat* (sympathy) *ziyáda hotí hai.* (*Taubatu-n-Nasúh.*) | |

| English. | Hindustani. | Notes. |
|---|---|---|
| **316.** You will have noticed in that book what insistence there is on (the duty of) sympathy for others. | *Hamdardí kí jaisí kuchh tákíd hai, tum ne us kitáb men̲ dekhá hogá.* (*Taubatu-n-Nasúh*). | This phrase *jaisá kuchh* occurs in sentence 265. |
| **317.** Sympathy for others is not only an essential of Christianity, it is an essential of humanity. | *Hamdardí shart-i-ísáiyat, balki shart-i-insániyat hai.* (*Taubatu-n-Nasúh*). | This meaning of *shart* occurs in sentence 277. |
| **318.** If he had not urged me I should never have gone. | *Agar isne isrár na kiyá hotá, to main̲ kabhí na gayá hotá.* | *Isrár* means pressing, urging, persistence; *isrár karná*, to press, to urge. |
| **319.** If the patient will not eat of his own accord, urge him to take a little, or all his strength will go. | *Agar bímár ápse na kháe, to isrár karke thoṛá sá usko khilá díjiyo, nahín̲ to uskí táqat játí rahegí.* | *Játá rahná* means to fail, to cease, &c. |
| **320.** He compelled me. | *Usne mujhko majbúr kiyá.* | |
| **321.** I was altogether at his mercy (*i.e.* "in his power"), and what I did, I did under compulsion. | *Main̲ to bilkull uske bas men thá: jo kuchh main̲ ne kiyá, majbúrí se kiyá.* | Note *majbúrí se* for "under compulsion." |
| **322.** He replied without hesitation that he would go. | *Usne be-ta,ammul jawáb díyá, ki achchhá, main̲ jáún̲.* | The usual meaning of *ta,ammul* is hesitation, or pause. Literally it means reflection. |

| English. | Hindustani. | Notes. |
|---|---|---|
| 323. After a considerable pause he replied, No, Sir, I cannot do this. | *Kuchh der tak ta,ammul karke jawáb díyá, ki nahín, Sáheb, yih kám main nahín kar saktá.* | |
| 324. Don't be in a flurry, don't be alarmed; no one will do anything to you. | *Haṛbaṛáo mat, ghabráo mat, tum se koí kuchh nahín karegá.* | |
| 325. It is not well to do anything in a flurry. | *Harbaṛí se kám karná achchhá nahín hai.* | It is important to notice the difference between *haṛbaṛí* and *utáole-pan*: the one means flurry, and the other, hurry. |
| 326. Work done in a hurry is never well done. | *Jo kám utáole-pan se kiyá játá, kabhí achchhá nahín hotá.* | |
| 327. This man's shop is not prospering, on the contrary it is going down. | *Is shakhs kí baṛhiyá dukán nahín hai, balki ghaṭiyá dukán hai.* | The two principal meanings of *balki* are "moreover," and "on the contrary." |
| 328. He says the river is slightly risen to-day; if it had fallen, the boat could never have gone. | *Wuh kahtá ki nadí ke pání men áj thoṛá sá baṛháo húá hai; agar ghaṭáo húá hotá, to kishtí kabhí nahín já saktí thí.* | As shown here, *baṛhná* and *ghaṭná* are opposites. |
| 329. This horse goes better down-hill than up. | *Ba nisbat chaṛhái ke yih ghoṛá utár men kuchh achchhá játá hai.* | *Chaṛhái ki nisbat se* (both forms meaning "as compared with") would be equally correct. |

| English. | Hindustani. | Notes. |
|---|---|---|
| **330.** Mediating between combatants does not always end pleasantly for the mediator. | *Laṛnewálon men bích-bicháo karná báẓí auqát darmiyání ke liye khair-anjám nahín hotá.* | It should be noted that though *waqt* in the singular is masculine, the plural *auqát* is feminine. *Báẓí auqát* means "occasionally," *aksar auqát* means "generally." |
| **331.** If I undertake this labour, what remuneration shall I get? | *Agar main yih mihnat uṭháún, to merí kyá ujrat hogí?* | |
| **332.** Unremunerated labour is distasteful to most people. | *Be-ujrat-wálí mihnat aksar logon ko ná-pasand hotí hai.* | |
| **333.** I am not going to undertake such an impossibility. | *Aisí anhoní ká bíṛá main nahín uṭhátá. (Taubatu-n-Nasúh.)* | *Bíṛá uṭháná* is a figurative expression, meaning to undertake, to make oneself responsible for. |
| **334.** He says that I approved of this practice, whereas, as a matter of fact I have always opposed it. | *Yih kahtá ki main is amal ká rawádár thá, hálánki main pahle se uská muzáhim ho rahá hún.* | *Hálánki* means literally, "the fact being that," and it answers to our "whereas, as a matter of fact," "whereas really," &c. |
| **335.** There was no comparison between his strength and that of his rival (or "opponent"). | *Uskí táqat aur uske haríf ke zor se pásang kí kuchh nisbat na thí.* (A quotation.) | This *pásang* idiom (*pásang* being the make-weight in a pair of scales) is a favourite one with native writers. It corresponds to our expressions, "to counterbalance," "to outweigh." In sentence 335 the word means "equality." |

| English. | Hindustani. | Notes. |
|---|---|---|
| **336.** The offence of which this sinner has been guilty is such, that the treasure of the whole world would fail to counterbalance it. | *Yih taqsír is gunahgár se sarzad húí, ki khazána tamám ąlam ká uske pásang men na chaṛhe.* (*Bágh-o-Bahár*). | *Sarzad hona,* to occur, to happen. |
| **337.** This man has outstripped all his rivals. | *Yih shakhs apne sab harífon se sabqat legayá hai.* | *Sabqat lejáná* means the carrying off by one competitor of something which several competitors have been striving for; hence "to outstrip," "to surpass." |
| **338.** England has in this matter outstripped all other countries. | *Inglistán ká mulk is bát men aur sab mulkon se sabqat legayá hai.* | |
| **339.** This colour which you see is not its natural colour, it is artificial. | *Yih rang jo tum dekhte ho, uská qudratí rang nahín hai, masnúį rang hai.* | Note *qudratí* and *masnúį.* |
| **340.** These people act in the way natural to them. | *Yih log apne qudratí taur par ąmal karte hain.* | |
| **341.** This is not his real name, it is an assumed one. | *Yih uská asl nám nahín hai, farzí hai.* | Note *farzí* for fictitious, assumed. |
| **342.** To bathe in the river underneath a high overhanging bank is a very dangerous practice. | *Ḍháng ke níche daryáo men nahâná bahut khatar-nák ąmal hai.* | *Ḍháng* means a high overhanging bank or cliff. |

| English. | Hindustani. | Notes. |
| --- | --- | --- |
| 343. Now that she has been relieved to some extent of household worries, she will be able to turn her attention to other matters. | *Ab jo khánadárí ke bakheṛon se wuh thoṛí bahut* (or "*kisí qadar*") *subuk-dosh húí hai, to aur kámon kí taraf mutawajjih ho sakegí.* | Note *bakheṛe* for "worries," and *subuk-dosh* for "relieved," or "rid of." |
| 344. This man's face has become wrinkled through age. | *Is ádmí ke chihre par buṛhápe ke sabab jhurriyán paṛ gaín hain.* | |
| 345. There is a fissure in that rock. | *Us chaṭán men shigáf hai.* | |
| 346. Stuff some pieces of cloth into the chink in the door, and place the bar across the window. | *Kiwáṛ ke darz men kuchh ṭukre kapṛe-latte ṭhos deo, aur khiṛkí men ḍanḍe ko aṛá do.* | *Ṭhos dená,* to cram, to stuff in. *Aṛá dená* occurs in sentence 295. |
| 347. The ground about here is always moist. | *Is jagah kí zamín hamesha namnák rahtí hai.* | |
| 348. Mould gets on to things owing to the dampness of the ground. | *Zamín kí namnákí kí wajh se chízon par phaphundí lag játí hai.* | |
| 349. I am anxious that no one should get to know of this. | *Main cháhtá ki yih bát kisí par záhir na hone páwe.* | Note that the preposition in these sentences is not *ko* but *par.* |
| 350. So far, no one knows anything of the matter. | *Ab tak yih bát kisí par nahín khulí.* | |

| English. | Hindustani. | Notes. |
| --- | --- | --- |
| **351.** I feel sure there is not a soul in the town who does not know of it. | *Yaqín hai ki shahr men ek bhí nahín hai ki jispar yih bat áshkára na húí ho.* | Lit. To whom it is not manifest. |
| **352.** You should certainly apprise the Saheb of this. | *Tumko is bát se albatta Sáheb ko ágáh karná cháhiye.* | |
| **353.** Getting wind of this, the thief bolted. | *Is bát kí ágáhí pákar, chor bhág gayá.* | |
| **354.** Taking the average of the last five years, he found there had been an average rainfall in each year of about thirty inches. | *Pichhle pánchon sál ká ausat lagákar, usne daryáft kiyá, ki is hisáb se har ek sál men takhmínan tís inch kí bárish pari húí thí.* | Note *ausat* for 'average,' and *takhmínan* for 'about.' |
| **355.** Tell him to give an estimate of the probable cost of the work. | *Usse kahdo ki is kám kí lágat ká takhmína de.* | |
| **356.** His affairs are in great confusion at present: he hopes as soon as he has got them a little straight, to carry out your honour's order. | *Is waqt uske muámalát kí bari abtarí húí: wuh cháhtá ki kuchh sídhe aur rú-ba-ráh hojáen, to áp ká hukm ba-já lawegá.* | Note *abtarí* for "confusion," "disorder." |
| **357.** This man does not belong to our party, he belongs to the opposite (or 'rival') party. | *Yih ádmí hamáre thok ká nahín hai, hamáre haríſon ke thok ká hai.* | *Thok* means a party, set, or clique. |

| English. | Hindustani. | Notes. |
|---|---|---|
| **358**. The custom is not peculiar to this country; it is to be found in other countries also. | *Yih riwáj is mulk se khusúsiyat nahín rakhtá; aur mulkon men bhí páyá játá hai.* | |
| **359**. My brother won that game of chess; I was beaten. | *Us shatranj kí bází men merá bháí bází legayá, main hár gayá thá.* | |
| **360** The farmers are feeling very anxious about their crops just now, owing to the want of rain. | *Kisán logon ko bárish na hone ke sabab apní khetiyon ke liye is waqt au-desha bahut hai.* | |
| **361**. With the exception of this man, no one opposes this. | *Ba-juz is shakhs ke aur koí is bát ká máni nahín hotá hai.* | *Ba-juz* followed by *ke*, "with the exception of." |
| **362**. Instead of milk he gave me water. | *Ba-jáe dúdh ke usne mujhko pání díyá.* | *Ba-jáe* followed by *ke*, "instead of." |
| **363**. These are very straightforward people, and upright in their dealings. | *Yih bahut sídhe-sádhe log hain, aur beohár ke khare.* | It may be interesting to note that while *khaṛá* spelt with the hard or dotted "ṛ" means upright, in the sense of "erect," *khará* spelt with the ordinary "r" means upright in practice. *Beohár* is a good word for "business dealings." |
| **364**. There is nothing to be afraid of. Go to the Saheb and state your case to him without misgiving. | *Ḍarne kí bát nahín hai, Sáheb ke pás jáo aur be-khaṭke apná hál bayán karo.* | |

| English. | Hindustani. | Notes. |
|---|---|---|
| 365. The people about here are in constant dread of this man. | *Yahán ke logon ke dilon men is ádmí ká har waqt dagh-dagha rahtá hai.* | |
| 366. The people in this neighbourhood use horses for ploughing, not bullocks. | *Is gird-nawáh ke log hal jotne men ghoṛe ká isti'mál karte hain, bail ká nahín.* | |
| 367. I put him up the whole of the time that he stayed in Calcutta. | *Jitne din wuh Kalkatte men ṭhahrá, main ne usko apne ghar men ṭhahrá rakhá thá.* | *Ṭhairná* and *ṭhairáná* is the spelling adopted by some. |
| 368. The ungrateful fellow has forgotten all the benefits conferred on him by the Saheb. | *Saheb kí sab neamaten is nimak-harám ne bhulá dín hain.* | |
| 369, After a while he managed to become more or less intimate with the people of the place. | *Kuchh din ke bád wahán ke logon se us ne thoṛá bahut irtibát baham pahúncháyá.* | *Irtibát* means terms of intimacy. |
| 370. The good news has come from the police-station that the ringleader of this gang has at last been caught. | *Tháne se yih khush-khabarí ái hai, ki is giroh ká sarghana ab pakṛá húá hai.* | Note *sarghana* for "ringleader." |
| 371. It was raining cats and dogs when he reached my house. | *Jiswaqt wuh mere ghar pahúnchá, menh múslá dhár barastá thá.* | |

| English. | Hindustani. | Notes. |
|---|---|---|
| 372. Why did you do this without letting the Saheb know? | *Sáheb kí be-ittilá yih kám tum ne kyún kiyá?* | *Be-ittilá* is the correct way of expressing this. |
| 373. There are quantities of water collected in the low places. | *Nashebon men ḍher pání jama hogayá hai.* | Note *nasheb* and *ḍher.* |
| 374. Keep this by you until you need it; it is sure to come in useful some day. | *Is ko zarúrat ke waqt tak tum apne pás rakho; ek roz zarúr kár-ámad hogá.* | *Kár-ámad honá* is simply another form of *kám áná.* |
| 375. I am not a free agent in the matter, I am bound by the Saheb's order. | *Is men merá kuchh ikhtiyár nahín hai, main Sáheb ke hukm ká páband hún.* | *Páband* means "bound by," or "devoted to." |
| 376. This is mere conventionality, nothing else. | *Yih sirf rasm kí pábandí kí bát hai, aur kuchh nahín.* | |
| 377. He does this simply because it is the fashion to do it, and yet he considers it meritorious. | *Wuh sirf rasm kí pábandí hí se yih kám kartá, phir jáe-sawáb samajhtá hai.* | |
| 378. She was in this state of suspense (fear and hope) for three days, she then got tidings of her husband's safety. | *Is khauf wa rijá men tín roz tak rahí, bád uske uske shauhar kí salámatí kí khabar áí.* | |

| English. | Hindustani. | Notes. |
|---|---|---|
| **379.** He can't make up his mind whether to do it or not to do it. | *Is bát ke taraddud meṉ hai, ki áyá karná cháhiye yá nahíṉ karná cháhiye.* | *Taraddud* means irresolution: *ki áyá* means "whether." |
| **380.** He is now grown up, and independent of me. | *Ab wuh jawán húá, aur mujh se be-niyáz.* | Note *be-niyáz* for "independent." |
| **381.** They say that justice was not done in this case, but that on the contrary there was a miscarriage of justice. | *Log kahte haiṉ ki is muqaddame meṉ insáf nahíṉ húá. balki be-insáfí húí thí.* | Here we have *balki* in the sense of "on the contrary." *Haqq-rasání* and *haqq-talafí* are substitutes for *insáf* and *be-insáfí.* |
| **382.** The paragraph (or passage) which the pleader cited in his speech, did not really apply to the case at all. | *Wuh fiqra ki jiská vakíl ne apní taqrír meṉ hawála díyá thá, dar asl is muqaddame meṉ mutlaq á,id nahíṉ hotá thá.* | *Hawála dená,* to cite as authority; *taqrír,* speech; *á,id honá,* to be applicable, or relevant to. |
| **383.** This magistrate is a bribe-taker, and a great perverter of justice. | *Yih hákim rishwat le-newálá hai, aur haqq-talafí bahut kartá hai.* | |
| **384.** These people are utterly wanting in appreciation. | *Yih log qadar-dání se bilkull be-bahra haiṉ.* | Note *be-bahra* and *be-nasib,* both meaning "wanting, deficient." *Árí* (spelt with an *ain*) is another word for devoid or destitute of, or "free from." |

| English. | Hindustani. | Notes. |
|---|---|---|
| 385. They are also wanting in a sense of what is right. | *Haqq-shinásí se bhí be-nasíb hain̲.* | |
| 386. Without doubt this man is the rightful owner of this property. | *Be-shakk yih ádmí is mál ká haqq-dár hai.* | |
| 387. He himself admits the reasonableness of this. | *Is bát kí mạqúliyat ká wuh k͟hud qá,il hai.* | |
| 388. All who have seen this thing, without exception, bear witness to its excellence. | *Jitne logon̲ ne is chíz ko dekhá hai, sab ke sab uskí ụmdagí par gawáhí dete hain̲.* | Note *ụmdagí* for "excellence." |
| 389. What an excellent decision! | *Kyá ụmda tạjwíz húí!* | |
| 390. I can do nothing in this matter; I have tried plan after plan, and not one of them answers. | *Is bát men̲ mujh se kuchh ban nahín̲ paṛtá; tadbír par tadbír main̲ ne nikálí, magar ek se bhí kám nikaltá nahín̲.* | Note *ban paṛná* and *kám nikalná.* |
| 391. Well then, you won't try severity, and gentleness doesn't answer; so at last we come to this, that nothing can be done (or "so the case is hopeless.") | *Bhalá, phir sak͟htí karoge nahín̲, aur narmí se kám nikaltá nahín̲; ák͟hir wuhí bát húí, ki honá huwáná kuchh nahín̲ hai.* (*Taubatu-n-Nasúh.*) | *Honá huwáná nahín̲ honá* means that the case is hopeless. |

| English. | Hindustani. | Notes. |
|---|---|---|
| **392**. It never even entered his head (lit. "mind") that he was himself the person spoken of. | *Yih bát uske zihn men̲ bhí nahin̲ guzrí, ki k͟hud usíki nisbat yih kahá gayá ho.* | Note *zihn* for "mind." |
| **393**. He has no legal right whatever to interfere in this matter. | *Is bát men dak͟hl dene ká wuh hargiz majáz nahín̲ hai.* | *Majáz* means legally entitled, or competent. |
| **394**. On inquiry it turned out that it was the hero Bikramájit, but no one could realize that since he had left a considerable time had elapsed. | *Pursish ahwál se málúm húá ki bír Bikramájít hai, lekin use nikle muddat jo guzar ga,í thí pahcháná na játá thá.* (*Áráish-i-mahfil*). | Use *nikle*. See sentences 4 and 5 and the notes thereon. The meaning here is, that it seemed no time whatever since he had left. |
| **395**. After serving the Government for twenty years, he has now retired into private life. | *Bís baras tak sarkár kí k͟hidmat-guzárí kí; ab wuh alag ho baiṭhá hai.* | |
| **396**. After years of friendship, these two have now fallen out. | *Barson̲ kí dostí ke bád, ab yih donon̲ ápas men̲ bigaṛ baiṭhe hai.* | This use of *baiṭhná* with another verb should be noted: it implies continuance. |
| **397**. This boy failed ("did not succeed") in his examination. | *Yih laṛká imtihán men̲ kámyáb nahin̲ húá.* | *Kámyáb honá*, *surk͟hrú honá*, and *uhdabará honá*, all mean "to succeed." *Surk͟hrú* (red-faced) suggests our own phrase, "flushed with success." |

| English. | Hindustani. | Notes. |
|---|---|---|
| **398**. The pleader did not win his case, on the contrary he lost it. | *Vakíl us muqaddame men surkh-rú nahín niklá, balki zich húá thá.* | *Zich honá*, to be worsted, or beaten. |
| **399**. The demon could not get the better of him, so he bolted. | *Deo usse uhda-bará na húá, aur bhágá.* (*Áráish-i-Mahfil.*) | |
| **400**. If my plans succeed, I shall make a lot of money. | *Merí tadbíren pesh-raft hon, to bahut sá rúpíyá háth áwegá.* | We have had *pesh-raft* before, in sentence 117. |
| **401**. Those people must be crowing over our failure. | *Wuh log hamárí ná-kámyábí par shádiyána bajáte honge.* | |
| **402**. The father of the boy is very jubilant over his son's success. | *Larke ká báp apne bete kí kámyábí par bahut ríjhtá hai.* | |
| **403**. This man is always grumbling at his lot, though as a matter of fact he is far better off than others. | *Yih ádmí apne nasíb par hamesha kurkurátá hai, hálánki ba nisbat auron ke uská nasíb kahín bihtar hai.* | See note to 334 on meaning of *hálánki*. |
| **404**. This man never tells the truth even by accident. | *Yih ádmí kabhí bhúlkar bhí sach nahín boltá.* | *Bhúlkar bhí* exactly answers to our "even by accident," in the sense of "through inadvertence." |
| **405**. Daily exercise is necessary for health. | *Roz kí riyázat tandurustí ke liye zarúr hai.* | |

| English. | Hindustani. | Notes. |
|---|---|---|
| 406. Through old age both his intellect and strength are beginning to fail. | *Buṛhápe ke sabab uskí aql aur táqat donon̲ zá,il hone lagín̲.* | *Zá,il honá*, to fail, to diminish, to be on the decline. |
| 407. Being quite young, when he saw this ruffian standing before him, he was extremely frightened. | *Azbaski kam-umr thá, jab us muṭh-mard ko apne sámne khaṛá dekhá, to bahut hí ḍar gayá.* | *Azbaski* means "owing to," or "in consequence of." |
| 408. If you make it your object at all times and in all things to please the Saheb, I feel sure you will shortly be promoted. | *Agar tum har waqt aur har bát men̲ Sáheb kí khushnúdí se kám rakhoge, to yaqín hai ki thoṛe din men̲ tumhárí taraqqí hogí.* | *Kisí bát se kám rakhná* means to aim at that particular thing. |
| 409. Always bear in mind that without labour and effort promotion is not to be looked for. | *Is bát par hamesha khiyál rahe, ki baghair mihnat aur koshish ke taraqqí mutaswwir hí nahín̲.* | Lit. "Let it always be borne in mind." |
| 410. This thing is so spoilt that it can never come right again. | *Yih chíz aisí bigaṛ gaí, ki ab sudhar nahín̲ saktí.* | *Bigaṛná*, to go wrong.<br>*Sudharná*, to get right again. |
| 411. It has got spoilt it is true, but it must be put right again as far as possible. | *Bigaṛ to ga'í hai, lekin jahán̲ tak ho sake usko phir sudhárná cháhiye.* | *Sudhárná*, to put to rights, to rectify. |
| 412. Examine your money, and see whether it is right or not. | *Apná rúpiya sahej lo, durust hai yá nahín̲.* | *Sahejná* means to examine, in the sense here given. |

| English. | Hindustani. | Notes. |
|---|---|---|
| **413.** He is putting his affairs in order just at present. | *Iswaqt wuh apne umúr ko sanwár rahá hai.* | *Sanwárna* means to adjust, to arrange, to put in order. |
| **414.** This is a very easy matter. | *Yih to bahut sahl kám hai.* | |
| **415.** This man is left-handed, but so strong that he can lift a weight of five maunds with ease. | *Yih ádmí báen-hathá hai, magar aisá zoráwar ki pánch man ká wazn sahaj se uṭhá saktá hai.* | *Sahaj se* means easily, or with ease. |
| **416.** At last his incapacity became so very apparent, that he had to be dismissed. | *Ákhir uskí na-rasáí aisí záhir hoga,í, ki usko barkhást karná paṛá.* | *Ná-rasáí* means incapacity, "not being up to the mark," as we say. |
| **417.** Did not I warn you from the first that this man was wanting in ability? | *Pahle se main ne tumhen jatá diyá na ki yih ádmí kam-isti'-dád hai?* | *Isti,dád* means ability, capacity. |
| **418.** His brother is a man of extraordinary ability. | *Uske bhái kí parle darje kí liyáqat hai.* | *Parle darje ká* has exactly the meaning of "extraordinary." |
| **419.** This is my last resource. | *Yih merí háre darje kí tadbír hai.* (*Taubatu-n-Násuh.*) | *Háre darje kí tadbír* answers also to our "forlorn hope." |
| **420.** This is a first-class shop. | *Yih to awwal darje kí dukán hai.* | 416 and 417 are from the *Áráish-i-mahfil.* |
| **421.** Of a truth, that which is to be will be. | *Sach hai ki hone-wálí bát bin húe nahín rahtí.* | *Bin húe nahín rahní* means to be inevitable, and *nazar* |

| English. | Hindustani. | Notes. |
| --- | --- | --- |
| **422.** Such clouds of dust arose that both earth and sky were hidden. | *Gard wa ghubár is qadar uṛá ki zamín o ásmán nazar áne se rahgayá.* | *áne se rahjáná,* to be obscured, or hidden. Note that *zamín* and *ásmán* are treated as forming one common whole, so that the verb is in the singular. This is very common in Hindustani. |
| **423.** A third said something else, but no one really knew for certain (*ba-tahqíq*) how he had got there. | *Tísrá aur kuchh kahtá thá, magar kisíko ba-tahqíq má-lúm na húá ki wuh kyúnkar wahán par áyá.* | |
| **424.** It is quite evident from his way of speaking that he is not a man of this country, but a foreigner. | *Uskí tarz i kalám se sáf záhir hai ki wuh is mulk ká nahín hai, kisí ghair mulk ká ádmí hogá.* | *Tarz* means form, tenor, style. |
| **425.** I feel certain from the way he describes it, that he could never have seen what took place with his own eyes. | *Uskí tarz i bayán se mujhko yaqín hai ki is májará ko isne apní ánkhon se kabhí nahín dekhá hogá.* | *Májará* means an occurrence, "that which happens." |
| **426.** He has caught a very big fish today; it has very large scales, and it got caught by the gills. It had swallowed the bait. | *Áj isne ek bahut baṛí machhí pakṛí hai; uske sihre baṛe baṛe, aur uske galphare men bansí lagí thí. Chára nigal gaí thí.* | *Sihrá* is the word for a fish's scale, and *galphará* the word for a fish's gills. |
| **427.** He is a man of middling height and middling size; his father is a very stout man, and his brother a slight man. | *Wuh hai ausat qadd wa ausat badan; uská báp hai dohrá badan, aur uská bhái ikahrá badan.* | *Dohrá badan* means literally double-bodied, and *ikahrá badan* single-bodied. |

| English. | Hindustani. | Notes. |
|---|---|---|
| **428.** The soil here is sandy, for this reason water quickly gets absorbed. | *Yahán kí zamín retílí hai, is wajh se pání us men jaldí se khaptá hai.* | *Khapná* means to sink into, to be absorbed, and also to fit into (something else). |
| **429.** The wretched creatures had such outlandish names, that they would not fit into Kalim's verse, do what he would. | *In kambakhton ke nám aise ṭeṛhe the, ki Kalím ke saje men kisí ḍhab se nahín khapte the.* | 429 is from the *Taubatu-n-Nasúh.* |
| **430.** The water in this river is shallow, not deep. | *Is daryáo ká pání chhichhlá hai, gahrá nahín.* | Note *chhichhlá* for shallow. |
| **431.** Notwithstanding its shallowness, very large fish are caught in it. | *Bá-wujúd chhichhláí pání ke baṛí baṛí machhliyán us men pakṛí játí hain.* | Sentences generally take the Persian form of construction, as here, after words like *bá-wujúd, ba-mújib,* &c. |
| **432.** If the meshes of the net are too large, the smaller fish make their escape through them. | *Jál ke kháne ziyáda baṛe hone se chhoṭí machhliyán un men se nikal játí hain.* | The ordinary Hindustani form here would be, *pání kí chhichhláí ke sáth.* |
| **433.** Blotting paper absorbs the ink. | *Jázib kághaz siyáhí ko jazb kar letá hai.* | *Jazb honá* and *khapná* are equivalents. |
| **434.** Tell the merchant to send the goods in a cart that I bought to-day. | *Saudágar se kahdo ki wuh jins jo main ne áj kharídí thín, gáṛí men karke bhej de.* | Note that the idiom is *gáṛí men karke,* not *rakhke.* Whether we use *kharídná* or *mol lená* is entirely a matter of choice. |

| English. | Hindustani. | Notes. |
|---|---|---|
| **435.** These books reached me through a friend. | *Yih kitáben ek dost kí márifat mere háth pahúnchí hain.* | *Márifat, wasíla,* and *zaria,* and their uses, should all be noted. |
| **436.** This post was conferred on me by Government through the intervention of a friend. | *Ek dost ke wasíle se yih mansab sarkár se mujh ko ináyat húá hai.* | When a vowel has a dot under it the letter is an *'ain.* |
| **437.** He has no ostensible means of subsistence. | *Iská koi záhirí wasíla ma'ásh ká nahín hai.* | *Ma'ásh* means livelihood; hence *bad-ma'ásh,* of bad livelihood. |
| **438.** He sent the Saheb news of the matter by letter. | *Usne khatt ke zarie se is bát kí khabar Sáheb tak pahúncháí.* | |
| **439.** Does your honour know if this person is really connected with the Government? | *Is shakhs ká sach-much sarkár se tawas-sul hai na, áp ko málúm hai?* | *Tawassul* means connection. |
| **440.** He openly declares his intention of having his revenge for this. | *Wuh barmalá kahtá hai, ki is bát ká main zarúr in-tiqám lúngá.* | Note *barmalá* for "openly," or "publicly." |
| **441.** We have doubtless not yet got hold of the real facts of the case. | *Bilá shubha is bát kí aslí máhiyat abtak nahín khulí hai.* | *Máhiyat* means the "essence," the "real character or nature," of a thing. |

| English. | Hindustani. | Notes. |
|---|---|---|
| **442.** This man drags his wife about by the hair of her head. | *Yih ádmí apní 'aurat ko jhonṭon se* (or *jhoṭe se*) *ghasíṭtá hai.* | *Jhonṭá* (used either in the singular or in the plural, as here) means the whole hair of the head. The addition of the word *sir* is unnecessary. *Jhoṭá*, without the "n," is often used. |
| **443.** He tries to win the hearts of some, and to worm the secrets out of others. | *Báẓon kí dil-joí kartá hai, aur báẓon kí ráz-joi bhí kartá hai.* | *Dil-joí* means "heart-seeking," and *ráz-joí*, "secret seeking," as we say, "pumping." |
| **444.** He has also been seeking redress from the Court for four months. | *Chár mahíne se adálat se chára-joí bhí kartá hai.* | |
| **445.** The Court admits (the justice of) your claim; what it objects to is your taking the law into your own hands. | *Adálat tumháre dáwe ko taslím kartí hai, magar yih e'tiráz kartí hai, ki tum ne kyún khud-hákimí kí?* | *E'tiráz* means objection. Note the meaning and force of *khud-hákimí*. |
| **446.** What difference is there between such a man and a beast? None whatever. | *Aise ádmí se haiwán tak kyá farq? Kuchh bhí nahín.* | |
| **447.** Seeing his wife standing up, his sister lying down, and his two sons running, he wondered what could be the matter. | *Apní 'aurat ko khaṛá, apní bahin ko paṛá, aur apne do beṭon ko dauṛtá, dekhkar, usne ta'ajjub kiyá, ki yih kyá hál húá?* | Note that the effect of *ko* after a noun is to do away with both gender and number, so far as the succeeding participle or adjective is concerned, |

| English. | Hindustani. | Notes. |
|---|---|---|
| **448.** This water was very muddy before, it has now become clear, but there is a lot of sediment at the bottom. | *Pahle yih pání bahut gadlá thá, ab to nithrá hogayá hai, lekin uskí tah men̲ talchhaṭ bahut paṛí hai.* | this being invariably in all such cases in the masculine singular. |
| **449.** The bottom of the large earthen jar is broken. | *Baṛe maṭke ká pendá ṭúṭá hai.* | Note that *pendá* and *pendí* are the words for the bottoms of articles of this description according to their size. |
| **450.** The water was so hot that it has broken away the bottom of the tumbler. | *Pání aisá garm thá, ki uskí tezí se gilás kí pendí ṭúṭ niklí hai.* | |
| **451.** He was for some time in a faint, but he has now come round again. | *Wuh kuchh der tak g̲h̲ashí men̲ rahá, lekin ab phir ifáqe men̲ áyá hai.* | *Ifáqe men̲ áná* means to recover from a faint, or from sickness. |
| **452.** He has had a relapse. | *Uskí bímárí ne ạud kiyá hai.* | *Ạud karná* means "to return." It is spelt with an *'ain*. The literal meaning is, "his sickness has returned." |
| **453.** Shall I tie this loose or tight? | *Main̲ isko dhílá bándhún̲ yá kaske bándhún̲?* | |
| **454.** It has now become the regular thing for him to go to the town every morning, and to return home again in the evening. | *Ab yih mạ́múl ṭhahrá, ki roz fajr ko wuh shahr játá, aur phir shám ko ghar par átá.* | *Mạ́múl* means a personal habit or custom. It may or may not be followed by others. *Dastúr* may either have this limited, or a more extended, meaning. |
| **455.** According to his usual habit, he went out to-day for an airing at five o'clock. | *Apne mạ́múlí taur par áj pánch baje ke waqt wuh hawá kháne gayá thá.* | |

| English. | Hindustani. | Notes. |
|---|---|---|
| **456.** Enter this item in the day book in red ink. | *Yih raqam roznámche men lál roshnáí se darj kar do.* | Note that *lál siyáhi* would be a contradiction in terms. *Roshnáí* also means ink. |
| **457.** The whole of the papers are in the office. | *Jumla kághazát daftar-kháne men hain.* | |
| **458.** He closed his eyes. | *Apní ánkhen múnd kar lín.* | *Múndná* is the usual word for the closing of the eyes. |
| **459.** Shut the folding doors. | *Kiwáron ko bher do.* | *Bherná* means to bring two things together, as two folding doors, for instance; and *bhirná*, their being so brought together. |
| **460.** The folding doors are shut already. | *Kiwár to bhire húe hain.* | |
| **461.** The old woman scours her pots and pans so that they shine like silver. | *Burhiyá apne básan bartan ko yún mánjtí hai, ki chándí kí tarah* chamakte hain.* | *Mánjná*, to scour. * Pron. *tareh.* |
| **462.** Her daughter took a winnowing basket and began winnowing the corn. | *Uskí betí chháj leke ghalle ká bhúsá usáne lagí.* | *Ghalla* and *anáj* both mean corn or grain. The contracted form *náj* is also very common. |
| **463.** He has a granary on his premises. | *Uske ghar men ek ambár anáj ká hai.* | |
| **464.** He has just bought a new sickle. | *Ek to nai darántí abhí mol lí hai.* | |

| English. | Hindustani. | Notes. |
|---|---|---|
| 465. His daughter is engaged to my brother. | Uskí betí mere bháí kí mangetar hai. | *Mangetar* is the word for "betrothed," whether it be man or woman. |
| 466. Why should not these two persons be joined together? | In do sha<u>kh</u>so<u>n</u> kí kyú<u>n</u> waslat na ho? | |
| 467. I have heard that this man makes a good deal out of his mill. | Mai<u>n</u> ne suná hai ki yih ádmí apní ásiyá se bahut nafa uṭhátá hai. | |
| 468. When the ground is dry, it quickly drinks in the rain. | Jab zamín súkhí húí, to bárish ko jald pí játí hai. | |
| 469. Water is quickly absorbed in dry ground. | Jab zamín súkhí húí, to pání us me<u>n</u> jald lín hojátá hai. | *Jazb honá, lín honá,* and *khapná* are all synonymous. |
| 470. A law of nature. | <u>Kh</u>ilqat ká qá,ida. | |
| 471. When the sight gets weak, it is well to use glasses. | Jab basárat me<u>n</u> zọf á játá, to chashmak ká isti'mál karná bihtar hai. | When a vowel has a dot under it the letter is an 'ain. |
| 472. This woman has two little children, and her cow has a calf. | Is 'aurat ke áge do chhoṭe bachche hai<u>n</u>, aur uskí gáe ke níche ek bachhrú hai. | This distinction of *áge* and *níche* between human beings and animals should be noted. *Ke pás* is not the idiom here. |
| 473. To lead is the work of the teacher, and to follow is the work of the disciple. | Peshrawí karná ustád ká kám hai, aur pairawí karná shágird ká kám. | |

| English. | Hindustani. | Notes. |
|---|---|---|
| 474. At present he is prosecuting his case in Court. | Bilfẹl wuh adálat meṉ apne muqaddame kí pairawí kartá hai. | |
| 475. It is not yet known what the defendant's defence will be. | Abtak málúm nahíṉ mudda,áleh kí kyá jawáb-dihí hogí. | |
| 476. This man has no force of character; he is very easily led by others. | Yih ádmí mom kí nák hai; jald dúsroṉ kí mutába'at kartá hai. | Lit. "is a nose of wax"—a proverbial expression. |
| 477. Indeed some go so far as to say that he is not really an Englishman at all. | Chunánchi bázlog yih bhí kahte hai ki yih asl Angrez bhí nahíṉ hai. | Chunánchi may also be translated "for example," "for instance." |
| 478. There are two versions of this affair: some say that this man himself began it, while others say that the other man first struck him. | Is bát kí do riwáyateṉ haiṉ: koí log kahte ki pahal isíne kí; phir aur log kahte ki nahíṉ, dúsre shakhs ne pahle isko márá thá. | Pahal karná means here "to be the aggressor." Note riwáyat for "version." |
| 479. The doctor says that such a wound could never have been caused by such a weapon. | Dáktar Sáheb kahtá hai, ki aise hathyár se aisá zakhm kabhí nahíṉ á saktá thá. | Note the idiom in this sentence. Gháo is another word for wound. The words for "wounded" are gháil and zakhmí. |
| 480. He has no assets (or property) whatever, so how can the debt be recovered? | Iskí jáedád hai nahíṉ, phir qarze ká rúpiya kaháṉ se áwegá? | |

| English. | Hindustani. | Notes. |
|---|---|---|
| 481. Don't let him out of your sight for an instant. | *Apní ánkhon se ek lamha ojhal mat hone do.* | Note *ojhal honá.* |
| 482. I had not the moral courage to ask him. | *Mujhko itná yárá na thá ki usse púchhún.* | |
| 483. These people are not well off, they are very poor. | *Yih log ásúda to nahín hain, muflis hain.* | *Ásúdá honá* means to be well or comfortably off. |
| 484. Bring some cloth from the cloth merchant's, some of a lilac colour, some of a purple colour, some of a light green, and some of a light blue colour. | *Bazzáz ke yahán se kaprá lete áiyo, kuchh túsi rang ká, kuchh kákrezí rang ká, kuchh dhání rang ká, aur kuchh ásmání rang ká.* | *Dhání* means the colour of growing rice. Another word for *kákrezí* (plum colour) is *údá.* |
| 485. How is it possible for such an obvious thing to escape the observation of any one? | *Aisi moṭí bát, kyá mumkin ki kisí kí nazar se poshída rahe?* | *Poshída* means hidden, concealed. |
| 486. I took the things from him without examining them. | *Baghair dekhe bhále main ne un chízon ko uske háth se le liyá.* | |
| 487. He put all the books in their proper places. | *Usne sab kitáben ṭhikáne se rakhí thín.* | *Ṭhikáná* means a limited space set apart for a special purpose. |
| 488. By this arrangement you will escape the bother of travelling. | *Is bandobast se tum safar ke harj-marj se bachoge.* | |

| English. | Hindustani. | Notes. |
|---|---|---|
| **489.** He is always talking about his patriotism and loyalty, but he shows very few signs of either. | *Hamesha yih apní watan-dostí aur daulat-khwáhí ká dam bhartá hai, magar ásár uske kam dikhátá hai.* | *Dam bharná* means to talk or boast about a thing. "Either" is not translated here, as *uske* includes it. |
| **490.** The air is impeded by the great number of buildings. | *Imáraton kí kasrat se hawá bár pátí hai.* | Note *bár páná*, to be impeded. |
| **491.** On my poking in the ground with a bit of pointed stick, I turned up a coin. | *Ek ṭukre nokdár lakṛí se jo main ne zamín kurelí thí, to ek sikka niklá thá.* | *Kurelná* means to poke or prod with something small. |
| **492.** He gave me a prod in the side with the end of his stick. | *Apní lakṛí ke húre se usne merí kokh men khod diyá.* | *Húrá* is the word for the end of a stick. *Kokh* is the word generally used for "side." |
| **493.** The bullet did not hit the mark; it went ricochetting away. | *Golí nisháne men na lagí; ṭappe khá khákar chalí gaí.* | *Ṭappá* is the word for the bound of a ball. |
| **494.** Only look at the deer, how he is bounding! | *Hiran ko dekhiye, kuláncheṉ kaisá mártá hai!* | |
| **495.** This woman is so beautiful that all the other women are jealous of her. | *Yih 'aurat aisí khúbsúrat hai, ki aur sab 'auraten uspar rashk khátí hain.* | *Rashk* means jealousy or envy; *rashk kháná*, to be jealous or envious. |
| **496.** Analysis will show of what ingredients this medicine is compounded. | *Tajazzí se málúm hogá ki yih dawá kaun se juzvon se murakkab hai.* | |

| English. | Hindustani. | Notes. |
|---|---|---|
| **497.** In all the flower-beds in my garden flowers of various kinds are blooming. | *Mere chaman kí sab kiyáriyon men phúl mukhtalif qismon ke phúl rahe hain.* | *Chaman* is a flower-garden, and *kiyárí* a flower-bed. |
| **498.** This bridge is suspended by its two ends; it rests on nothing between; from the one side (of the river) to the other it has absolutely no support (*or* prop). | *Yih pul donon siron se mu'ạllaq hai; bích men kisí chíz par nahín ṭiktá; us pár se leke is pár tak ṭek zarrá bhí nahín hai.* | Note this description of a suspension bridge—*Mu'ạllaq*, *ṭikná*, *ṭek*, &c. |
| **499.** This man outstripped his rival in the race, and carried off the prize. | *Dauṛ men isne apne haríf ko píchhe ḍálá, aur bází legayá.* | Note *píchhe ḍálná*, to outstrip, and *píchhe paṛná*, to fall behind. |
| **500.** His rival has lost heart at having fallen behind, and says he shall not run again. | *Uská haríf píchhe paṛne ke sabab badhausila hogayá hai, aur kahtá ki phir nahín dauṛegá.* | |
| **501.** It is incumbent on (*or* the duty of) every man, of whatsoever country he be, to honour his parents. | *Har ek ádmí par, go wuh kisí mulk ká kyún na ho, farz hai ki apne má báp kí ịzzat kare.* | This peculiar idiom from *go* to *na ho* should be noted. |
| **502.** All the money I have with me will not suffice to pay for this. | *Mere pás ká kull rúpiya iskí qímat ko kifáyat na karegá.* | *Kifáyat karná* to suffice. |

| English. | Hindustani. | Notes. |
|---|---|---|
| **503**. I see a thousand difficulties in this matter. | *Is bát men̲ main̲ hazár diqqaten̲ dekhtá hún̲.* | |
| **504**. I threw my arms round him from behind. | *Main̲ ne píchhe kí taraf se uskí kaulí bhar lí.* | An idiom to be noted. |
| **505**. The girl was singing in the house and the birds in the trees. | *Laṛkí ghar men̲ gá rahí thí, aur darak͟ht͟on̲ par chiṛiyán̲ bhí chahchahá rahí thín̲.* | |
| **506**. The pain was so severe that he could not bear it. | *Dard aisá shadíd* (or *sak͟ht*) *thá ki wuh uskí táb na lá saká.* | *Táb láná*, to bear, to endure = *bardásht karná.* |
| **507**. He was so stiff that he could not hold himself straight. | *Akṛáṭ ke sabab wuh sídhá nahín̲ ho saktá thá.* | Lit. "on account of stiffness." |
| **508**. In the technical language of accountants any writing in an account is called a *raqam*. | *Mutasaddiyon̲ kí istiláh men̲ koí likháwaṭ jo hisáb men̲ kí játí hai raqam kahlátí hai.* | *Istiláh* means technical language or phraseology. |
| **509**. This word does not occur in ordinary conversation. | *Yih lafz rozmarre kí bol-chál men̲ nahín̲ átá.* | |
| **510**. What instruction can be got from this person? He is utterly illiterate. | *Is shak͟hs se kyá tạlím ho saktí hai? Wuh to ummí mahz hai.* | *Ummí* means illiterate, totally uneducated. *Mahz* means mere, sheer, utter; and it generally comes after the noun it |

| English. | Hindustani. | Notes. |
|---|---|---|
| **511.** Mere talking to him will do no good; unless he is punished he will never mend. | *Usko nirá samjháná kuchh fáida nahín; baghair sazá diye húe wuh kabhí sudharegá nahín.* | qualifies. It is also used as an adverb, and it then generally comes before the noun or object. |
| **512.** The Saheb has accepted his apology. | *Sáheb ne uskí mázúrí qabúl kar lí hai.* | *Mázúrí*, *mázarat*, and *uzr-khwáhí*, all mean "apology." |
| **513.** The arrow-head buried itself between his two shoulder-blades. | *Tír kí gánsí uske donon khauwon ke bích gaṛ gaí.* | *Khauwá* is shoulder-blade. Note these different "points," &c. |
| **514.** The point of his spear entered my thigh, and the point of my sword broke off on his shield. | *Uskí barchhí kí ání merí rán men khub ga,í aur merí talwár ká píplá uskí ḍhál par ṭúṭ gayá.* | Other names for "spear" are *bhálá*, *ballam*, and *neza*. |
| **515.** The point of the story is this, that it was not really a man but a monkey. | *Hikáyat* (or *kahání*) *ká hásil yih hai, ki dar asl ádmí nahín thá, bandar thá.* | |
| **516.** The bullet struck him in the left temple. | *Golí uskí báenwálí kanpaṭí men lag gaí.* | *Kanpaṭí* is the word for "temple." |
| **517.** He has sprained his right ankle. | *Uske dahnewále ṭakhne men moch á gayá hai.* | Note *ṭakhná* for ankle. |
| **518.** He is foaming at the mouth. | *Uske munh se jhág niklá húá hai.* | |
| **519.** He has lung disease, and his spleen is also out of order. | *Usko phephṛe ká maraz hai, aur tillí bhí durust nahín hai.* | |

| English. | Hindustani. | Notes. |
| --- | --- | --- |
| **520.** He does this simply for the sake of appearances. | *Sirf logon̲ ke dikháne ko yih kartá hai.* | |
| **521.** There is a haze over the hills at present. | *Is waqt paháṛon̲ par dhundh paṛá húá hai.* | |
| **522.** The roofing of this bungalow has cost me three hundred rupees. | *Is bangle kí chháoní ke úpar merá tín sau rúpiya k̲h̲arch hogayá hai.* | |
| **523.** Multiply ten by five, and you get fifty. | *Das ko pánch se zarb kar lo, to pachás húá.* | |
| **524.** Divide twenty-five by five, and you get five. | *Pachís ko pánch se taqsím kar lo, to pánch húá.* | |
| **525.** Deduct twenty from sixty and you get forty. | *Sáṭh se bís minhá kar lo, to chálís húá.* | *Wazạ karná* also means to deduct. |
| **526.** Add eighteen to twelve, and you get thirty. | *Aṭhárah aur bárah ká mízán kar lo, to tís húá.* | |
| **527.** I get into this state at times. | *Kabhí kabhí aisí hálat mujh par tárí hotí hai.* | *Tárí honá* is an idiom to be noted. |
| **528.** He is enjoying himself at present to his heart's content. | *Is waqt wuh apní k̲h̲átir-k̲h̲wáh * dil bahlátá hai.* | *A less refined way of expressing this is *peṭ bharkar.* |
| **529.** He completely lost his head under examination. | *Istifsár ke waqt uske hawáss uṛgae.* | |

| English. | Hindustani. | Notes. |
|---|---|---|
| **530.** I have borrowed this book from a friend. | *Yih kitáb main ne ek dost se áriyatan lí hai.* | *Áriyatan lená* does not apply to the borrowing of money. |
| **531.** On my saying this they all pricked up their ears. | *Mere yih kahne par sab ke kán khare hogae.* | |
| **532.** Some one broached this subject also at the same meeting. | *Usí jalse men kisí ne yih bát bhí chherí thí.* | *Chherná* means, among other things, to touch, to handle, to broach, &c. |
| **533.** I waited an hour for him, but he did not come. | *Ek ghante tak uská intizár kiyá, par nahín áyá.* | |
| **534.** He has an impediment in his speech. | *Uskí zabán men lugnat hai.* | This word is spelt *luknat* in the dictionaries, but *lugnat* seems to be the pronunciation. |
| **535.** On my taking a good look at it, I found that it was not new but second-hand. | *Main ne ghaur karke jo dekhá, to málúm húá ki istí'málí hai, nayá nahín hai.* | *Istí'málí* means literally "used." |
| **536.** This building requires repair; either repair it or pull it down. | *Yih makán marammat-talab hai; khwáh marammat karo, khwáh mismár kar dálo.* | *Talab* as an affix is common; it means requiring, calling for, &c. |
| **537.** This matter demands consideration. | *Yih bát ghaur-talab hai.* | |

| English. | Hindustani. | Notes. |
|---|---|---|
| **538.** Your advancement will be in proportion to your efforts. | *Jis qadar tum koshish karo, usí qadar tumhárí taraqqí hogí.* | *Qadar* is a word much used in the senses here given, extent, proportion, &c. |
| **539.** He is somewhat better to-day. | *Áj kisí qadar árám húá hai.* | Understand *usko* after *qadar.* |
| **540.** Engaging him in conversation, he got him to his house. | *Usko báton men parcháe húe apne ghar tak pahúncháyá.* | *Parchúná* means to engage another in conversation. |
| **541.** On the pretext of going to get something from the bazaar he made his escape. | *Bázár men jins kharídne ká bahána karke wuh bhág gayá.* | *Mol lená* can always be substituted for *kharídná,* if preferred. |
| **542.** There is great discrepancy between their two accounts. | *In donon ke bayán men ikhtiláf bahut hai.* | |
| **543.** If these two by any chance meet suddenly in the street, they commence fighting. | *Kahín gali men agar kisí waqt in donon ká muṭh-bheṛ hogayá, to ápas men laṛ paṛe.* | Note that in describing an imaginary case Hindustanis always use the past tense, and not, as we do, the present. |
| **544.** When the show was over, all the people left the place. | *Tamáshá jab khatm húá, to sab log wahán se chal paṛe.* | |
| **545.** Make this stick tapering. | *Is lakṛí ko gáo-dum kar do.* | *Gáo-dum* (tapering) means literally a cow's tail. |

# SECTION IV.

## Family Relationships, &c.

| English. | Hindustáni. | Notes. |
|---|---|---|
| 546. My paternal grandfather is an infirm old man, and my paternal grandmother a decrepit old woman. | *Merá dádá za,íf búṛhá hai, aur merí dádí fartút buṛhiyá húí.* | *Húí* is used in the second place here simply to avoid tautology. |
| 547. My maternal grand-parents are also in their dotage. | *Mere náná nání bhí saṭhiyá gae hain̲.* | Note the preference given to the masculine form when masculine and feminine nouns are conjoined in the same sentence. |
| 548. His paternal uncle is not truthful, and his paternal aunt is a great backbiter. | *Uská chachá rástgo nahín̲ hai, aur uskí phúphí baṛí chug̲h̲al-k̲h̲or hai.* | Another word for backbiter, tell-tale, &c., is *lutrá.* |
| 549. My maternal uncle has no occupation, and my maternal aunt squints. | *Mere mámú ká koí kám dhandá nahín̲ hai, aur merí mausí bhingí hai.* | Note that *phúphí* and *mausí* are respectively sisters to *chachá* and *mámú.* |
| 550. My father's brother's sons and his mother's brother's sons are at enmity with each other. | *Mere chachere bháí aur uske mamere bháí ek dúsre se ạdáwat rakhte hain̲.* | |

| English. | Hindustani. | Notes. |
|---|---|---|
| 551. My father's sister's daughters and my mother's sister's daughters are on close terms of intimacy. | *Merí phupherí bahinen aur merí mauserí bahinen ápus men bahut rabt-zabt rakhtí hain.* | |
| 552. This old woman is not my own mother, she is my step-mother. | *Yih burhiyá merí bemát hai, sagí má nahín hai.* | |
| 553. This man is not his full brother, he is his step-brother. | *Yih ádmí uská sautelá bhái hai, sagá bhái nahín hai.* | Also *bemát bhái.* |
| 554. This woman is my half-sister. | *Yih 'aurat merí sautelí bahin hai.* | Also *bemát bahin.* |
| 555. His step-daughter is engaged to my step-son. | *Uskí rabíba mere rabíb kí mangetar hai.* | |
| 556. My son-in-law is a carpenter. | *Merá dámád barhaí hai.* | |
| 557. Just at present my daughter-in-law is thrumming the seeds out of the cotton. | *Bilfel merí bahú kapás ot rahí hai.* | Cotton in its undressed state is *kapás*, afterwards *rúí.* |
| 558. My nephew (sister's son) and his nephew (brother's son) are twisting rope. | *Merá bhánjá aur uská bhatíjá rassí bat rahe hain.* | The corresponding words for niece are *bhánjí* and *bhatíjí.* |

| English. | Hindustani. | Notes. |
|---|---|---|
| 559. My wife's brother is a skilful workman, but my sister's husband is very clumsy. | *Merá sálá kárígar ádmí hai, magar merá bahnoí bahut anáṛí hai.* | |
| 560. My father-in-law and my mother-in-law have fallen out. | *Merá susrá* (or *sasur*) *aur merí sás ápas meṉ bigṛe húe haiṉ.* | *Sás* is a Hindi word: the more polite Musalman calls his mother-in-law *khush-dáman.* |
| 561. This woman does not mix much with her husband's family. | *Yih 'aurat apne samdhiyáne wáloṉ se bahut miltí jultí nahíṉ hai.* | *Samdhiyáná* means father-in-law's family. |
| 562. Seeing that this woman is my brother's wife, it does not seem right to turn her out of the house. | *Jab ki yih 'aurat merí bháwaj hai, to usko ghar se nikál dená munásib nahíṉ málúm hotá hai.* | |
| 563. My husband's younger brother treats his wife very badly. | *Merá dewar apní jorú kí bahut bad-sulúkí kartá hai.* | |
| 564. My wife's sister's husband has come in for a legacy. | *Mere sáḍhú ko ek wirsa pahúnchá hai.* | |
| 565. My grandson has enlisted as a soldier, to my granddaughter's great regret. | *Merá nawása fauj meṉ bhartí húá hai, jiske sabab merí nawásí bahut afsos kartí hai.* | 565 gives the Urdú for grandson and granddaughter, and 566 the Hindi. |
| 566. My brother has no grandchildren. | *Mere bhái ke koí potá potí nahíṉ haiṉ.* | |

# SECTION. V.

## Some Legal and Official Phrases.

| English. | Hindustani. | Notes. |
|---|---|---|
| 567. My enemy has brought a case against me to-day in the Criminal Court. | *Áj mere dushman ne ek muqaddama mere úpar faujdárí men ruj̣ú kiyá hai.* | *Faujdárí*, or *faujdárí ạdálat*, is the Criminal Court; *díwání*, or *díwání ạdálat*, the Civil Court. |
| 568. His complaint appears to be groundless. | *Uská istighása be-bunyád mạlúm hotá hai.* | *Istighása* is the word for a criminal complaint, and *mustaghís* for a complainant. |
| 569. The complainant declares that he had plenty of witnesses, but that the police have corrupted them. | *Mustaghís bayán kartá, ki mere gawáh bahut the, magar polís ne unko toṛ liyá hai.* | *Toṛ lená*, to corrupt, to tamper with. |
| 570. The Magistrate directed that the case should be heard when both parties were present. | *Hákim ká yún irshád húá, ki jab donon faríq házir honge, tab muqaddama suná jáegá.* | *Faríq* is the word for "party" in any kind of case. The plural is *faríqain*. See sentence 576. |
| 571. The accused is at present in the custody of the police, the inquiry not being yet completed. | *Bilfeḷ mulẓim polís kí hirásat men hai, tahqíqát abtak tamám nahín húí.* | Note *hirásat* for "custody," and *mulzim* for "accused." |

| English. | Hindustani. | Notes. |
|---|---|---|
| **572.** There are three under-trial prisoners in the lock-up. | *Hawálát men̲ tín to asámí hain̲.* | *Asámí* means an under-trial prisoner. |
| **573.** He has brought this complaint out of retaliation for my claim against him in the Civil Court. | *Main̲ ne jo uske úpar díwání men̲ dạ́wá kiyá thá, usíke palṭe men̲ ab usne yih nálish kí hai.* | *Nálish* is a much more common word for complaint than *istig̲h̲ása*, but it has no necessary connection with a Court of justice. For a claim or suit in the Civil Court the word is *dạ́wá*. |
| **574.** His witnesses do not corroborate his statement. | *Uske gawáhon̲ kí gawáhí uske bayán kí tá,íd nahín̲ kartí.* | |
| **575.** Owing to the defendant's having absconded, the summons could not be served. | *Muddaạleh * kí mafrúrí ke sabab saman kí tạmíl nahín̲ ho sakí.* | * I have written this word as it is pronounced, and not as a guide to the spelling of it, which should be studied. *Tạmíl* (from *ạmal*) means "execution" or "service." |
| **576.** The parties have made it up between themselves, and the case has therefore been dismissed. | *Faríqain ápas men̲ razámand hogae, chunánchi muqaddama k̲h̲árij kiyá gayá hai.* | |
| **577** One of the accused was sentenced to imprisonment, the other for want of proof was discharged. | *Ek mulzim kí nisbat hukm qaid ká húá, dúsrá mulzim sabút na hone kí wajh se rihá hogayá.* | *Mulzim* comes from *ilzám*, accusation, charge. The word for "criminal" is *mujrim*, from *jurm*, an offence, a crime. |
| **578.** Did the plaintiff appear in person or by a pleader? | *Muddaí asálatan házir húá, yá wakálatan?* | |

| English. | Hindustani. | Notes. |
|---|---|---|
| 579. My claim is for damages. | *Merá dáwá harje ká hai.* | |
| 580. You will have an opportunity of rebutting this later on. | *Iskí tardíd karne ká mauqa tumko píchhe milegá.* | *Tardíd*, rebutting (from *radd*). |
| 581. On the defendant's being cross-examined the real facts came out. | *Jab muddaáleh se jireh ke suwál kiye gae to asl bát khul gaí.* | *Jireh ká suwál* means a "wounding" or "damaging" question; it is the technical term for cross-examination. |
| 582. The jailor is an awe-inspiring man, so that he keeps the prisoners in subjection. | *Jel ká dárogha rob-dár ádmí hai, iswáste qaidí log usse dabte hain.* | |
| 583. The police superintendent is a firm man, and his subordinates fear him. | *Polís ká mohtamim zabardast ádmí hai, uske má-taht ke log usse darte hain.* | *Má-taht* means literally "that which is under," hence subordinate. |
| 584. The head of the office is a man of ability, and manages the office well; the under clerks also do all that he tells them. | *Sarrishtadár sáheb-i-isti'dád hai, aur sarrishte ká kám achchhí tarah chalátá hai; amla bhí uske khúb farmánbardár rahtá hai.* | *Amla* is the collective term for office-clerks, and, like our word "staff," is in the singular. |
| 585. The Court will rise at 4 o'clock. | *Adálat chár baje ke waqt barkhást hogí.* | |
| 586. There is no eye-witness of the occurrence. | *Wáridát ká koí gawáh chashm-díd nahín hai.* | |

| English. | Hindustani. | Notes. |
|---|---|---|
| **587.** Two witnesses state that they know nothing. | *Do gawáh lá-ịlmí bayán karte haiṉ.* | *Lá-ịlmí* means ignorance of any particular fact. |
| **588.** Defendant has applied for a delay of five days. | *Muddaạleh ne pánch roz kí muhlat mángí.* | |
| **589.** The case will be adjourned for five days. | *Muqaddama pánch roz tak multawí rakhá jáegá.* | |
| **590.** Plaintiff has petitioned for the case to be transferred to the higher Court. | *Muddaạ́ ne darkhwást kí ki muqaddama úparwálí ạdálat ko muntaqil kiyá jáe.* | *Muntaqil*, transferred, from *intiqál*, a transfer. |
| **591.** His petition has been refused. | *Uskí darkhwást námanzúr húí.* | |
| **592.** His statement that he was assaulted by an old woman is contrary to reason. | *Uská bayán ki ek buṛhiyá ne uspar hamla kiyá thá, khiláf-i-qaiyás hai.* | |
| **593.** There are two cases for to-day, one of highway robbery and one of arson. | *Áj ke do muqaddame haiṉ, ek to rahzaní ká aur ek to átashzaní ká.* | |

# SECTION VI.

## Some Hindustani Proverbs.

| English. | Hindustani. | Notes. |
|---|---|---|
| **594.** Words of counsel and admonition should be administered in private: who can hear (or "who will listen to") a parrot's voice in the room where the drums are beaten? | *Pand aur nasíhat kí báte<u>n</u> nirále me<u>n</u> sunání cháhiye: naqqár-<u>kh</u>áne me<u>n</u> túti kí áwáz kaun sunegá?* | The second part of this sentence gives the proverb. *Nirále me<u>n</u>* is Hindi; the Urdú equivalent is *<u>kh</u>alwat me<u>n</u>*. |
| **595.** To be bitten by a dog as you are getting on to a camel! | *Únṭ chaṛhe aur kuttá káṭe!* | Means what we call "taking a mean advantage." |
| **596.** What can he who has never had a broken chilblain on his foot know of the suffering of another? | *Jiskí na phaṭí ho biwáí, so kyá jáne píṛ paráí?* | We learn sympathy through personal suffering. |
| **597.** The bullock did not jump, the sack on its back did; who ever saw such a sight as this? | *Bail na kúdá, kúdí gon; yih tamáshá dekhe kon?* | A hit at those who pretend to be wiser, or cleverer, than their teachers. |
| **598.** What does a monkey know of the taste of undried ginger? | *Bandar kyá jáne áde ká swád?* | 598 and 599 answer to the Latin, *Ne sutor ultra crepidam.* |

| English. | Hindustani. | Notes. |
|---|---|---|
| **599.** What does an oilman know of the price of perfume. | *Telí kyá jáne atr ká bháo?* | |
| **600.** Lal Bujhakkar and no one else can understand this: may not a deer with mill-stones tied to its feet have bounded here? | *Yih to bújhe Lál Bujhakkar, aur na bújhe ko,e: páon men chakkí bándhkar mat harná kúdá ho,e?* | Lal Bujhakkar is synonym for "wiseacre." He and his friends, never having seen an elephant in their lives, come upon the footprints of that animal in the mud, and this is how he accounts for them. |
| **601.** No milk-woman ever says that her own *dahi* (clotted milk) is sour. | *Gwálin apne dahí ko khaṭṭá nahín kahtí.* | |
| **602.** A cat is a tiger in a jungle of small bushes. | *Jharberí ke jangal men billí sher.* | Compare "the little tyrant of his fields" in Gray's Elegy. |
| **603.** The dog's tail was shut up (lit. remained) in the blow-pipe for twelve years, but when it was taken out again, it was just as crooked as ever. | *Kutte kí dum phukní men bárah baras rahí, lekin jab báhar nikálí, to ṭeṛhí kí ṭeṛhí niklí.* | Corresponds to the Scripture simile, "Can the Ethiopian change his skin, or a leopard his spots?" |
| **604.** Like a washerman's dog, neither of the house, nor of the *ghaut*. | *Jaise dhobí ká kuttá, na ghar ká na gháṭ ká.* | Applied to any one who has no settled place of abode, an Anglo-Indian, for instance. |
| **605.** The tiger and the goat drink together at the same *ghaut*. | *Sher aur bakrí ek gháṭ pání píte hain.* | Implies a system of government so perfect that one thing dare not harm another. |

| English. | Hindustani. | Notes. |
|---|---|---|
| **606.** He has not even a thatch to his house, and his name is Dhanpat! (*i.e.* lord of wealth). | *Ghar par phús nahín, aur nám Dhanpat!* | |
| **607.** The dogs bark, and the traveller goes on his way. | *Kutte bhaunkte, aur musáfir chalá játá.* | Means that we ought not to be put out, or stopped in our course, by petty annoyances. |
| **608.** A guest like our life we shall not get a second time. | *Jí saríkhá páhuná na mile dújí bár.* | A Hindi saying. |
| **609.** The string is burnt, but the twist is in it still (has not gone). | *Rassí jalí, par bal na gayá.* | Same application as in 603. |
| **610.** Proclamation by beat of drum going on in the town, and (all the while) the child is under her arm! | *Ḍhanḍhorá shahr men aur laṛká baghal men!* | We sometimes think we have lost a thing, when all the while it is about our person or close to us. |
| **611.** The thief has a straw in his beard. | *Chor kí dáṛhí men tinká.* | Crime is often detected through oversights on the part of the criminal. |
| **612.** He can neither read nor write, and his name is Muhammad Fazil! (fázil=learned). | *Paṛhe na likhe, aur nám Muhammad Fázil!* | The *na* between *paṛhe* and *likhe* in this sentence does duty for both. |

| English. | Hindustani. | Notes. |
|---|---|---|
| **613.** Having eaten seventy rats, the cat has now gone on a pilgrimage to Mecca. | *Sattar chúhe kháke, billí hajj ko chalí.* | Making the most of both worlds. |
| **614.** To devour molasses and abstain from sweet cakes ! | *Guṛ kháná aur gulgulon̲ se parhez karná !* | To strain at a gnat and swallow a camel. |
| **615.** Among blind men the one-eyed man is a king. | *Andhon̲ men̲ káná rájá.* | |
| **616.** A leech will not fasten on to a stone. | *Patthar ko jon̲k nahín̲ lagtí.* | Toadies confine their attentions to those from whom they hope to get something. |
| **617.** He had no sooner had his head shaved than hail began to fall. | *Sir mun̲ḍáte hí ole paṛe.* | |
| **618.** The spot-eyed man is (a rogue) in a hundred, the one-eyed man (a rogue) in a thousand, and the man who squints (a rogue) in a lakh and a quarter. | *Sau men̲ phúlí, hazár men̲ káná, sawá lákh men̲ ainchá táná.* | The word "rogue" is not expressed in the Hindustani, but the meaning of the proverb is that here given. |

*N.B.*—Two noteworthy proverbs occur at page 40, Nos. 255 and 256.

# SECTION VII.

## Extracts from the Text-books, &c.

| English. | Hindustani. | Notes. |
|---|---|---|
| **619.** No correspondence even has ever passed between us and you. | *Hamáre tumháre to kabhí khatt-o-kitábat bhí na thí.* | Understand *darmiyán* after *tumháre.* Nos. 619-625 are from the *Ikhwán-us-safá.* The principle I have followed in translating these extracts is, that each language should keep to its own idiom. |
| **620.** Elephants, horses, camels, asses, and a number of other animals, who had always roamed unrestrained through the jungles and deserts, feeding wherever they liked, and wherever they found it, on the greenest and freshest pasture, and no questions asked, now had their shoulders galled and pits made in their backs through continuous labour night and day, and let them scream and cry out ever so much, what heed would their human lordships ever pay to them? Numbers of wild animals | *Háthí, ghoṛe, únṭ, gadhe, aur bahut se jánwar, ki sadá jangal bayábán meṉ shutur-i-bemahár phirte the, jaháṉ jí cháhtá achchhá hará sabza dekhkar charte, koí púchhnewálá na thá; so unke kándhe rát din kí mihnat se chhilga,e, píṭhoṉ meṉ ghár paṛ ga,e; harchand bahut sá chíkhte chingháṛte, par ye hazrat insán kab kán dharte? Aksar wahshí khauf-i-giriftárí se dúr-dast jangaloṉ meṉ bháge; tá,ir bhí apná baserá chhoṛ, bál-bachchoṉ ko sáth le, inke des se uṛánchhú hoga,e.* | |

| English. | Hindustani. | Notes. |
|---|---|---|
| through fear of capture fled to remote jungles; birds also, leaving their resting-places and taking their young ones with them, took their flight from their country. | | |
| **621.** Do not you know that correctness of deportment (lit. sitting down and rising up) is the peculiar characteristic of kings, and that ugliness and deformity (crookedness) are the distinguishing marks of slaves. | *Tum nahín jánte ki durustí nishast-o-barkhást kí khaslat bádsháhon kí hai, aur badsúratí wa khamídagí ạlámat ghulámon kí?* | |
| **622.** The queen-bee asked, In what way do the angels render obedience? He replied, In the same way as the five senses render obedience to the reason, *i.e.* they require no direction or correction. The queen-bee said, Be pleased to describe in detail. The king replied, In ascertaining for | *Yạsúb ne kahá, Firishton kí itá,ạt kis taur par hai? Kahá, jistarah hawáss-i-khamsa nafs-i-nátiqa kí itá,ạt karte hain, tahzíb o tạdíb ke muhtáj nahín. Yạsúb ne kahá, Isko mufassal farmáiye. Bádsháh ne kahá, ki hawáss-i-khamsa nafs-i-nátiqa ke wáste mahsúsát kí daryáft wa mạlúm karne men* | *Yạsúb ne kahá* translated literally would be, "The king-bee said." Orientals regard the insect as a male and not as a female. The king with whom the queen bee is conversing in this passage is the king of the jinns. |

| English. | Hindustani. | Notes. |
|---|---|---|
| the reason the nature of things perceived or felt the five senses have no need of commands and prohibitions: any particular thing the nature of which it (*i.e.* the reason) seeks to ascertain, they without hesitation or delay distinguish from other things and convey to the reason. In the same way the angels are occupied in rendering obedience to God. | *muhtáj amr o nahí ke nahín hain. Jis shai kí daryáft karne ke liye wuh mutawajjih hotá hai, we be-ta,ammul wa bilá tákhír usko dúsrí shai se mumtáz karke, nafs-i-nátiqa ko pahunchá dete hain. Isí tarah* firishte Khudá kí itá,at aur farmánbardárí men masrúf rahte hain.* | *Pron. *tareh.* |
| **623.** The fact as regards the physicians is this, that through having recourse to them disease is made worse. Things which generally cure a sick person they tell him to abstain from. If they would only leave him to nature the patient would get well. Your priding yourselves therefore on (your) physicians and astrologers is | *Yihí hál tabíbon ká hai, ki unke yahán iltijá lejáne se bímárí ziyáda hotí hai. Jin chízon se ki maríz beshtar shifá pátá hai, unhín chízon se parhez batláte hain. Agar tabí,at par chhor dewen to bímár ko shifá howe. Pas, tabíbon aur nujúmiyon par tumhárá fakhr karná mahz humuq hai. Ham unke muhtáj nahín hain, kyúnki ghizá hamárí ek waze par* | In this passage the parrot is speaking as the representative of the birds in the controversy between the animals and man. *Iltijá* means an appeal for help or protection in times of difficulty or distress, hence *iltijá lejáná*, to have recourse to. *Maljá*, an asylum, a place of refuge, comes from the same root. |

| English. | Hindustani. | Notes. |
|---|---|---|
| sheer folly. We need none of them, because our food is of one kind, consequently we do not get ill, nor do we have recourse to physicians; we have nothing to do with beverages and confections. The way of the free is not to be dependent on any one; the way of slaves is to be always running off to everybody. | *hai, isíwáste ham bímár nahín̲ hote, tabíbon̲ ke yahán̲ iltijá nahín̲ lejáte, kisí sharbat aur májún se g̲h̲araz nahín̲ rakhte. Shewa ázádon̲ ká yihí hai, ki kisí se ihtiyáj na rakhen̲; yih taríqa g̲h̲ulámon̲ ká hai ki har ek ke yahán̲ daurte phirte hain̲.* | |
| **624.** There is great jealousy and hatred between dogs and cats. When dogs see a cat (*lit.* see her), they jump up from where they are and make such an onslaught on her, that if they caught her they would tear her to shreds. | *Kutte aur billí men̲ hasad wa bug̲h̲z rahtá hai. Kutte jiswaqt usko dekhte hain̲, apní jagah se jast karke istarah hamla karte hain̲, ki agar páwen̲ to chhíchhṛá chhíchhṛá karen̲.* | *Hasad* and *bug̲h̲z* here take the verb in the singular, as the two things are allied and form one common sentiment. |
| **625.** We are entitled (*or* have a right) to exercise lordly sway over these (creatures), and to exact from them | *Hamko sazáwár hai ki hukúmat-i-k̲h̲áwindána inpar karen̲, aur jo kám cháhen̲ unse len̲. In men̲ se jisne hamárí itá,at qabúl* | Here the spokesman is the man, and the opposite party the animals. *Hamko sazáwár hai* should be noted, and also |

| English. | Hindustani. | Notes. |
| --- | --- | --- |
| what work we choose. Whoever of them agrees to obey us is accepted of God, and whoever rebels against our commands, rebels, so to say, against God. | *kí, maqbúl Khudá ká húí, aur jo hamáre hukm se phirá, goyá Khudá se phirá.* | the use of the past tense in *qabúl kí, hukm se phirá*, &c. |
| **626.** On getting to the fort we went inside it. We found the buildings everywhere in ruins, but one huge well of masonry, though perfectly dry and without any water in it, we found intact. We went and stood by it. Meanwhile each of us, on looking at his clothes, noticed that they were greener than emeralds, though in reality they were white. On our coming out again from the fort they resumed their original appearance. | *Jab qile ke muttasil pahunche, andar gae. Já ba já makánát uske ṭúṭe páe, lekin ek patthar ká indárá niháyat kalán, par khushk, be-áb, jon ká ton dekhá. Uspar já khaṛe rahe. Itne men nigáh har ek kí jo apne apne kapṛon par paṛí, unko zumurrud se bhí ziyáda sabz dekhá, hálánki sufed the. Jab qile se báhar nikle phir jaise ke taise hogae.* | Extracts 626-631 are from the *Áráish-i-Mahfil.* See note to 334 on *hálánki.* |
| **627.** Accordingly the Rajah fastened a golden fish to a long pole and stuck it up in the maidan, and he had a large | *Algharaz rájá ne ek lambí lakṛí par sone kí machhlí bándh kar, maidán men usko khaṛá kiyá, aur ek baṛí deg tel se bharí* | The context requires that *algharaz* should here be translated "accordingly." |

| English. | Hindustani. | Notes. |
|---|---|---|
| cauldron filled with oil placed on a fire-place underneath it. He also caused an extremely strong stiff bow with arrows to be placed alongside it; and he made this condition, that whoever should draw this bow, and so shoot an arrow as to drop the fish from the pole into the cauldron, he would give him this girl in marriage and make him his son-in-law. The chiefs and rajahs who had come together for this purpose were all put to shame on that maidan; they could not fulfil the condition. These five brothers also were sitting in a corner like so many faqirs watching the spectacle. Whatever may have come into Arjun's mind, he took up the arrows and the bow, and so discharged a shaft that the fish was severed from the | *húí níche uske chúlhe par dharwádí. Sáth iske ek kamán bhí niháyat kaṛí, tír samet, pás uske rakhwá dí; aur yih shart kí, ki jo koí is kamán ko khainchkar aisá tír máre ki machhlí is lakṛí par se deg men̲ án-paṛe, usíke sáth is laṛkí ko biyáh dún̲ aur apní dámádí men̲ lún̲. Jitne ráo rájá ki is iráde par áe the, us maidán men̲ k̲h̲afíf húe; yih shart ba-já na lá sake. Ye pánchon̲ bháí bhí faqíron̲ kí mánind ek kone men̲ baiṭhe tamáshá dekh rahe the. Arjun ke jí men̲ jo kuchh áyá, tír o kamán uṭhákar, aisá hí ek tír márá ki wuh machhlí lakṛí par se judí hokar us deg men̲ á paṛí. Wonhín̲ Rájá Darpad kí beṭí Daropadí ko us dangal se legayá, aur dág̲h̲ hasrat ká unke tálibon̲ ke dil par degayá. Tamásháí uskí zoráwarí aur phurtí dekhkar bhaichak rah gae: kisíko jurat na* | |

| English. | Hindustani. | Notes. |
|---|---|---|
| pole and fell into the cauldron. He thereupon carried off Darpad's daughter Daropadi from the crowd, affixing the brand of chagrin on the hearts of her suitors as he did so. The spectators, on witnessing his strength and dexterity, were astounded; no one dared to oppose him. | *húí ki usse muqábala kare.* | . |
| **628.** At Mainpore there are 12,000 bighas of saffron cultivation. Truly they are well worth seeing and exploring. From the end of Baisakh and through the whole of Jeth the cultivators plough the land and make it soft, then they hoe every plot and make them ready for planting, and then they put in the saffron bulbs. Each plant bears eight flowers in succession; each flower has six petals | *Mainpúr meṉ bárah hazár bíghe zamín zạ́farán kí khetiyoṉ kí hai. Filwáqị qábil i díd wa láiq i sair. G͟haraz Baisákh ke ák͟hir se le sárá mahíná Jeth ká kishtkár hal chalá, zamín kọ narm kar, kudáloṉ se har ek qiṭạ uská qábil bone ke baná, zạ́farán ke gaṭṭhe bo dete haiṉ. Har paudhe meṉ áṭh phúl ba-tadríj phúlte haiṉ, pankhṛiyá har ek meṉ chha, rangat un meṉ sausní; darmiyán unke chha* | 12,000 bighas would be about 4000 acres. The word now generally used for cultivator in the N.-W. Provinces is not *kishtkár* but *káshtkár*. The author is presumably speaking here of meadow saffron. |

| English. | Hindustani. | Notes. |
|---|---|---|
| of a bluish colour, and in the centre of these six stamens, of which three as a rule are yellow and three red. It is from these that the saffron comes. | *tár, beshtar tín zard aur tín lál. Záfarán unhín kí hotí hai.* | |
| **629.** The tidal ebb and flow occurs at this place (a place called Bagulá) as it does at Calcutta. But in the twenty-ninth year of Akbar's reign, one day when one watch of the day remained, a most remarkable flood took place. The whole town was submerged. For five hours the storm raged and there was no abatement in the flood in the river. In addition to this the lightning flashed, the clouds thundered, and the rain poured. In the end two lakhs of living beings, animal and human, were swallowed up in the flood of mortality (*i.e.* perished). | *Juwár bhátá ba taur Kalkatte ke us maqám men bhí átá hai. Lekin Akbar ke untíswen sál i julúsí men, pahar din rahe ek roz ajab ek sail namúd húí. Tamám shahr dúbá. Gharaz pánch sá,at josh túfán ká rahá aur tamauwuj daryá ká na ghatá. Sáth iske bijlí chamká kí, bádal garjá kiye, menh barsá kiyá. Ákhir do lákh jándár haiwán o insán se sail i faná men gharq húe.* | Understand a preposition after *pahar din rahe,* "at the remaining of one watch." Note that the idiom is *ajab ek sail* and not *ek ajab sail.* For *bijlí chamká kí,* &c., see Sect. II. and notes. |

| English. | Hindustani. | Notes. |
|---|---|---|
| **630.** It is said that just about that time an earthquake took place, that there was thunder and lightning without any clouds, and that a star burst from the sky in the most appalling manner and went careering through the environs of Hastinapur. Wild animals came into the villages, and jackals came into the bazaars and howled in broad daylight; vultures uttered their cries at the doorways of the houses; water-lilies bloomed on the trees; the trees bore fruit out of season; cows gave birth to young donkeys; indeed most of the animals bore young of alien species. | *Kahte hain ki us-waqt bhúnchál áyá, aur rád wa barq bidún abr ke numáyán húe, aur ek tárá kamál haibat se ásmán par se ṭúṭkar Hastinápúr kí atráf men phirá. Sahráí jánwar bastí men áe; gídaṛ bázáron men din-diye ákar chilláe; kargas gharon ke darwázon par bole; gul-i-nílofar darakhton par phúle; darakht be-mausim phale; gáe gadhe ká bachcha jani; balki aksar haiwánon se bachche ghair jins paidá húe.* | These somewhat startling phenomena, the writer goes on to say, were interpreted by experts to mean that some dire calamity would shortly befall a famous family of ancient Hindu warriors, whose history he is giving, and this accordingly comes to pass. *Din-diyá* means daylight. Hastinapur is the name of ancient Delhi. |
| **631.** Owing to its (the river Indus) being narrow at this part, it flows with great force and noise, so much so that the sight of the onlooker becomes dazed; it | *Azbaski páṭ uská wahán chhoṭá hai, niháyat zor shor se bahtá hai, yahán tak ki dekhnewálon kí nigáh khíragí kartí hai; mutlaqan wa aslá nahín ṭhahrtí.* | In this fine bit of description the author is speaking of the Indus near Attock.<br>*Páṭ* is the word always used for the width of a river. |

| English. | Hindustani. | Notes. |
| --- | --- | --- |
| cannot fix itself for an instant. Through the violent agitation of the water the hearts of the alligators become water, while the breasts of the hills from the impact of the waves go to pieces. The ferry boats, through the rapidity of the current, are over from this side to that in the twinkling of an eye. | *Tamauwuj kí shiddat se nihangon ká jigar áb hojátá hai, aur paháron ká sína maujon ke sadme se ṭukre ṭukre.* *Guzáre kí náwen pání kí tezrawí se is kináre se us kináre turfat-ul-ain men pahúnchtí hain.* | *Azbaski*, as already remarked (sentence 407), means "owing to," "in consequence of." *Mutlaqan wa aslá* means literally "in the very least." |
| **632.** To attempt and to fail, and not to attempt at all, between these two things there is all the difference that there is between earth and heaven. | *Koshish men nákám rahná, aur mutlaqan koshish na karná, in do báton men zamín ásmán ká farq hai.* | Lit. "To fail in one's attempt," &c. 632-635 are from the *Taubatu-n-Nasúh.* |
| **633.** Although these people gave him no encouragement, the shameless fellow deliberately thrust himself upon them. To seat himself down with persons of high position was still more unbecoming in him. Watching all they did, he acquired all | *Agarchi wuh log usko munh nahín lagáte the, magar yih be-ghairat zabardastí unmen ghustá thá. Únchí haisiyat ke logon men baiṭhná uske haqq men aur bhí zabún thá. Unkí dekhá dekhí usne tamám ádaten amírzádon kí sí ikhtiyár kar rakhí thín, magar* | *Munh lagáná* means to show familiarity to an inferior. *Be-ghairat* means without self-respect. *Nibhná* means to last, to continue. *Unkí dekhá dekhí* means "following their example." |

| English. | Hindustani. | Notes. |
| --- | --- | --- |
| the habits of well-born people; but then he was not well-born, so how could it last? | *amírzádagí na thí, to kaise nibhe?* | |
| **634.** At the first children are more at home with their mothers (*i.e.* than with their fathers), and they pick up their mothers' peculiar ways. | *Bachche ibtidá men máon hí se ziyáda mánús hote hain, aur máon hí kí khú-bú pakaṛte hain.* | I have introduced Nos. 634 and 635 simply for the sake of *mánús* and *ná-mánús*, which are important. *Mánús* means literally familiar, accustomed to, and *ná-mánús* of course the opposite. |
| **635.** Nasuh wanted to take him (*i.e.* his son Kalim) along a new and unfamiliar road. | *Nasúh ek naí aur ná-mánús ráh par usko lejáná cháhtá thá.* | |
| **636.** This man was formerly a Chhatri by caste. At that time his name was Prag Singh; but fourteen years ago he became a Musalman in order to marry a Musalman woman. He walks in a remarkable way; at every step his knees seem to be turning outwards. When talking to any one, he fixes his eyes on the person's face | *Yih shakhs pahle qaum ká Chhatrí thá. Uswaqt uská nám Prág Singh thá; lekin arsa chaudah sál ká húá ki ek Musalmán aurat se nikáh kar lene kí gharaz se Musalmán hogayá. Ajíb taur se chaltá hai; har qadam par uske ghuṭne báhar ko phire húe málúm hote hain. Bát karne ke waqt ádmí ke chihre par ṭakṭakí bándhkar ghaur se dekhtá hai.* | This is from the N. W. Provinces Police Gazette. Note that *qaum* is the word for "caste," and that the idiom is *qaum ká Chhatrí*. Note also *ṭakṭakí bándhná*. |

| English. | Hindustani. | Notes. |
|---|---|---|
| and examines him attentively. | | |
| 637. One day a wag asked a barber's son, Have you ever shaved a monkey? He promptly replied, Well, up to the present no such opportunity has come in my way, but if your honour will sit down I will do my best. | Ek mas<u>kh</u>are ne ek roz ek hajjám ke laṛke se púchhá, Kyá, tú ne kabhí kisí bandar kí hajámat kí hai? Usne barjasta yih jawáb diyá: Abtak to koí mauqa aisá na paṛá, lekin agar áp bai<u>th</u>en to mai<u>n</u> koshish karú<u>n</u>. | This pleasing little anecdote was taken from an Indian newspaper. |

# SECTION VIII.

THE FOLLOWING ARE GIVEN AS A FEW AIDS TO MEMORY AND PRONUNCIATION.

| Rhymes. | Notes. |
| --- | --- |
| 638. The jailor says without your "*izn*"<br>He cannot keep this man in prison. | *Izn*, permission. *Ijázat* is the common word. |
| 639. The stain on cloth which men call "*dhabbá*"<br>Can't be got out with india-rubber. | See note to 31. |
| 640. I may be nothing but a dreamer,<br>But I really thought this was your "*ímá*." | Suggestion, hint. *Ishára* is the common word. |
| 641. Is it a fact that with a ruler<br>You struck this man upon the "*kúlá*"? | *Kúlá*, hip. |
| 642. I find that certain things keep cleaner<br>From being overlaid with "*míná*." | Enamel. |
| 643. Because from its top you see so far,<br>A lofty tower's "*jahán-numá*." | "Showing the world." Stress on last syllable. |
| 644. He cannot answer if he would,<br>And therefore he is "*dam-ba-khud*." | Mute, keeping his breath to himself. |

| Rhymes. | Notes. |
|---|---|
| 645. The thumb-screw, that most dreadful squeezer,<br>Was solely meant to inflict "*ízá*." | *Ízá* means pain, torture. |
| 646. 'Twas right of course to appease their hunger;<br>But why on *my* crop should you feed your "*dangar*"? | *Dangar* is the colloquial word for cattle: the book word is *maweshí*. |
| 647. From the haunts of men they have gone apart,<br>And now they are feeding on "*nabátát*." | Vegetables. (The book word.) |
| 648. My little man, if you are wise,<br>You will keep your hands from "*sila ná jáiz*." | Illegal gratification, bribe. (a legal term.) |
| 649. In every race he came in "*mírí*,"<br>And that is why he looks so cheery. | *Mírí* is the foremost in a race, and *phisaḍḍí* the hindmost. |
| 650. The ground, he says, was very muddy,<br>And that was how he got "*phisaḍḍí*." | |
| 651. He said he knew it was his coat,<br>(It seemed a queerish order,)<br>Because it had a scarlet "goat,"<br>But "goat," it seems, means "border." | *Goṭ* is the border of a garment. |
| 652. Tell me the word for stalk, my boy:<br>The boy replied, I won't.<br>(He knows the meaning of "cane," that boy :)<br>The word for stalk is "*bonṭ*." | There are several words for "stalk;" *bonṭ* is one. |

| Rhymes. | Notes. |
|---|---|
| 653. The word for "blade," be it sharp or dull,<br>Is nothing more nor less than "*phal.*" | The blade of a knife, &c. The handle is *bainṭá.* |
| 654. They told me he was very rich;<br>There'd come to him of late<br>Some "milk," they said: how could I tell<br>That "milk" meant "an estate"? | *Milk* is the proper word for a landed estate. |
| 655. He said with something of a brogue,<br>His voice had in it thickness—<br>That he was suffering from a "rogue."<br>It turned out "rogue" meant "sickness." | *Rog* is a common word for sickness or disease, especially in writing. |
| 656. Some men deride the notion of<br>A bird's being called a turtle:<br>Words unpolite I fear they'd use<br>If told that "ass" meant "myrtle." | *Ás* is Hindustani for myrtle. |
| 657. *Ụnfuwán i shabáb* is "the heyday of youth;"<br>Make a note of it, friend, you will find it's the truth. | "*U*" with a dot under it means that the letter is an *ain.* |
| 658. Rest now awhile, my pen, and take *árám;*<br>Thy work and mine have reached their *ikhtitám.* | *Ikhtitám,* completion. |

# VOCABULARY AND INDEX.

*N.B.*—"Index" here applies to those words only which have figures after them, indicating the sentences where they occur. In this vocabulary, when two or more words are given separated by commas, it means that they are all equally common; but if separated by a dash, thus —, that the first words are those in most ordinary use, and the subsequent ones those chiefly used by educated natives. The exact sense in which different words are used is shown in brackets. For pronunciation, &c., see "Introductory Note."

---

A *or* an, *ek.*
Abandon, *chhoṛ dená — tark karná.*
Abase, *zalíl karná.*
Abasement, *zillat.*
Abate (*v.n.*) *ghaṭná;* (*v.a.*) *ghaṭáná.*
Abatement, *ghaṭáo,* 328.
Abbreviate (abridge), *mukhtasar karná.*
Abbreviation (abridgment), *ikhtisár.*
Abet, *sahárá karná—iáṇat karná.*
Abetment, *madad—iáṇat.*
Abettor, *madadgár:* (in law) *muíṇ-i-jurm.*
Abhor, *nafrat karná, ... se dúr bhágná.*
Abhorrence, *nafrat, ghin.*
Ability, *liyáqat — istẹdád;* (power) *maqdúr.*
Able (capable), *qábil, láiq;* (to be able) *sakná.*
Abolish, *uṭhá dená, mauqúf kar dená.*
Abortive, *lá-hásil, akárat.*
Abound, *bahut honá, kasrat se honá.*
About (approximately), *koí, qaríb —takhmínan.*
About (concerning), ... *kí bábat, kí nisbat.*
About (round about), *ás-pás—ird-gird.*
Above, ... *úpar,* ... *ke úpar.*
Abreast, *barábar-barábar, ekhí barábar.*
Abridged, *mukhtasar.*
Abscess, *dummal.*
Abscond, *bhág jáná — farár honá,* 166, 167.
Absence, *ghair-háziri;* (separation) *judáí.*
Absent, *ghair-házir.*
Absolute, *mutlaq;* (complete) *sarásar.*

Absolutely, *mutlaqan*; (altogether) *bilkull.*
Absorb, *pí jáná—jazb karná.*
Absorbed, to be, *khapná, lín honá—jazb honá*, 428, 433, 468.
Absorbent, *jázib.*
Abstain from, ... *se parhez karná.*
Abstinent (abstemious), *parhezgár.*
Abstract (take out), *nikál lená.*
Abstract of an account, *goshwára.*
Absurd, *behúda.*
Absurdity, *behúdagí, wáhiyát.*
Abundance, *bahutáyat, rel-pel, kasrat.*
*In* Abundance (abundant), *bahut, dher, kasrat se.*
Abuse (bad language), *gálí, gálígalauj.*
Abuse (*v.a.*), *bhalá burá kahná, gálí dená.*
Abusive, *bad-zabán.*
Accede to, *qabúl karná, manzúr karná.*
Accent, *lahja.*
Accept, *le lená, qabúl kar lená.*
Acceptance, *pazíráí.*
Accepted, *maqbúl, pazírá*, 625.
Accessory (accomplice), *sáthí—hamráz*; (in law) *muín-i-jurm.*
Accident, (calamity) *hádisa*; (something unforeseen) *ittifáq.*
*By* Accident (unintentionally), *bhúl se*, 404.
Accommodation (convenience), *rafáhiyat*, 98.
Accompany, *sáth* (or *sang*) *chalná—hamráh honá.*
Accomplice, *sáthí, sharík.*
Accomplish, (carry out) ... *ko anjám dená*; (one's object) *bar láná.*
Accomplished in an art, to be, ... *men khúb salíqa rakhná.*
*Of one's own* Accord, *áp se áp, áp hí áp, áp se.*
According to, ... *ke muwáfiq—ke mutábiq, ke ba-músjib.*
Accost, *tokná.*
Account, (description) *bayán*; (money) *hisáb*; (on account of) *ke sabab*; (on this account) *isliye, iswáste.*
Accountable for, ... *ke zimme honá.*
Accumulate, (*v.a.*) *jama kar lená*; (*v.n.*) *jama ho jáná.*
Accumulation, *jamáo, dher.*
Accuracy, *durustí—sihhat.*
Accurate, *durust, thík—sahíh.*
Accusation, *shikáyat, nálish*; (false) *tuhmat.*
Accuse, ... *par nálish karná*; (falsely) *tuhmat lagáná.*
Accustom to (make familiar with), ... *se mánús karná.*
Accustomed to, ... *se mánús*, 634.
Ache (*v.n.*), *dukhná, dard karná.*
Ache (*n.*), *dard.*
Acid, (*adj.*) *khattá*; (acidity) *khatáí.*
Acknowledge, *iqrár karná, mán lená.*
Acknowledgment, *iqrár—etiráf.*
Acquaintance, *áshná, ján-pahchán*; (polite term) *muláqátí.*
Acquaintanceship, *ján-pahchán, áshnáí*, 243.
Acquainted with (a particular subject), ... *se wáqif.*
Acquire, *hásil karná, baham pahúncháná.*

Acquitted, *chhúṭ gayá, rihá ho gayá.*

Across, (athwart) *aṛá, benḍá,* 295, 346 ; (a river, &c.) *pár.*

Act (action), *kám—fel, ạmal.*

Action at law, (in general) *muqaddama* ; (civil) *dạ́wá.*

Active, *chálák.*

Activity, (quickness) *chálákí* ; (in business, &c.) *sargarmí.*

Acute (severe), *sakht, shadíd.*

Add up, *joṛ lená—mízán karná.*

Addicted to, ... *ká ạdí honá.*

Addition, (in arith.) *mízán* ; (increase) *izạ́fa.*

Address, (place of abode) *patá* ; (on a letter) *sarnáma,* 211.

Adept, *máhir, mashsháq.*

Adequate, *bahut, káfí.*

Adhere (stick), *chipakná, chipaṭná.*

Adjacent, *pás hí pás—muttasil.*

Adjourn, *multawí karná.*

Adjust, (put right) *saj sajáná, durust karná* ; (a debt) *adá karná, bhar dená.*

Adjusted (paid), *paṭá húá, adá húá.*

Adjustment (of a debt), *nikásí, adáí.*

Administration, *ạmaldárí.*

Administrator (ruler), *hákim, ạmaldár.*

Admire, ... *se girawída honá, ạzíz rakhná.*

Admiration, *pasandí, girawídagí.*

Admit, (concede) *mánná—taslím karná* ; (let in) *bhítar* (or *andar*) *áne dená,* 170, 172, 445.

Admittance, *dakhl, ghus-paiṭh.*

Admonish, *samjháná — nasíhat karná.*

Admonition, *samjháná—nasíhat,* 594.

Adopt (a child), *god lená, le pálná.*

Adopted (child), *le-pálak.*

Adorn, (the person) *singár karná;* (one's house, &c.) *árásta karná, sanwárná.*

Adulterate, ... *men milauní karná.*

Adulteration, *milauní.*

Advance, (go ahead) *áge baṛhná, qadam baṛháná* ; (of money) *peshgí.*

Advantage, *fáida.*

*To take* Advantage of (in a bad sense), *samajhná.*

N.B.—In this use of *samajhná,* the meaning is, "acting on the knowledge of," 111, 113.

Adventure (*n.*), *sarguzasht, wáridát.*

Adversity, *musíbat—tíra-rozí.*

Advertisement, *ishtihár.*

Advice, *saláh.*

Advisable, *saláh.*

Advise, *saláh dená.*

Adze, *basúlá.*

Affair, *bát, amr* (pron. *amar*).

Affect (to concern), ... *ká asar paṛná,* with *par* after the person or thing affected.

Affect (to pretend), ... *ká bhagal bharná.*

Affection, *muhabbat* ; (parental) *mámatá, láḍ-piyár.*

Afflicted (in affliction), *taklíf-zada, dukhit.*

Affliction, *dukh, musíbat.*

Afford—can't afford so much—*itná dene kí gunjáish nahín,* 175.

Affront (*n.*), *be-ịzzatí.*

Aforesaid, *mazkúr.*
Afraid, to be, *ḍarná—khauf honá.*
After, *ke píchhe, ke bąd.*
Afternoon, *do pahar ke bąd—sipahar.*
Afterwards, *uske bąd, uske píchhe;* (later on) *píchhe se.*
Again, *phir, dobára.*
Against, (in opposition to) *ke barkhiláf;* (against the wall) *díwár se.*
Agate (moss), *sijrí.*
Age, *ụmar.*
Aged, *buḍḍhá;* (woman) *buṛhiyá.*
Agent, *gumáshta;* (legal representative) *mukhtár.*
Aggravate (make worse), *aur kharáb karná,* 623.
Aggressive, to take the, *pahal karná,* 478.
Agitation, (shaking) *takán;* (popular) *shorish.*
Agony, *ązáb, jánkaní.*
Agree to, *rází honá.*
Agreeable (pleasant), *dil-pasand, suháwaná.*
Agreeably to, *ke muwáfiq.*
Agreement, (written) *iqrárnáma;* (concord) *ittifáq.*
Agriculture, *káshtkárí,* 189.
Aim at, *tákná, shist lagáná;* (seek to attain) ... *se kám rakhná,* 408.
Air, *hawá;* (tune) *rág.*
Alarm (*n.*), *ghabráhaṭ.*
Alert, on the, *chaukas—ámáda.*
Alias, (adj.) *ụrf;* (an alias) *ụrfí nám.*
Alien, *begána, bidesí;* (species) *ghair-jins,* 630.
Alienation, *mughàyarat.*
Alight, *utarná.*
Alike, *eksán—mushábih.*
Alive, *jítá—zinda;* (and kicking) *jítá jágtá.*
All, *sab, sárá—kull;* (all day) *din bhar, sáre din.*
Allay, *ṭhanḍá karná.*
Allegation, *bayán.*
Allegiance, *tábịdárí;* (to the sovereign) *daulat-khwáhí.*
Allegory, *tamsíl.*
Alleviate, *kam karná.*
Alleviation, *takhfíf.*
Alliance, (confederacy) *sázish;* (matrimonial) *nisbat.*
Alligator, *magar.*
Allow, *dená;* (admit) *mánná, qabúl karná.*
Allure, *lubháná—tahrís karná.*
Allusion, *ishára, zikr.*
Almanack, *jantrí.*
Almond, *bádám;* (shaped) *bádámí.*
Almost, *qaríb.*
Alone, *akelá—tanhá.*
Along with, *sáth, sang;* (together with) *samet.*
Aloof, to hold, *pare rahná—darkinár rahná.*
Already, (done already) *ho chuká;* (gone already) *já chuká.*
Also, *bhí.*
Alter, *badal karná, tabdíl karná.*
Alteration, *tabdíl.*
Alternate (one thing with another), *ápas men pher phár karná.*
Alternately, *bárí bárí se.*
Although, *agarchi, harchand;* (granting that) *go ki.*
Altogether, *bilkull—sarásar.*
Alum, *phiṭkirí.*
Always, *hamesha, har waqt.*

Ambassador, *elchí.*
Amber, *kahrubá.*
Ambition, *hausila*, 288.
Ambitious, *hausilamand*, 290.
Ambush, *ghát—kamín.*
Amends, *taláfí, badlá*, 100.
Amethyst, *kaṭailá.*
Amidst, *ke bích men—ke darmiyán.*
Amuse oneself, *dil bahláná*, 528.
Amusement, *dil-lagí*, 192.
Analogy, *mushábahat.*
Analysis, *tajazzí*, 496.
Ancestors, *bápdáde.*
Anchor, *langar* ; (to cast) *langar ḍálná.*
Ancient, *qadím, qadímí.*
Anecdote, *qissa.*
Angel, *firishta.*
Anger, *ghussa.*
Angry, *khafá, ghussa.*
Anguish, *shikasta-dilí.*
Animal, *jánwar.*
Animate (having life), *jándár*, 182
Ankle, *ṭakhná*, 517.
Anniversary, *sál-girih.*
Announce, *záhir karná.*
Annoy, *diqq karná, chheṛná.*
Another, *dúsrá, aur—dígar.*
Answer (*v.a.*), *jawáb dená* ; (to succeed) ... *se kám nikalná*, 390, 391.
Ant, *chiúnṭí.*
Antagonist, *haríf.*
Anxiety, *fikrmandí, be-qarárí.*
Anxious, *fikrmand, be-qarár.*
Any, *koí, kuchh.*

*N.B.*—Things that form parts of a quantity, as rupees, grain, &c., take *kuchh* before them; things that are complete in themselves, as books, &c., take *koí.*

Anyhow (not properly), *lashṭampashṭam.*
Anything, *kuchh.*
Anywhere, *kahín.*
Apart, *alag—ạláhida.*
Apathy, *sahlangárí*, 127.
Aperient (*n.*), *julláb.*
Apiece — two apiece, three apiece, *do do, tín tín.*
Apology, *mạzúrí, ụzr-khwáhí*, 512.
Appalling, *haibatnák, bhayának*, 630.
Apparatus, *sámán.*
Apparently, *dekhne men, záhir men.*
Appear, (become visible) *dikhái dená, nazar áná* ; (to seem) *mạlúm honá.*
Appearance, *súrat* ; (for the sake of appearances) *logon ke dikháne ko*, 520.
Appendix, *zamíma.*
Appetite, *bhúkh—ishtihá.*
Applaud, ... *kí shábáshí karná*, 242.
Applause, *shábáshí.*
Apple, *seb.*
Application, *darkhwást.*
Apply (for) *darkhwást karná* ; (as a plaster) *lagáná.*
Apply (be relevant to), *ạid honá, lagná.*
Apply to (fitly as an epithet), ... *par sádiq áná.*
Appoint, *muqarrar karná.*
Appointment, (to an office) *taqarrurí*; (the office itself) *ụhda, mansab* ; (engagement) *wạda.*
Apprentice, *shágird.*
Apprise (warn, &c.), *jatá dená—ágáh karná*, 352.

Approve, (sanction) *manzúr karná*; (approve of) *ká rawádár honá*. Example: I do not approve of gambling, *main júá khelne ká rawádár nahín hún*.
Arbitration, *sálisí*.
Arbitrator, *sális*.
Arbitrators, *panch, pancháyat*.
Argue, *bahs karná* (pron. *baihs*), *hujjat karná*.
Argument, *hujjat*.
Argumentation, *mubáhasa*.
Arm, *bánh, bázú*; (to arm oneself) *hathyár bándhná*.
Armed, *hathyár-band*.
Arms (weapons), *hathyár*.
Army, *fauj—lashkar*.
Arrange (adjust), *sajáná, durust rakhná*, 413.
Arrangement (regular order), *tartíb*.
Arrangements, *bandobast*.
Arrant scoundrel, *pakká badmaásh*.
Arrest, (*v.a.*) *giriftár karná*; (*n.*) *giriftárí—mákhúzí*, 168.
Arrival, *ámad*, also the verb *áná* used substantively.
Arrive, *pahúnchná, á jáná*; (polite term) *wárid honá*.

*N.B.*—In announcing an arrival *pahúnch jáná* or *á jáná* is always used.

Arrow, *tír*; (arrow-head) *gánsí*.
Arsenal, *silah-kháná*.
Art, *fann*.
Artful, *híla-báz—fitratí*.
Article, *chíz*; (in a paper, &c.) *mazmún*.
Artifice, *híla-bahána*.
Artificial, *banáyá húá—masnúí*, 339.
Artillery, *top-kháná*.
Artisan, *kárígar*.
Artist, *musawwir*.
Artless, *bholá—sáda*.
As, *jaisá*; (since) *jo ki, chún ki*; (when) *jiswaqt*; (as soon as) *jiswaqt*; (as though) *ki goyá*.
Ascend, *úpar charhná*.
Ashamed, *sharminda*.
Ash-coloured, *khákistarí*.
Ashes, *rákh*.
Ask, *púchhná*; (ask for) *mángná*.
Assault (*v.a.*), ... *par hamla karná*.
Assembly, *majlis*.
Assent to everything, *har ek hán men hán miláná*.
Assessment, *lagán*.
Assets, *jáedád*, 480.
As yet, *ab tak—hanoz*.
Assign (cause for, &c.), *qarár dená*, 283.
Assist, *madad dená, kí madad karná*.
Assistance, *madad—imdád*.
Assumed (fictitious), *farzí*, 341.
Astonished, *muta'ajjib*.
Astonishment, *ta'ajjub*; (matter for) *ta'ajjub kí bát*.
Astute, *tez-fahm*.
At all (whatever), *bhí*, 16, 17, *bilkull*.
At last, *ákhir men—ákhirkár*.
At once, *abhí, jhatpat—fauran*.
At present, *bilfel*, 557.
Atheist, *dahriyá*.
Attached (devoted) to, ... *se girawída*; (to become so) ... *se jí lagná*.

Attack (*v.a.*), ... *par hamla karná.*
Attempt, *qasd karná, koshish karná.*
Attend to, *mutawajjih honá*, 130.
Attention, *tawajjuh—iltifát.*
Attentive (to one's work, &c.) to be, *dil lagáná.*
Attorney, *mukhtár.*
Attribute to, ... *se mansúb karná.*
Attribute (quality), *sifat*, 182.
Auction, *nílám*; (a bid at one) *bolí.*
Aunt, (paternal) *phúphí*; (maternal) *mausí—khála.*
Authority, *ikhtiyár.*
Autumn, *kharíf.*
Autumnal, *kharífí.*
Avarice, *lálach—hirs-wa-hawá.*
Avaricious, *lálchí—harís.*
Average (*n.*), *ausat*; (to strike one) *ausat lagáná*, 354, 427.
Average (middling), *ausatí.*
Avoid, ... *se bachná*; (shun) ... *se dúr rahná*; (avoid observation) *nazar bacháná.*
Awake, (*v.n.*) *jágná*; (*adj.*) *jágtá.*
Awaken (*v.a.*), *jagáná.*
Aware of, to be, *ko malúm honá —ágáh honá.*
Away, (absent) *ghair házir*; (to go away) *chalá jáná*; (to take away) *lejáná.*
Awe-inspiring, *robdár*, 582.
Awkward, (unskilful) *anárí*; (as an animal) *bhadesalá.*
Awkwardness (want of skill), *anárpan.*
Awl, *sutárí.*
Awning, *namgíra.*
Axe, *kulhárí.*
Axle, *dhurá.*
Babbler, *bakwásí—yáwa-go.*
Bachelor, *kúárá—ná-katkhudá.*
Back, *píth*; (the rear) *pichhwárá.*
Backbite, *chughlí khánú.*
Backbiter, *lutrá—chughul-khor*, 548.
Backbiting, *chughlí — chughul-khorí.*
Backbone, *ríṛh.*
Backdoor, *chor-khiṛkí.*
Bad, *burá, kharáb—bad*; (to go bad) *bigaṛ jáná.*
Badge, *chaprás*; (on turban, &c.) *taghma.*
Badly, *burí tarah se* (pron. *tareh*), *bure taur par.*
Baffle, *haráná, bátil karná.*
Bag, *thailí*; (large) *thailá.*
Baggage, *asbáb, chíz-bast.*
Bail (the person), *zámin, házir-zámin.*
Bail, (security) *zamánat*; (on bail) *zamánat par.*
Bailiff, *sazáwal.*
Bait (for fish), *chára.*
Bake, *pakáná.*
Baker, *roṭí-wálá.*
Balance, (of account) *báqí*; (make-weight) *pásang.*
Balcony, *chhajjá—bálá-khána.*
Bald, *chandlá, ganjá.*
Baldness, *chandlápan.*
Bale, *gaṭṭhá.*
Bale (out water), *ulíchná.*
Ball, (for playing with) *gend*; (bullet) *golí.*
Bandage, *paṭṭí.*
Banging (of a door, &c.), *ṭakkar*, 150.
Banishment, *jilá-watani.*
Bank, (of river) *kinára*; (part for walking on) *paṭrí.*

Banker (native), *mahájan.*
Bankrupt, *dewáliyá* ; (to become so) *dewálá nikalná*, 102, 103.
Bankruptcy, *dewálá.*
Banner, *jhandá.*
Banquet, *ziyáfat.*
Banyan-tree, *bar.*
Bar (of a cage), *kámp*, 225.
Barb (of a hook or arrow), *ánkrí.*
Barbarous, *janglí—wahshí.*
Barber, *náí, hajjám.*
Bard (Hindu), *bhát.*
Bare, *nangá* ; (mere) *khálí, sirf.*
Barely (time to, &c.), *mushkil se, diqqat se.*
Bargain (*v.a.*), *saudá karná*, 217.
Bargaining (*n.*), *saudá*, 217.
Bark (of a tree), *bakkal*, 183.
Bark (as a dog), *bhaunkná.*
Barley, *jau.*
Barrel, (cask) *pípá* ; (of gun) *nalí.*
Barren, *bánjh* ; (land) *kallar.*
Barrier, (obstruction) *háil* ; (to act as one) *háil honá*, 187, 188.
Barter (*v.a.*), *adlá-badlí karná.*
Barter (*n.*), *adlá-badlí.*
Bashful, *sharmgín, mahjúb.*
Bashfulness, *hijáb, láj.*
Basin, *chilamchí.*
Bask in the sun, *dhúp tápná.*
Basket, *tokrí* ; (large) *tokrá.*
Bat, *chamgudrí, chamgiddar* ; (flying-fox) *bádur.*
Bath, *ghusal* ; (room) *ghusal-khána.*
Bathe, *naháná, ghusal karná.*
Bathe (another), *nahláná, ghusal dená.*
Battalion, *paltan.*
Batter (with a club, &c.), *chhetná.*
Battle, *laráí.*
Bay (colour), *kumait*, 232.
Bayonet, *sangín.*
Be (*v.n.*), *honá.* Be quick! *jaldí karo!*
Bead, *pot, dána.*
Beak, *chonch.*
Beam (wooden), *karí, lathá, dharan.*
Bean, *báqlá.*
Bear (animal), *ríchh, bhálú.*
Bear (endure), *kí bardásht karná, kí táb láná*, 29, 506.
Bear (in mind), *khiyál rahná* ; (lit. to be borne in mind), 409.
Bear (as a tree), *phal láná.*
Bearer, (servant) *bahrá* ; (of a letter, &c.) *hámil.*
Beard, *dárhí.*
Beast, *jánwar.*
Beat, *márná, pítná* ; (at play) *jítná* ; (to be beaten at play) *hár jáná.*
Beautiful, *khúbsúrat, sundar.*
Beauty, *khúbsúratí, khúbí.*
*The* Beauty of it is, &c., *lutf yih hai, ki.*
Because, *kyúnki, is liye ki, is wáste ki* ; (forasmuch as, *az baski*).
Because of, *ba-sabab, ke sabab se.*
Beckon, *háth se ishára karná.*
Become, *hojáná* ; (look nice) *zeb dená.*
Become (to befit), *sajná, phabná.*
Bed, (bedstead) *palang* ; (bedding) *bistará, bichhauná.*
Bedding (for a horse), *bichálí.*
Bedroom, *sone ká kamará, palang ká kamará.*

Bedstead (used by all classes), *chárpái.*
Bee, *shahd kí makkhí.*
Beetroot, *chuqandar.*
Befitting, *ba já, munásib.*
Before, *pahle, peshtar;* (in the presence of) *ke sámhne, ke rúbarú;* (ahead) *áge, agárí.*
Beforehand, *áge se.*
Beg, (for alms) *bhíkh mángná;* (entreat) *minnat karná.*
Beggar, *bhikhárí, bhikmangá, ṭukar-gadá.*
Begin, *shurú karná, lagná.*

*N.B.*—The preceding verb is always inflected before *lagna*, but never before *shurú karná.*

Beginner (tyro), *mubtadí.*
Beginning (*n.*), *ibtidá, shurú.*
Behalf, *haqq men.*
Behave, (generally) *chál chalná*, preceded by *nek* or *burí* according to the behaviour; (on a particular occasion) *pesh áná*, 114.
Behaviour (in general), *chál-chalan.*
Behind, (*prep.*) *ke píchhe;* (in the rear) *píchhe;* (to fall behind) *píchhe parná.*
Believe (*v.a.*), *báwar karná, yaqín karná;* (to feel sure) *yaqín honá.*
Bell, *ghanṭá;* (on a bullock's neck) *ghanṭálí.*
Bellmetal, *kánsá.*
Bellow (or low), *rámbhná.*
Bellows, *dhaunkní.*
Belly, *peṭ.*
Bellyband (saddlery), *peṭí.*
Belong to, *ká honá;* (to me) *merá hai.*
Beloved, *piyárá — mahbúb;* (fem.) *piyárí—mahbúba.*
Below, (*prep.*) *ke níche, ke tale;* (down below) *níche.*
Belt, (waist) *diwálí;* (cross) *partalá.*
Bench, *takhta.*
Bend, (as a stick) *lachakná;* (*v.a.*) *lachkáná.*
Bend, (forward) *jhukná;* (over or downwards) *nihúrná.*
*To cause to* Bend *or stoop, jhukáná.*
Bend (in a river), *bánk.*
Beneath, (*prep.*) *ke níche, ke tale;* (*adv.*) *níche.*
Benediction, *duá-nek.*
Benefactor, *munim;* (great benefactor) *khudáwand-i-neamat.*
Beneficial, *mufíd, fáidamand.*
Benefit, *fáida;* (conferred) *ihsán, neamat.*
Benevolent, *mihrbán.*
Bent, (crooked) *ṭeṛhá;* (inclination) *mailán.*
Bequeath, *wasiyat karná.*
Bequest, *wasiyat, hiba.*
Berry, *dána.*
Beseech, *minnat karná, girgiráná.*
Besides these, *inke siwá, siwá inke.*
Best, *sab se achchhá.*
Bestow, *bakhsh dená, ináyat karná.*
Bet (*n.*), *bází, shart;* (to bet) *bází* or *shart lagáná.*
Betel-nut, *supárí;* (the leaf) *pán.*
Better than, ... *se achchhá, se bihtar;* (better still) *aur achchhá.*
Betray (a secret), *pardadarí karná.*

Betrayal (of a trust), *khiyánat.*
Betrothed (man or woman), *mangetar*, 465, 555.
Between, *ke bích men—ke darmiyán.*
Beverage, *sharbat.*
Bewail, ... *par nála karná.*
Beware of, ... *se khabardár raho.*
Beyond, ... *se pare, kí parlí taraf*, 94, 110.
Bid adieu to, *salám karná*, 227.
Big, *bará.*
Bile, *pitt* or *pittá.*
Bilious, *safráí.*
Bill, (account) *hisáb*; (of exchange) *hundí*; (of sale) *bainámа.*
Bind, *bándhná.*
Binding (of a book), *jild.*
Bird, *chiriyá.*
Birth, *paidáish.*
Birthday, *janam-din—sál-girih.*
Birthplace, *janam-bhúm — zádbúm.*
Bit, *tukrá—purza*; (a little bit of) *zarrá sá*; (horse's bit) *dahána.*
Bite, *kátná, kát kháná.*
Bitter, *karwá.*
Bitterness, *karwáhat—talkhí.*
Black, *kálá—siyáh.*
Blacken, *kálá karná.*
Blacking, *siyáhí.*
Blackguard, *badzát, badmásh.*
Blackness, *siyáhí.*
Blacksmith, *lohár.*
Bladder, *masána.*
Blade (of knife, &c.), *phal*, 653.
Blame, (reprove) *malámat karná*; (not to blame, *adj.*) *be-qusúr.* Who is to blame? *kiská qusúr hai?*
Blamelesss, (innocent) *be-qusúr*; (as a life) *be-aib.*
Blank (*adj.*), *sáda.*
Blanket, *kammal.*
Blaspheme, *kufr bakná.*
Blasphemous (as language), *kufr-ámez.*
Bleat, *mimiyáná.*
Bleed, *lohú* (or *khún*) *járí honá.*
Blemish, *aib, nuqs.*
Blend (*v.n.*), *mil jáná.*
Bless, (invoke blessing) *duá dená*; (bestow blessing) *barakat dená.*
Blind, *andhá*; (of one eye) *káná.*
Blister (*n.*), *phapholá—ábila*, 183.
Block (of wood), *kunda.*
Blockhead, *ahmaq* (pron. *aihmaq*), *ghámar.*
Blood, *lohú, khún.*
Bloodshed, *khúnrezí.*
Bloodstone, *pitauniá.*
Bloody, *lohú-lahán, khún-álúda.*
Bloom (*v.n.*), *phúlná, khilná*, 497.
Blot, Blotch, } *dágh*
Blot-out, *mitá dálná*, or *dená.*
Blotting-paper, *siyáhí ká kághaz.*
Blow (*n.*), *chot, chapet*; (with the fist) *mukká, ghúsá.*
Blow, (with the mouth) *phúnkná*; (as the wind) *chalná.*
Blow-pipe, *phukní*, 603.
Bludgeon, *sontá, lath.*
Blue, *nílá*; (light) *ásmání rang.*
Blunder, *khatá, bhúl.*
Blunt, *kund, bhotá.*
Blush, *khijlat utháná.*
Boar (wild), *janglí súar.*
Board, *takhta.*
Boast of, (glory in) *par fakhr karná*, 623.

Boat, *náo, kishtí*; (small) *dengi.*
Boatman, *malláh.*
Bodily, (whole) *sábit ká sábit.*
Body, *badan.*
Bog, *dhasan, daldal.*
Boggy, *daldalá.*
Boil, *ubalná, khaulná—josh márná*; (*v.a.*) *ubálná.*
Boil (sore), *phorá.*
Boiling water, *phúṭá pání.*
Bold, *diler, be-bák.*
Boldly, *nidharak—dilerána.*
Bolt, *chhiṭkaní.*
Bond, *bandhan*; (agreement) *tamassuk.*
Bondage, *ghulámí, pábandí*; (captivity) *asírí, qaid.*
Bone, *haḍḍí.*
Book, *kitáb.*
Boon, *neamat.*
Booty, *lúṭ—ghanímat.*
Borax, *sohágá.*
Border (of garment), *goṭ—sanjáf*, 654.
Border (edge), *kinára.* Borders (limits), *sarhadd.*
Bore (make holes), *barmáná, chhedná.*
Bore (to weary), *maghz cháṭná.*
Born, *paidá húá.*
Borrow, (an article) *máng lená, udhár lená*; (money) *qarz lená*, 530.
Bosom, *chháti—sína.*
Both, *donon dono.*
Both parties, *donon taraf*; (in a suit) *fariqain.*
Bother, (trouble) *taklíf, harj-marj*, 488; (*v.a.*) *diqq karná.*
Bottom, (of a basket, &c.) *talí*; (of a tumbler, &c.) *pendí*; (of a jar, &c.) *pendá*; (of a river) *tah, tháh*, 449, 450.
*We've not got to the* Bottom of this, *iskí asliyat nahin khulí.*
Bough, *ḍálí, ṭahní.*
Bound (of a ball), *ṭappá*, 493.
Boundaries, *sarhadd.*
Boundary, *siwáná, hadd*; (ridge between fields) *ḍaul.*
Bound by, *pá-band*, 375.
Bounding (of a deer), *chaukaṛí, kulánch*, 494.
Boundless, *be-hadd—be gháyat.*
Bounty, *faiyází.*
Bow (*n.*), *kamán, dhanuk.*
Bow (*v.n.*), *jhukná.*
Bowels, *antṛí.*
Bowl (for drinking), *belá—bádiya.*
Box, *sandúq*; (small) *ḍibbá*; (very small) *ḍibiá.*
Boy, *chhokṛá, laṛka, launḍá.*
Boyhood, *laṛakpan.*
Bracelet, *kaṛá, chúṛí, kangan.*
Braces, *gális.*
Brackish, *khárá.*
Brackishness, *shoriyat.*
Braid, *fíta*; (*v.a.*) *gúndhná.*
Brain, *dimágh, maghz*; (Hindi) *bhejá*; (disease of) *khalal-dimághí.*
Bran, *chokar.*
Branch, *ḍálí, ṭahní.*
Branch-canal, *rájbáhá.*
Brand (*v.a.*), *dágh dená.*
Brasier *kaserá, ṭhaṭherá.*
Brass, *pítal*; (of brass) *pítal ká, pítlá.*
Brave, *diláwar, jawán-mard.*
Bravery, *diláwarí, jawán-mardí.*
Bravo! *shábásh!*
Brawl, *jhagṛá-ragṛá, qaziya.*
Bray (*v.n.*), *renkná.*

Bread, *roṭí.*
Breadth, *chauṛaí, chauṛán.*
Break, (*v.a.*) *toṛná* ; (*v.n.*) *ṭúṭná, ṭúṭ jáná.*
Break of day, *pau phaṭne ká waqt, bhor, taṛká.*
Break into a house (by digging), *naqab lagáná.*
Break out (as a fire), *lagná.*
Break the news to, *se gosh-guzár karná.*
Breast, *chhátí, sína.*
Breast high, *chhátí-bhar.*
Breast-work, *fasíl.*
Breath, *sáns, dam.*
Breathe, *sáns lená, dam lená.*
Breathless, *be-dam.*
Breed (*n.*), *zát, nasl.*
Breed (engender), *paidá karná.*
Breeding (good breeding), *tahzíb.*
Breeze, *hawá.*
Brethren (brotherhood), *bháí-band, birádarí.*
Brevity, *ikhtisár.*
Bribe (*n.*), *rishwat, ghús,* 383.
Brick (*n.*), *ínṭ* ; (brickwork) *ínṭgárí* ; (brick-kiln) *pajáwa* ; (broken brick) *roṛá.*
Bride, *dulhin.*
Bridegroom, *dulhá.*
Bridge, *pul* ; (making one) *pul-bandí.*
Bridle, *lagám.*
Brief, *mukhtasar* ; (in brief) *gharaz.*
Bright, *roshan* ; (as a polished boot) *chamakdár* ; (as a light) *tez.*
Brighten, *chamakdená, chamká-dená.*
Brightness, *roshní, chamkáhaṭ.*

Brim, *kinára, lab.*
Brimful, *labálab, labrez.*
Brimstone, *gandhak.*
Brine, *shoriyat.*
Bring, *láná, le-aná* ; (bring about) *wuqú men láná* ; (bring forth, produce) *paidá karná* ; (bring forward) *darpesh karná* ; (bring up rear) *pálná, parwarish karná* ; (bring to light) *barámad karná.*
Brink, *kinára, lab.*
Brittle, *názuk, mihín.*
Broach (a subject), *chheṛná,* 532.
Broad, *chauṛá* ; (emphatic) *chauṛá-chaklá.*
Broadcloth, *bánát* or *banát.*
Brocade, *kimkhwáb, tásh, bádalá.*
Broil (*v.a.*), *bhúnná.*
Broken, *ṭúṭa, phúṭá.*
Broken-hearted, *dil-shikasta.*
Broken-heartedness, *shikasta-dilí.*
Broker, *dallál.*
Brokerage, *dallálí.*
Brood (litter, &c.), *jhol.*
Brook, *nálá.*
Broom, *jháṛú.*
Broth, *shurwá.*
Brother, *bháí.*
Brow (forehead), *máthá, pesháni.*
Browbeat, *dhamkí dená, ghurkí dená.*
Brown, (as hair) *bhúrá* ; (dark-brown—a horse) *mushkí,* 232.
Bruise, (*n.*) *choṭ* ; (*v.a.*) *kuch-alná.*
Bruised, *rang nílá hogayá.*
Brutal (cruel), *be-rahm.*
Brutality (cruelty), *be-rahmí.*
Brute, *jánwar—haiwán.*
Bubble (*n.*), *bulbulá.*

Bucket, (stable) *bálti*; (for drawing water) *ḍol*; (large leathern, for irrigating) *charas*.
Buckle, *baksúá*.
Bud, *kali—ghuncha*.
Bud (*v.n.*), *konpal nikalná, kaliyáná*.
Buffalo, (male) *bhainsá*; (female) *bhains*.
Buffoon, *maskhara, bhánḍ*, 184.
Buffoonery, *maskharagí*.
Bug, *khaṭmal*.
Build, *chunáná, banáná—taʻmír karná*, 43, 98.
Building, *imárat*.
Bulb, *gaṭṭhá*, 628.
Bulk, *moṭái*.
Bull, *sánṛ* or *sánḍ*.
Bullet, *golí*.
Bullfrog, *meghá*.
Bullock, *bail*.
Bullock-cart, *chhakṛá*.
Bump, *súján, waram*; (permanent) *gilṭí*.
Bumptious, *sir-chaṛhá*.
Bunch, *lachchhá, guchchha*, 65.
Bundle, *poṭlí, gaṭhrí*; (small) *buqcha*.
Burden, *bojh, bhár*.
Burdensome, *bhárí*; (to be) *bhárí lagná*; (a person) *par bojh dená*.
Burglary, *naqab-zaní*.
Burial, *dafan-kafan*; (burial-ground) *qabaristán*.
Burn, (*v.n.*) *jalná*; (*v.a.*) *jaláná*.
Burnish, *chamkáná, jhalkáná*.
Burst (*v.n.*), *phúṭná*; (as clothes through tightness) *masakná*.
Bury, *gáṛ dená, miṭṭí dená—dafn karná*.
Bush, *jháṛ*; (small bushes) *jhunḍ*.
Bushy, *lachchhedár, guchchhedár*, 306.
Business, *kám*; (trade, &c.) *károbár*, 190. What business of yours? *tumko kyá wásta?* 172.
Bustle (fuss), *dauṛ-dhúp*.
Busy, (at work) *mashghul*; (not at leisure) *kuchh kám hai*.
But, *par, lekin, magar*; (except) *siwá*.
Butcher, *qasáí*.
Butter, *makkhan*.
Butterfly, *títri, titlí*.
Button, *ghunḍí, buṭám*.
Button-hole, *káj*.
Buy, *mol lená, kharídná*.
Buyer, *kharídár*.
Buying and selling, *kharíd-o-farokht*.
Buzz, *bhinbhináná, gúnjná*.
By-and-by, *abhí, thoṛí der men*.
By chance, *ittifáq se—ittifáqan*.
By degrees, *áhiste áhiste, rafta rafta*.
By no means, *kabhí nahin, hargiz nahin*.
By-path, *pagḍanḍí*.
Bystanders, *log jo khaṛe hain* (or *the*).

Cabbage, *kobí*.
Cackle, *kuṛkuṛáná*.
Cackling, *kuṛuk*.
Cage, *pinjrá—qafas*.
Cajole, *phusláná, dam dená*.
Cajolery, *phusláhaṭ, dambází*.
Calamity, *áfat, bipat*.
Calculate, *hisáb karná*.
Calculation, *hisáb*.
Calendar (month, &c.), *shamsí*.

Calf, (small) *bachhrú;* (large) *bachhrá;* (of leg) *pindlí.*
Calico, *kapásí kaprá, chhínt.*
Call, *buláná;* (call out to, or for) *áwáz dená, pukárná.*
Call (give name to), *nám rakhná, kahná.*
Called (so and so) to be, *kahláná.*
Callous, *be-dard, sakht.*
Callousness, *be dardí, sakhtí.*
Calm, (*adj.*) *khátir jama;* (*n.*) *níwá—sukún.*
Calmness, *khátir-jamaí—etidálí.*
Calumniate, *tuhmat lagáná, badnám karná.*
Calumniator, *muftarí.*
Calumny, *buhtán, túfán.*
Camel, *únt—shutur.*
Camp, *dere* (lit. tents), *paráo.*
Camphor, *káfúr.*
Camping-ground, *paráo.*
Can (to be able), *sakná.*
Canal, *nahr.*
Cancel, *mansúkh karná,* 155.
Candid, *sáf-dil, be-riyá.*
Candidate, *ummedwár.*
Candle (wax), *mom-battí.*
Candlestick, *shama-dán.*
Candour, *kusháda-dilí, be-riyáí.*
Cane, *bent;* (to cane) *bent lagáná.*
Cannibal, *mardum-khor.*
Cannon, *top;* (cannon-ball) *golá.*
Canoe, *dengí.*
Canopy, *sáyabán.*
Canter, (*v.n.*) *poyán chalná;* (*v.a.*) *sarpat dauráná,* 303.
Cantonments, *chháoní.*
Canvas, *tát.*
Cap, *chhotí topí.*
Capable (qualified), *qábil, láiq.*
Capacity (ability), *liyáqat—istedád;* (function) *haisiyat,* 417, 418, 584.
Capital (pecuniary), *púnjí, sarmáya.*
Capricious, *talauwun-mizáj.*
Capsize, *ulat jáná, tale-úpar jáná.*
Captious, *nukta-chín, harf-gír.*
Captivate (charm), *moh lená, fárefta karná.*
Captivated, *farefta.*
Captivating, *dil-fareb, dil-rubá.*
Captive, *asír, bandhúá, qaidí.*
Captivity, *qaid, asírí.*
Capture, *giriftárí;* (*v.a.*) *giriftár karná.*
Caravan, *qáfila.*
Carbuncle, (gem) *shab-chirágh;* (sore) *phorá.*
Carcass, *lásh.*
Cards, (playing) *tás*—(the game) *ganjífa,* 223.
Care (*n.*), *parwá, fikr;* (to take) *khabardár honá.*
*Take* Care of (keep carefully), ... *kí khabardárí karná;* (a sick person, &c.) ... *kí khabargírí karná.*
Care for, (like) ... *men jí lagná;* (not to care to do a thing) *manzúr nahín honá.*
Careful, *khabardár.*
Carefully, *khabardárí se, hoshyárí se,* 67.
Careless, *gháfil.*
Carelessly, *ghaflat se, gháfilí se.*
Carelessness, *ghaflat, gháfilí.*
Caress (*v.a.*), *piyár karná.*
Cargo, *bojháí—bár.*
Carnal, *nafsání.*
Carouse (*v.a.*), *mai-noshí karná.*
Carpenter, *barhaí.*
Carpet, *farsh, darí.*

Carriage, *gáṛí*; (hackney) *ṭheká gáṛí*; (close) *pálkí gáṛí*; (for troops) *bárbardárí*.
Carrot, *gájar*.
Carry, (along) *háthmen liye jáná*; (away) *uṭhá lejáná*; (carry off) *le-bhágná*; (carry out) *bajá láná*.
Carry, (as a donkey, &c.), *ḍhoná*.
Cart, *gáṛí*; (dog-cart) *ṭamṭam*; (bullock-cart) *chhakṛá*.
Cartman, *gáṛíwán*.
Cartridge, *kártús*; (cartridge-bag) *tosdán*.
Case, (covering) *ghiláf*; (of a watch) *ḍhakan*.
Case, (matter) *bát*, *amar*; (circumstances) *hál*; (state your case) *apná hál batláo*; (condition) *hálat*.
Case (in Court), *muqaddama*.
*In any* Case (at all costs), *ba har súrat*, *ba har hál*.
Cash, *naqd*, *naqdí*; (to sell for) *naqd bechná*, 105.
Cask, *pípá*.
Cast, (to throw) *ḍálná*; (as metal) *ḍhálná*.
Cast down, (overthrow) *de ḍálná*. (This is a much more forcible expression than "*ḍál dená*.")
Caste, *zát*; (class) *qaum*, 636.
Castle, *qilạ*, *gaṛh*.
Castor-oil, *renḍí ká tel*.
Castrate, *khasí karná*.
Castrated (a horse), *akhta*.
Cat, *billí*; (tomcat) *billá*.
Catalogue, *fihrist*.
Cataract, *jhál*.
Catastrophe, *áfat*, *bipat*.
Catch (catch hold of), *pakaṛná*.
Catch fire, ... *men ág lágná*.
Cat's-eye, *lasaniyá*.
Cattle, *dangar* — *maweshí* 266, 646.
Cattle-road, *gohar*.
Cauldron, *deg*, 627.
Cauliflower, —*phúl-kobí*.
Cause, *sabab*—*wajh* (pron. *wajeh*).
Cause (to produce), *paidá karná*.
Caution, *kharbardárí*, *hoshyárí*—*ihtiyát*; (want of) *be-ihtiyátí*.
Caution (to warn), *khabardár karná*, *jatá dená*.
Cautious, *khabardár*, *hoshyár*.
Cautiously, *hoshyárí se*, *dekh bhálke*.
Cavalry, *risála*; (soldier) *sawár*.
Cave (cavern), *ghár*, *guphá*.
Cavil, *ạib pakaṛná*.
Caviller, *hujjatí*—*harf-gír*.
Cavilling, *ạib-joí*, *harf-gírí*.
Cavity, *khol*.
Cease, *se háth uṭháná*, ... *se báz áná*; (as wind or rain) *tham jáná*, *band honá*.
Ceiling, *chhat*.
Celebrate (keep), *ạmal men láná*.
Celebrated, *mashhúr*, *námwar*.
Celebrity, *námwarí*; (a person) *námwar shakhs*.
Celestial, *ásmání*—*samáwí*.
Cell, *hujra*.
Cement (mortar), *gach*.
Cemetery, *qabaristán*.
Censure, (reproof) *malámat*; (*v.a.*) *malámat karná*.
Census, *mardum-shumárí*.
Cent. (five per cent.), *pánch rúpiya saikṛá*.
Central *bích men*—*darmiyání*.
Centre, *bíchon-bích*—*wasat*, *markaz*.
Century, *sadí*.

Ceremonious, *pur takalluf;* (a person) *takalluf-mizáj.*
Ceremony, (punctiliousness) *takalluf;* (absence of) *be-takallufí.*
Certain, (indisputable) *yaqíní;* (to feel certain) .. *ko yaqín honá*, 89.
Certainly, (of course) *albatta, be-shakk;* (without fail) *zarúr.*
Certainty, *yaqín—tayaqqun.*
Certificate, *sanad;* (servant's) *chiṭṭhí.*
Chaff, *bhúsá;* (to banter) .. *kí chiṛ nikálná.*
Chagrin, *hasrat*, 627.
Chain, *zanjír;* (surveyor's) *jaríb.*
Chair, *chauki, kursí.*
Chairman, *mír-majlis.*
Chalk, *kharí miṭṭí.*
Challenge (*v.a.*), *bíṛá ḍálná, lalkárná.*
Chance, *ittifáq;* (by chance) *ittifáq se.*
*By any* Chance (or possibility), *kahíṉ.*
Change, (*n.*) *tabdíl;* (vicissitude) *inqiláb.*
Change, (*v.n.*) *badal* or *tabdíl honá;* (*v.a.*) *badal* or *tabdíl karná;* (money) *tuṛáná*, also *bhunáná*, or *bhunwáná.*
Changeable, *talauwun-mizáj, búqalamún*, 273.
Channel (of communication), *sabíl.*
Chapter, *báb.*
Character, (reputation) *nám;* (general behaviour) *chál-chalan;* (of good character) *nek-nám;* (of bad) *badnám.*
Characteristic (*n.*), *khaslat, khássiyat*, 621.

Charcoal, *koelá.*
Charge, (trust) *supurdagí, hawála;* (in your charge), *tumháre supurd;* (if a prisoner) *tumháre hawále.*
Charge (to enjoin), *tákíd karná.*
Charity, (alms-giving, &c.) *khairát.*
Charm, (personal) *dilrubáí;* (of scenery, &c.) *lutf;* (without charm) *be-lutf, be-kaifiyat.*
Charming, *dilchasp;* (a person) *dilrubá.*
Chase, (*v.a.*) *ragedna*, ... *ke píchhe lagná;* (on foot) .. *ke píchhe dauṛná.*
Chase (pursuit), *raged, ta'áqub.*
Chasm, *shigáf, darár.*
Chaste, *pársá;* (a woman) *pákdáman.*
Chastise, *sazá dená.*
Chastity, *pákízagí, pársáí.*
Chatter (as a monkey), *kikiyáná.*
Cheap, *sastá.*
Cheapness, *sastáí—arzání.*
Cheat, (*v.a.*) *ṭhagá lená, daghá dená;* (*n.*) *farebí, daghá-báz.*
Cheated (taken in), *ṭhagá gayá, fareb kháyá.*
Cheating, (*n.*) *ṭhagáí—daghá;* (at play) *kaj-bází.*
Check, (*v.a.*) *rokná;* (put a stop to) .. *ká insidád karná.*
Cheek, *gál—rukhsár;* (boldness) *be-bákí, ḍhiṭháí.*
Cheeky (bold), *be-bák, ḍhíṭh.*
Cheer, (to gladden) *ká dil khush karná;* (to comfort) *dilásá dená.*
Cheerful, *khush-mizáj—khanda-peshání.*
Cheese, *panír.*

Cheque, *hundí*.
Chess, *shatranj*, 223.
Chest, *chhátí*, *sína*; (box) *sandúq*.
Chestnut (colour), *surang*, 232.
Chew, *chabáná*.
Chief, (head) *sardár*; (of a gang) *sarghana*; (principal) *sadar*; (as a reason, &c.) *asl*.
Child, *bachcha*.
Childhood, *bachpan*, *larakpan*.
Children (of a family), *bál-bachche*, *larke-bále*.
*To be* Chilled (or numbed), *ṭhiṭhir lagná*.
Chimney (of fire-place), *dúdkash*.
Chin, *ṭhuḍḍí*.
Chink, *darz*, 207, 346.
Chisel, *rúkhání*.
Choice, *ikhtiyár*; (precious) *chokhá*, *nafís*.
Choke, (*v.n.*) *dam* (or *sáns*) *ruk jáná*; (*v.a.*) *dam* (or *sáns*) *rokná*.
Choked (bunged up), *jabad gayá*.
Cholera, *haiza*.
Choose, (select) *chun lená*, *chhánṭná*; (to do a thing), *ikhtiyár karná*.
Chronic (disease), *bigṛá húá—dáimí*.
Church, *girja-ghar*; (the assembly) *kalísiya*.
Churn (*v.a.*), *mathná*.
Circle, *dáira*, *gherá*.
Circular, *gol—mudauwar*.
Circulate, *ghumáná*.
Circulation (of the blood, &c.), *sailán*.
Circumcision, *khatna*.
Circumference, *gher*, *gherá—gird*.
Circumstance (occurrence), *wáridát*, *wuqúa*.
Circumstances, *hál*, *hálat*, *súrat*; under the circumstances, *is súrat men*.
Cistern, *hauz*.
Citizen, *báshinda*, *shahrí*.
Citron (shaddock), *chakotara*.
City, *shahr*.
Civil, (polite) *milansár—khalíq*; (not military), *mulkí*.
Civility, *milansárí—khush-akhláqí*.
Civilization (not barbarism), *ádmiyat*, 311, 312.
Civilize, *ádmiyat men láná*.
Civilized (to become), *ádmiyat men áná*, *ádmiyat pakaṛná*.
Claim, (*n.*) *dáwá*; (*v.a.*) *dáwá karná*.
Claimant, *dáwídár*, *muddaí*.
Clandestinely, *chhipá-chhipí*, *bálá-bálá*.
Clap (of thunder), *kaṛak*.
Clap (the hands), *tálí bajáná*.
Clasp (in the arms), ... *kí kaulí bhar lená*, 504.
Class, (order) *darja*; (social) *qaum*; (in school) *jamá'at*.
Clause, *jumla*, *fiqra*.
Claw, *changul*; (claws) *panja*.
Clay, *chikní miṭṭí*.
Clean, *sáf*, *safá*; (*v.a.*) *sáf karná*.
Cleanliness, *safáí*; (purity) *pákízagí*.
Clear, (evident) *záhir*; (as the sky) *sáf*; (as water) *nithrá*, 448.
*To be* Cleared up (a matter),... *kí safáí honá*.
Clearing up (of a thing), *tasfiya*, 97.
Clemency (in practice), *karam-bakhshí*.
Clerk (native), *muharrir*.

Clever, *chatur—rasá;* (expert) *chálák-dast.*
Cleverness, *chaturáí—rasáí;* (skill) *chálák- dastí.*
Client, *mutawakkil.*
Climate, *áb-o-hawá.*
Climb, *úpar charhná.*
Cling to, *ko lipaṭ jáná,* or *pilich jáná.*
Clock, *gharí.*
Clockmaker, *gharí-sáz.*
Clod, *ḍhelá.*
Close to me, *mere-pás hí;* (close by, close at hand) *pás hí pás.*
Close (v.a.), *band karná;* (v.n.) *band honá.*
·Close intimacy, *garm-suhbat.*
Close together, *pás-pás,* 185.
Cloth, *kaprá.*
Cloth-merchant, *bazzáz.*
Clothes, *kapṛe—libás.*
Clouds, *bádal—abr;* (covering the sky) *ghaṭá.*
Clove, *laung.*
Club, *sonṭá, laṭh.*
Clue, (to whereabouts) *patá;* (to a crime) *patá, surágh,* 209, 210.
Clumsy (unskilful), *anáṛí,* 559.
Clutch, *pakaṛ lená,...par panja márná.*
Coachman, *kochwán.*
Coal, *koelá.*
Coarse, *moṭá, gáṛhá.*
Coast, *lab-i-daryá, kinára.*
Coat, *kurtá* or *kurtí.*
Coax, *chumkárná.*
Cobra, *kálá sámp.*
Cock, (domestic) *murgh;* (male) *nar.*
Cockroach, *tilchaṭṭá.*
Cocoanut, *nariyal.*
Coffee, *káfí—qahwa.*

Coffin, *tábút.*
Cog (of a wheel), *dántí.*
Coil (n.), *bal, kundal, kundlí.*
Coin, *sikka.*
Cold, (adj.) *ṭhanḍá;* (n.) *jáṛá, sardí.*
Cold (catarrh), *sardí—zukám.*
Collapse (v.n.), *baiṭh jáná.*
Collar, (horse) *halqa;* (female ornament) *hanslí.*
Collar-bone, *hanslí* or *haslí.*
Collect, *jamạ karná;* (in one place) *ikaṭṭhe karná.*
Collection (subscription), *chandá, úgahní.*
Collector of revenue (native), *tahsíldár.*
College, *madrasa.*
Collision, *ṭakkar;* (with another person) *muṭh-bheṛ.*
Collusion, *sázish.*
Colonize, *ábád karná, basáná.*
Colony *mạmúra, nau-ábádí.*
Colour, *rang, rangat;* (natural colour) *qudratí rang.*
To come out in one's true Colours, ...*kí qalạí khul jáná,* 193.
Colt, *bachherá—ná-kand.*
Column (pillar), *sutún, khambá.*
Comb, *kanghí;* (cock's) *kes, kalghí.*
Come, *áná;* (come along) *chalá áná;* (come down) *utarná;* (come out) *nikalná;* (come to hand) *milná;* (come in sight) *nazar áná;* (to arrive) *ájáná.*
To Come up to (equal),...*kí ṭakkar ká honá;* (no one to come up to him here), *yahán uskí ṭakkar ká koí nahin hai.*
Comely, *chhabílá, khúbsúrat.*
Comfort, (ease) *árám;* (v.a.) *tạsallí dená.*

Comfortable, *árám ká*, or *árámí*.
*In* Comfortable *circumstances*, *ásúda-hál*.
Command, (*n.*) *hukm*; (*v.a.*) *hukm dená*, or *hukm karná*.
Commence, *shurú karná*.
Commencement, *shurú*.
Commend, *saráhná*, *tárif karná*.
Commendable, *tárifí*, *tárif keláiq*.
Commerce, *saudágarí—tijárat*.
Commercial, *saudágarí*.
Commission, (warrant) *sanad*; (order) *farmáish*; (on goods) *dastúrí*.
Commit, (perpetrate) *karná—ká irtikáb karná*; (for trial) *supurd karná*.
Common, *ámm*.
Common place, *be-lutf*, *be-kaifiyat*.
Commotion, *khalbalí—shorish*.
Communicate, *kahná*, *khabar dená*.
Communication, *khabar*, *ittilá*.
Compact (*adj.*), *thos*; (agreement) *ahd*.
Companion, *sáthí—rafíq*, 80, 167.
Companionship, *rifáqat*.
Company (assembly of people), *jamáat*, *majlis*.
Compare (with), ... *se muqábala karná*.
*As* Compared *with*, *ba-nisbat*; as compared with last year, *ba-nisbat pár sál ke*.
Comparison, *muqábala*; (in comparison with him) *uske muqábale men*, *uske áge*.
Compass (mariner's), *qutub-numá*.
Compasses, *parkár*.
Compassion, *shafaqat*.
Compel, *majbúr karná*, 320.
Compensation, *muáwaza*.
Competent, *láiq*, *qábil*; (legally, to do a thing) *ká majáz honá*, 393.
Compete, *lágá lágí men sharík honá*.
Competition, *lágá lágí*.
Complain (against another), ... *kí shikáyat karná*, *ke úpar nálish karná*.
Complaint, *shikáyat*, *nálish*; (in Court) *istighása*, 266, 568, 573.
Complainant (in Court), *mustaghís*.
Complete, (*adj.*) *púrá*, *tamám*; (*v.a.*) *púrá karná*.
Completed, to be, *púrá honá*, *ho-jáná*, *ho lená*.
Completion, *ikhtitám*, 658.
Complexion, *rang*, *rangat*.
Compliance, *razámandí*.
Complication, *ech-pech*.
Compliments (formal), *ádáb*; (to a superior) *taslímát*.
Comply, *qabúl karná*, *rází honá*; (carry out) *bajá láná*.
Composition, *tarkíb*, 496.
Compress, (*v.a.*) *dabáná*; (cram in) *thos dená*.
Compulsion, *majbúrí*; (under) *majbúr*, 321.
Compulsory (indispensable), *lázimí*, *zarúrí*.
Comrade, *rafíq*.
Conceal, *chhipáná — poshída rakhná*.
Concealed, *chhipá húá—poshída*.
Concealment, *chhipáo — poshídagí*, *darpardagí*.
Concede (a point), *mán jáná*, *taslím karná*.
Conceit (vanity), *khud-pasandí*.
Conceited (vain), *khud-pasand*.

Concern, (business) *károbár;* (anxiety) *andesha;* (no concern of your's) *tumhárá kuchh wásta nahin hai.*
Concerned (anxious), ... *ko andesha húá—muztarib.*
Concerned in (implicated), *sharík.*
Concise, *mukhtasar.*
Concisely, *mukhtasar taur par.*
Conclude, (finish) *khatm karná;* (infer) *qaiyás karná.*
Conclusion (end), *tamámí;* (inference) *qaiyás.*
Concoction (made up story), *banáwat.*
Concourse, *bhír—hujúm.*
Concur (in or with), *ittifáq karná.*
Concurrence, *ittifáq.*
Concurring (two persons), *muttafiq.*
Condemn, *gunahgár* (or *mujrim*) *thahráná;* (sentence) ... *ká hukm dená.*
Condemned (to imprisonment), *qaid ká hukm húá.*
Condition, *hál, hálat;* (status) *haisiyat,* 177.
Condition (stipulation), *shart,* 627.
Conditional, *shartiya.*
Condolence, *mátam-pursí.*
Conducive to, ... *ká mumidd.*
Conduct, (behaviour) *chál-chalan;* (*v.a.*) *le-chalná.*
Confess, *iqrár karná.*
Confession, *iqrár.*
Confidant, } *rázdár.*
Confidante, }
Confidence, *bharosá, ásrá.*
Confident, to be, *ko yaqín honá.*

Confined (or restricted) to, ... *par munhasir,* 270.
Confines (limits), *sarhadd.*
Confirm (an order), *bahál rakhná.*
Confiscate, *zabt karná, qurq karná,* 307.
Conflict, (war) *laráí;* (of opinion) *ikhtiláf.*
Confront, *ke sámhne karná, ke rúbarú karná.*
Confuse (bewilder), *ghabráhat men dálná.*
Confused (bewildered), to be, *ghabráná, ghabrá jáná.*
Confusion, (disorder) *abtarí;* (to get into) *usal-pusal jáná.*
Confutation, *ibtál.*
Confute, *radd karná.*
Congeal, *jam jáná.*
Congratulate, *mubárakbád kahná.*
Congratulation ... *mubárakbádí—tahniat.*
Congregate, *jama honá.*
Conjecture, (*n.*) *qaiyás, ihtimál;* (*v.a.*) *qaiyás karná.*
Conjurer, *jádúgar.*
Connect (*v.a.*), *jorna, miláná.*
Connecting link (or bond), *rábita.*
Connection, *ta'alluq, íláqa,* 160, 439.
Connive at, *ánákání dená—chashmposhí karná.*
Conquer, *jítná,* .. *par ghálib áná.*
Conquered, *maghlúb.*
Conquest, *fath* (pron. *fateh*).
Conscience, *zamír.*
Conscientious, *diyánatdár.*
Conscientiousness, *diyánatdárí.*
Conscious of, to be, *málúm honá.*
Consecutive, *mutawátir, lagátár.*
Consent (*n.*), *razámandí, qabúl.*

Consent, (*v.a.*) *rází honá, qabúl karná;* (say yes) *hámí bharná,* 254.
Consequence, *natíja, phal;* (of no consequence) *kuchh muzáyaqa nahin;* (in consequence of this) *ba sabab iske.*
Consequently, *chunánchi.*
Consider, *sochná, ghaur karná.*
Consideration, *ghaur.*
Consign, *sompná.*
Consistency (in conduct), *ek-rangí.*
Consolation, *tasallí.*
Console (*v.a.*), *tasallí dená.*
Conspicuous, *namúdár.*
Conspiracy, *sázish, bandish.*
Conspire, *sázísh karná.*
Constancy (fidelity), *wafádárí.*
Constant (oft repeated), *mutawátir,* 291.
Constantly, *hamesha, har waqt.*
Constellation, *burj.*
Consternation, *ghabráhat.*
Constitute (establish, &c.), *qarár dená, thahráná.*
Constitution (nature), *tabíat.*
Construct, *banáná.*
Construction, *banáwat—sákht.*
Consult, . . *se mashwara karná.*
Consultation, *mashwara.*
Consume, *kharch karná.*
Consumed (by fire), *bhasam.*
Consumption (expenditure), *kharch.*
Contact, *lagáo—ittisál.*
Contagion, *siráyat.*
Contagious (infectious), *muta'addí.*
Contain, (hold) ... *men samáná* (or *atná*); lit. "to be contained in."
Contamination, *chhút—álúdagí.*
Contemporary, *ham-asar.*
Contempt, *hiqárat.*
Contemptible, *haqír, zalíl.*
Contemptuously, *hiqárat se.*
Content (satisfied), *rází — ser-chashm.*
Contention, *takrár, jhagrá.*
Contentment, *razámandí, — qanáat.*
Contents (of a letter, &c.), *mazmún.*
Contiguous, *muttasil.*
Continual, *harwaqt ká.*
Continually, *harwaqt.*
Continuance, *thahráo, mudáwamat.*
Continuation (supplement), *tatimma.*
Continue, *rahná, rah jáná, thahar jáná.*
Contraband, *ná-jáiz.*
Contract (to shrink), *simat jáná, sukar jáná.*
Contract (for work, &c.), *theká;* (in writing) *iqrárnáma.*
Contractor, *thekádár.*
Contradict, *khiláf kahná.*
Contradictory, (discrepant) *mukhtalif;* (two things to be)—*men ikhtiláf honá.*
Contrary (to), *ke barkhiláf—ke baraks.*
Contrary to reason, *khiláf-i-qaiyás,* 592.
*On the* Contrary, *barkhiláf iske.*
Contravention, *inhiráf.*
Contribute, *apná hissa dená.*
Contribution (individual), *hissa.*
Contrivance, *tadbír.*
Contrive, *tadbír lagáná.*
Control (restrain), *zabt karná.*
Convenience, } *subhítá.*
Convenient, }

Conventionality, *rasm kí pábandí*, 376, 377.
Conversation, *bát-chít, guft-gú.*
Convey, *pahúnchháná.*
Convict (*v.a.*), *mujrim ṭhahráná.*
Convict (prisoner), *qaidí.*
Convicted, *mujrim ṭhahrá.*
Convince, *qáil karná.*
Convinced, *qáil-máqúl.*
Coo (as a dove), *guṭakná.*
Cook, (*n.*) *báwarchi*; (*v.a.*) *pakáná.*
Cool down (subside), *ṭhanḍá hojáná—faro hojáná*, 235.
Copper, *támbá.*
Copy, (*v.a.*) *naql karná*; (*n.*) *naql.*
Coquette, *ashwa-gar, náz-pesha.*
Coral, *múngá.*
Cord, *ḍor, ḍorí, rassí.*
Cordiality, *garmjoshí.*
Core, *darúna.*
Corkscrew, *pech-kash.*
Corn *anáj, ghalla*; (for horses) *dána.*
Corner, *koná.*
Correct, (*adj.*) *ṭhík, durust*; (*v.a.*) *durust karná.*
Correction, *isláh*; (receiving it) *isláh-pazír.*
Correspondence, *khatt-o-kitábat*, 619.
Corroborate, *kí táíd karná.*
Corroboration, *táíd.*
Corrupt (to tamper with), *toṛ lená*, 569.
Cost (expense), *lágat*, 43, 99.
Costly *besh-qímat, qímatí.*
Costume, *bhes—libás.*
Cotton, (raw) *kapás*; (prepared) *rúí*, 557.
Cough, (*n.*) *khánsí*; (*v.n.*) *khánsná.*
Count (*v.a.*), *ginná, gin lená.*
Countenance (*n.*), *munh, chihra—bashara.*
Counterfeit, (*adj.*) *jálí*; (coin) *khoṭá—talbísí.*
Country, *mulk, des, sarzamín.*
Courage, *diláwarí, himmat*; (to summon up courage) *jí ko mazbút karná, himmat bándhná.*
Of Course, *albatta, be-shakk, aur kyá?*
Court (yard), *sahn, ángan.*
Court, (of justice) *adálat*; (the building) *kachahrí.*
Court (regal), *darbár.*
Courteous, *milansár — khush-akhláq.*
Cousin, *See* "Family Relationship" Section, pp. 80, 81.
Cover (*v.a.*), *ḍhámpná, ḍhakná, ḍhánkná.*
Cover, (*n.*) *ḍhakná*; (pot-lid) *ḍhakní, sarposh.*
Covet (*v.a.*), ... *ká lálach karná.*
Covetous, *lálchí—harís.*
Cow, *gáe*; (cowherd) *gwálá.*
Coward, *ḍarpok—buzdil*, 285.
Cowardice, *buzdilí*, 286.
Crab, *kenkṛá.*
Crack (*v.n.*), *phaṭná, chaṭakná.*
Crack (*n.*), *darz, phaṭá.*
Crafty, *híla báz—fitratí.*
Cram in, *ṭhos dená, anṭwáná.*
Cramp, *ainṭh—tashannuj.*
Crash (*n.*), *dhaṛám, dhaṛáká.*
Crawl (as an insect), *rengná.*
Crazy, *báolá.*
Creak (as a boot, &c.), *marmaráná*; (as a bed) *machmacháná.*
Cream, *malái.*
Crease (*n.*), *shikan, chunnat.*
Create, *paidá karná.*
Creator, *kháliq.*

Creature, *makhlúq*, (pl.) *makhlúqát*.
Credible, *etibár ke qábil*.
Credit, (reliance) *etibár*, *bharosá*; (to sell on) *udhár bechná*, 105.
Creditor, *qarz-khwáh*, 246.
Creed (belief), *etiqád*.
Creep (as an insect) *rengná*.
Creeper, *latá*, *bel*, *belí*.
Crest, *kalghí*; (device) *taghma*.
Crested, *kalghí-dár*.
Crevice, *shigáf*, *phatá*.
Crime, *gunáh—jurm*.
Criminal, *gunahgár—mujrim*; (criminal case) *faujdárí muqaddama*; (Criminal Court) *faujdárí adálat*.
Crimson (*adj.*), *qirmizí*, *súhá kusumbhá*.
Cripple, *langrá*; (in the hands) *lúlá*; (without hands) *tundá*.
Crisis (in an illness), *buhrán*.
Crisp, *khasta*.
Crispness, *khastagí*.
Criticise, *nukta-chíní karná*.
Crocodile, *magar*, *ghariyál*.
Crooked, *terhá*, *tirchhá*.
Crop, *khetí—ziráat*.
Cross, (peevish) *chirchirá*; (sulky) *magrá*.
Cross (a river), *pár jáná*, 63.
Cross-bar, *arbangá*.
Cross-examine, *jireh ká suwál karná*.
Cross-grained (crabbed), *kaj-khulq*.
Cross-purposes, *kaj-fahmí*.
Cross-roads, *chau-maháni*.
Crouch, *dabak baithná*.
Crow (*n.*), *kauwá*, *kág*.
Crowbar, *khantí*.
Crow over (anyone), *kisí ke úpar shádiyána bajáná*, 401.
Crowd, *bhír*; (surging or moving crowd) *hujúm*.
Crown (monarch's), *táj*.
Crown (of the head), *chandiyá*.
Crucible, *kuthálí*, *ghariyá*.
Cruel, *be-rahm*.
Cruelty, *be-rahmí*.
Crumble (*v.n.*), *chúr chúr honá*; (*v.a.*) *chúr chúr karná*.
Crumple (*v.a.*), *dal-masal karná*.
Crush (*v.a.*), *kuchalná*.
Cry, (*v.n.*) *roná*; (cry out) *chilláná*.
Crystal, *billaur*.
Cucumber, *khírá*, *kakrí*.
Cud (to chew the), *jugálí karná*, 269.
Cudgel (to belabour), *kundí karná*.
Cultivate, *jotná*.
Cultivation, *khetí-bárí—ziráat*.
Cultivator, *kisán*, *káshtkár*.
Cunning, *aiyár*, *siyáná*, *fitratí*.
Cunning (*n.*), *aiyárí*, *failsúfí*.
Cup (small, metal), *katorá*.
Cure (*v.a.*), *changá karna*, *achchhá karná*.
Cure (*n.*), *shifá*.
Cured, *achchhá lichchhá*, *bhalá changá*.
Curiosity (rarity), *saughát*.
Curl (ringlet, &c.), *zulf*, *kákul*.
Current (stream), *dhár*, *dhárá*.
Current (in use), *chaltí*, *járí*.
Curse (*v.a.*), *kosná*, ... *par lánat karná*.
Curse (*n.*), *kosá*, *lánat*.

Curtain, *parda*; (musquito curtains) *masahrí*.
Cushion, *gaddí*.
Custody, (of a prisoner) *hirásat*; (of property) *hifázat*.
Custom, (popular) *dastúr*, *rasm*, *riwáj*; (personal habit) *mámúl*, 138, 139, 228.
*Manners and* Customs, *ráh-o-rasm*.
Customary (usual), *mámúlí—ráij*.
Cut (*v.a.*), *káṭná*.
Cypress, *sarv*.

Dagger, *khanjar*, *kaṭár*.
Daily (*adj.*), *rozmarre ká*.
Damage, (*n.*) *nuqsán*, *zarar*; (*v.a.*) *bigáṛná*, *zarar pahúncháná*.
Damaged, *dághí*, *bigṛá húá*.
Damaging (as evidence), *muzirr*, 159.
Damp, *gílá—namnák*, 348.
Dampness, *gíláí—namnákí*, 348.
Danger, *khatra*.
Dangerous, *khatarnák*, 67.
Dark, *andherá*.
Dark-brown (a horse), *mushkí*, 232.
Darken, *andherá karná*.
Darkness, *andhiyárá*, *andherá*.
Darn (*v.a.*), *rafú karná*.
Dash (tinge), *damak*, 233.
Dash down, *de paṭakná*, *de márná*.

*N.B.*—These are much more forcible expressions than *paṭak dená*, &c. would be.

Dashed to pieces (shattered), *chaknáchúr*.
Date, (of month, &c.), *táríkh*; (fruit) *khajúr*, *chhuhárá*.
Daughter, *beṭí*.
Dawn, *bhor*, *taṛká*, *subh* (pron. *subeh*).
Day, *din*, *roz*.
Day before yesterday, } *parson*.
Day after to-morrow, }
Day and night, *rát-din*.
Day-book, *roznámcha*, 456.
Daybreak, *bhor*, *pau phaṭne ká waqt*.
Day by day, *roz ba roz*.
Daylight, *din-diyá*, 630.
*In the* Daytime, *din ko*.
Dazed (stunned) to be, *sannáṭe men rahná*, 631.
Dazzled, to be, *chaundhiyáná*.
Dead, *mará húá*; (anything dead) *murda*.
Deadly, *muhlik*; (deadly enemy) *dushman-i-jání*; (deadly wound) *zakhm-i-kárí*.
Deaf, *bahrá*.
Dear (beloved), *piyárá*, (fem.) *piyárí*.
Dear (expensive), *mahngá*.
Death, *maut*—(euphemistically) *intiqál*.
Debarred (excluded) from, ... *se mahrúm*, *se khárij*, 191.
Debate (*n.*) *mubáhasa*.
Debris (of a house, &c.), *malbá*, 99.
Debt, *qarza*.
Debtor, *qarzdár*.
Decamp (make off), *chal dená*, 78, 80.
Decay, (*n.*) *zawál*; (*v.n.*) *záil honá*.
Deceased, *matwafá*.
Deceit, *dhoká*, *fareb*.
Deceitful, *farebí*, *daghábáz*.
Deceive, *dhoká dená*.
Deceived, to be, *fareb kháná*, *fareb men áná*.

Declaration, *izhár.*
Decline, (refuse) *inkár karná;* as the day, &c.) *ḍhal jáná.*
Decorate, *árásta karná, sanwárná.*
Decoration, *árástagí.*
Decrease, (*v.n.*) *ghaṭ jáná,* (*n.*) *ghaṭáo.*
Decrepit, *fartút,* 546.
Deduct (*v.a.*), *minhá karná,* 525.
Deed (document), *dastáwez,* 196.
Deep, *gahrá.*
Deep-seated, *jigarí,* 239.
Deer, *hiran.*
Defame, *badnám karná, baṭṭá lagáná.*
Defeat, (an opponent) *haráná;* (an army) *shikast dená.*
Defeated, (to be) *hár jáná;* (an army) *ghúnghaṭ kháná.*
Defect, *ạib, nuqs.*
Defective, *náqis.*
Defence (in a law-suit), *jawábdihí,* 475.
Defenceless, *láchár.*
Defend (stick up for), ... *kí himáyat karná.*
Defendant, *mudda'ạleh.*

*N.B.*—For legal and official phrases, see from 567 to 593.

Defender (protector), *hámí.*
Defer (postpone), *multawí rakhná.*
Deference, *lihẩz.*
Deficiency, *kamí—kotáhí.*
Defile, *mailá karná, nápák karná.*
Defilement, *álúdagí, nápákí.*
Definite, *muqarrar, muqarrarí.*
Deformed, *ṭeṛhá—khamída.*
Deformity, *ṭeṛháí—khamídagí,* 621.
Degree, (extent) *qadar;* (in some degree) *kisí qadar.*

Delay (*n.*), *der, derí.*
Delay (*v.a.*), *derí karná, der lagáná.*
Deliberately, *soch-samajhkar, ján-bújhke.*
Delicate, *názuk, sukhwár.*
Delicious, *mazedár, lazíz.*
Deliciousness, *lazzat.*
Delight, *khushí—masarrat.*
Delighted, *bahut khush—masrúr.*
Delightful, *dilkushá, dilchasp.*
Delirium, *sarsám.*
Deliver, *chhuṛáná;* (make over) *sompná, supurd karná.*
Deliverance, *chhuṭkárá, naját.*
Delude, *dhoká dená.*
Delusion, *dhoká, fareb.*
Demand, (*v.a.*) *talab karná, mángná;* (*n.*) *talabí.*
Demolish, *ḍhá dená—mismár karná,* 536.
Demon, *bhút, dev.*
Demonstrate, *záhir karná.*
Demoralize, *bigáṛ dená.*
Demoralized, *bigṛá húá, miṭṭi kharáb hogaí,* 84, 86.
Denial, *inkár,* 115.
Dense (as jungle, &c.), *ghaná—gunján,* 296.
Deny, *inkár karná, mukar jáná.*
Depart, *chalá jáná, rawána honá.*
Department, *ịláqa—sígha.*
Departure, *rawánagí,* 246.
Depend (rely on), ... *par bharosá rakhná.*
Dependent on (as life on food), ... *par mauqúf,* 189, 190.
Deportment, *nishast-o-barkhást,* 621.
Deposit, (*v.a.*) *amánat rakhná;* (*n.*) *amánat.*

Deposition (evidence), *bayán, gawáhí.*
Deprive of, *le lená.*
Deprived of, ... *se mahrúm, se khárij.*
Depth, *gahráí, gahrá-pan.*
Derived from, ... *se milá, ... se hásil húá.*
Deranged, (in disorder) *abtar;* (mentally) *pareshán.*
Descend, *níche utarná.*
Descent, *utár.*
Describe, *bayán karná.*
Description, *bayán, kaifiyat.*
Desert (wilderness), *bayábán.*
Desert place, *wírán jagah.*
Desire, (*v.a.*) *cháhna;* (*n.*) *khwáhish, cháhat.*
Desirous of, to be, ... *ká mushtáq honá.*
Desist from, ... *se háth utháná, se dastbardár honá.*
Despair, (*n.*) *máyúsí;* (in despair) *máyús.*
Despatch (send off), *rawána karná.*
Despatched (sent off), *rawána húá.*
Despise, *náchíz samajhná, haqír jánná.*
Destination, *manzil-maqsúd.*
Destiny, *nasíb, taqdír.*
Destitute, *muflis, muhtáj.*
Destroy, *barbád karná, ghárat karná;* (waste) *záya karná.*
Destruction, (of life) *halákat;* (of property) *ghárat, bar-bádí.*
Detach, *judá karná, alag karná.*
Detailed description, *mufassal bayán,* 622.
Details, *tafsílen.*
Detain, *rok rakhná.*
Detect, *daryáft karná.*
Detective, *surághí.*
Detention, *rok-tok.*
Determination (resolve), *musammam iráda.*
Determine (to resolve), *dil men thánná.*
Devoid of, ... *se khálí, ... se be-bahra.*
Dew, *os—shabnam.*
Dexterity, *chálák-dastí.*
Dexterous, *chálák-dast.*
Diagnosis, *tashkhís.*
Diagram, *naqsha.*
Dialect, *bolí.*
Diameter, *qutar.*
Diamond, *hírá.*
Diary, *roznámcha.*
Dictionary, *lughat.*
Diet, *ghizá, khurák.*
Difference, *farq,* 446.
Different, *mutafarriq, mukhtalif.*
Difficult, *mushkil—dushwár.*
Difficulty (trouble), *diqqat, mushkil,* 503.
Digestion, *házima,* 224.
Diligence, *koshish—sargarmí.*
Diligent, *sargarm, mihnatí.*
Dimensions, *lambáí-chauráí.*
Diploma, *sanad.*
Direct, *sídhá—ba ráh-i-rást.*
Direction, *taraf—simt;* (address) *patá.*
Direction (command), *irshád.*
Directions (instructions), *hidáyat.*
Disaffected, *bad-khwáh.*
Disaffection, *bad khwáhí.*
Disagreement, *ná-ittifáqí.*
Disallow, *ná-manzúr karná.*
Disappear, *gháib honá, champat honá.*

Disappoint, *ná-ummed karná, hawá baţáná.*
Disappointment, *ná-murádí.*
Disapprove, *ná-pasand karná, ... ko ná-pasand honá.*
Disaster, *áfat.*
Discharged (a prisoner), *chhúţ gayá, rihá húá.*
Disciple, *shágird.*
Discipline (military) *tálím-o-qawáid*; (school) *tádib.*
Disclosure, *inkisháf, isrár.*
Disconnected, *be-ta'alluq.*
Discontent, *nárází.*
Discontented, *náráz.*
Discount (*n.*), *baţţá.*
Discover, *daryáft karná.*
Discovery, *daryáft.*
Discrepancy, *ikhtiláf*, 542.
Discriminate, *tamíz karná.*
Discrimination, *imtiyáz.*
Discussion, (friendly) *guftgú*; (argument) *bahs* (pron. *baihs*).
Disease, *bímárí—maraz*, 623, 655.
Diseased, *bímár, rogí.*
Disentangle, *suljháná.*
Disfavour, to fall into, *nazaron se girná.*
Disgrace, *ruswáí*; (indignity) *be-izzatí.*
Disgrace (put to shame), *ruswá karná.*
Disgrace (cause for shame), *nang-o-ár.*
Disguise (oneself), *bhes badalná, libás tabdíl karná.*
Disguise (*n.*), *tabdíl-i-libás.*
Dishevelled hair, *bikhare húe bál.*
Disinclination, *ná-pasandí, daregh.*
Disinterested, *be-gharaz.*
Dislike, (*v.a.*) *ná-pasand karná*; (*n.*) *ná-pasandí.*
Dismiss (a servant), *mauqúf karná, barkhást karná.*
Disobedience, *ná-farmání.*
Disobedient, *ná-farmán.*
Disorder (confusion), *abtarí*, 563.
Disparage, *baţţá lagáná.*
Display (ostentation), *ţháţh, dikháwá.*
Displease, *ná-khush karná.*
Displeased, *ná-khush—barham.*
Displeasure, *ná-khushí, khafgí.*
Dispute (*n.*), *takrár, bahs* (pron. *baihs*).
Disregard of orders, *udúl-hukmí.*
Disrespect, *be adabí.*
Disrespectful, *be-adab.*
Dissolve, *gholná*; (be dissolved) *ghul jáná.*
Distance (from one place to another), *fásila*, 230. He has come from a great distance *kále kos se áyá hai.*
Distant, *dúr*; (far distant, remote) *dúr-dast.*
Distasteful (unpalatable), *ná-gawár*, 151.
Distinct, *judá, alag.*
Distinguish (one thing from another), *mumtáz karná*, 622.
*To make a* Distinction, *farq karná.*
Distribute (portion out), *bánţná—taqsím karná.*
Distribution, *taqsím.*
Distrustful, *bad-etiqád.*
Disturbance (rising), *balwá, danga-fasád.*
Ditch (moat), *khandaq, khái.*
Ditto, *aizan.*
Division (in arith.), *taqsím*, 524.
Divulge, *fásh karná.*
Document, *dastáwez*, 196.
Dog, *kuttá.*

Dog-cart, *ṭamṭam.*
Donkey, *gadhá.*
Door, *darwáza;* (folding-doors) *kiwár.*
Dose (of medicine), *khurák.*
Dotage, to be in one's, *saṭhiyáná,* 547.
Double, *dohrá;* (twofold) *doguná, dúná.*
Doubt, *shakk, shubha.*
Doubtful (suspicious), *mushtabih,* 106.
Doubting (incredulous), *shakkí.*
Downhill, *utár,* 329.
Drag along, *ghasíṭná,* 442.
Dread (alarm), *dahshat—daghdagha,* 365.
Dream, (*n.*) *khwáb;* (to dream) *khwáb dekhná.*
Dreary (no sound or sign of life), *sunsán.*
Dregs, *síṭhí.*
Drip, *ṭapak parná.*
Dripping wet, *shor-bor, tar-ba-tar.*
Drizzling rain, *phúṉhí, phúhár.*
Drop (fall off, as fruit, &c.), *jhar jáná.*
Dropsy, *jalandhar.*
Drown (*v.n.*), *ḍúbke marná.*
Drowsiness, *únghái—ghunúdagí.*
Drum, *ḍhol, tambúr.*
Dry, *súkhá—khushk.*
Dry land, *khushkí.*
Duly (in a fitting manner), *achchhí tarah se, jaisá ki cháhiye.*
Dumb, *gúngá.*
Dun (colour), *samand,* 232.
Dun (to importune), *taqázá karná.*
Duplicate, *musanná.*
Duplicity, *do-rangí.*
Durability, *derpáí.*
Durable, *derpá.*
Dusk, *muṉh andherá.*
Dust, *gard, dhúl, khák.*
Duty, *farz; e.g.* It is your duty to do this, *yih karná tum par farz hai.*
Dye, *rangná;* (the beard) *khizáb karná.*
Dyer, *rangrez.*
Dysentery, *áṉv ki bímárí.*

Each, *har, har ek.*
Eager, *sargarm, shauqín.*
Ear, *kán.*
Early, *sawere.*
Early dawn, *pau phaṭne ká waqt,* 305.
Earn, *kamáná.*
*To be in* Earnest (not joking), *satbháo se kahná,* 238.
Earnest money, *bai'ána.*
Earnings, *kamáí.*
Earring, *bálí.*
Earthenware, *sifálí.*
Earthquake, *bhauṉchál—zalzala,* 630.
Ease (facility), *ásání.*
Easily, *ásání se, sahaj se,* 415.
Easily led (no character), *mom kí nák* (lit. "a nose of wax"), 476.
East, *púrab, mashriq.*
Easterly, *purwá.*
Easy, *ásán, sahl.*
Eaves, *oltí.*
Eavesdropper, *jásús.*
Ebb and flow, *jawár bháṭá—madd-o-jazr,* 629.
Ebullition, *josh, joshish.*
Echo, *sadá,* 145.
Eclipse, *gahan.*

Economical, *salámat-rau.*
Economy, *salámat-raví.*
Ecstasy, *wajd.*
Eddy, *bhanwar.*
Edge (of a sword, &c.), *dhár.*
Edged tool, *dhárwálá hathyár.*
Edifice, *imárat.*
Educate, *tarbiyat karná, tálím dená.*
Education, *tarbiyat, tálím.*
Efface, *mitá dená.*
Effect, (*n.*) *asar, tásír;* (consequence) *natíja.*
Effective (efficacious, &c.), *kárgar —bá-asar.*
Effeminate, *aurat-mard.*
Effervesce, *josh márná.*
Effervescence, *joshish.*
Efficient, *qábil.*
Effort (endeavour), *koshish,* 247, 409, 632, 637.
Effrontery, *gustákhí.*
Eh? *kyún jí?*
Either (followed by "or"), *yá to.*

Example.—Either finish the work or leave it, *yá to kám púrá karo, yá chhor do.*

Eject, *nikál dená.*
Elapse, *guzar jáná.*
Elastic, *lachakdár.*
Elated, *bágh-bágh, harakhmán.*
Elbow, *kuhní.*
Elected (to an office), *muntakhib.*
Election (to an office), *intikháb.*
Elegant (as a building, *e.g.*), *khushnumá.*
Elementary (primary), *ibtidáí.*
Elevate, *únchá karná.*
Elevation (height), *bulandí.*
Eloquent, *fasíh—balígh.*
Eloquence, *fasáhat, balághat.*
Elsewhere, *aur kahín.*
Elude, *kaniyá jáná.*
Emaciated, *dublá, lághar.*
Emancipate, *ázád karná.*
Embankment, *pushta-bandí.*
Embark, *jaház par charhná.*
Embarrass, *mushkil men dálná.*
Embarrassment, *janjál — hais bais.*
Embezzle, *tasarruf karná, hazm kar lená.*
Embezzlement, *taghallub.*
Emblem, *nishán, alámat.*
Emboldened, to be, *hausila honá,* 287.
Embrace, *gale lagáná.*
Embroidery, *chikankárí, gulkárí.*
Embroil, *uljháná.*
Emerald, *zumurrud, panná,* 626.
Emerge, *nikalná, nikal áná.*
*In an* Emergency, *zarúrat ke waqt men.*
Emetic, *qai lánewálí dawá.*
Emissary, *harkára.*
Emotion, *iztiráb, dil kí joshish.*
Emphasis, *isrár;* (emphatically) *isrár se.*
Employ, *kám men lagáná, naukar rakhná.*
Employment (service), *naukarí.*
Empty (*adj.*), *khálí, súná.*

Note.—*Súná* means empty in the sense of "void."

Emulate, *hiská karná.*
Emulation, *hiská, ghairat.*
Enable, *táqat dená.*
Enamel, *míná,* 642.
Enamoured (of anyone), *kisí ká farefta honá.*
Encampment, *paráo.*
Enceinte, *do-pastá, hámila.*

Enchanting (charming), *dil-chasp, dilrubá.*
Enchantment, *jádú—sihr.*
Enclose, *gher lená, iháta karná.*
Enclosure, *chár-díwárí, iháta.*
Encounter (meet), *muqábala honá, muláqát honá.*
Encourage (incite), *targhíb dená.*
Encouragement (incitement), *targhíb.*
Encroach, *mudákhalat karná.*
Encroachment, *mudákhalat.*
End, (of a road, &c.) *sirá;* (of a business) *anjám;* (of a writing, speech, &c.) *ikhtitám.*
*To put an* End (to anyone), *kisí ká kám tamám karná;* (to an affair) *band kar rakhná.*
Endanger, *khatre men dálná.*
Endurance, *bardásht, tahammul.*
Enemy, *dushman, bairí.*
Energetic, *sargarm, chálák.*
Energy, *dhun, chálákí.*
Engage (a servant, &c.), *muqarrar karná.*
Engaging another in conversation, *báton men parcháná,* 540.
Engagement (appointment), *wáda.*
Engender, *paidá karná.*
Engine, *kal.*
Engrave, *khodná—kanda karná.*
Enhance, *ziyáda karná, barháná.*
Enigma (riddle), *muammá, pahelí.*
Enjoin (insist on), *tákíd karná;* (a less common but very good word is *qadaghan karná*).
Enjoy (a thing), *kisí chíz se mutamatti honá.*
Enjoyment (of a thing), *tamattu.*
Enjoy oneself, *dil bahláná,* 528.
Enlighten, *roshan karná.*
Enlist (as a soldier), *bhartí honá,* 565.
En masse (as one man, &c.), *ek lakht.*
Enmity, *adáwat, dushmaní.*
Enough, *bas, káfí.*
Entangle, *phasáná, uljháná.*
Entanglement, *uljherá, phansáo.*
Enter, (*v.n.*) *bhítar* (or *andar*) *jáná* (or *áná*), *ghusná, dákhil honá.*
Enter (in a book, &c.), *darj karná.*
Enterprise, *mansúba.*
Enthusiasm, *sargarmí.*
Enthusiastic, *sargarm.*
Entire, *samúchá, sábit;* (bodily) *sábit ká sábit.*
Entirely (altogether), *bilkull, sarásar.*
Entitled to, *sazáwár, mustahaqq.*
Entrance, *dakhl, ghus-paith.*
Entreat, *minnat karná.*
Entry (in a book), *raqam.*
Envious (jealous), *rashkí.*
Environs, *atráf, gird-nawáh,* 630.
Envoy, *elchí.*
Envy, *hasad, rashk.*
Epidemic, *marí, wabá.*
Epilepsy, *mirgí.*
Epitome, *mújaz.*
Equable, *motadil.*
Equal, *barábar;* (an equal) *ham-sar.*
Equality, *barábarí, takkar;* (in position) *hamsarí.*
Equity, *insáf.*
Equivalent (*quid pro quo*), *badlá, iwaz.*

Era, *zamána*, *sáká*.
Erase, *miṭá dená*; (with a knife, &c.) *chhılná*.
Erect, (*adj.*) *khaṛá*; (*v.a.*) *khaṛá karná*.
Err, *bhúl karná*, *ghaltí karná*, *khatá karná*.
Erroneous, *ghalat*.
Error, *ghaltí*; (in spiritual things) *gumráhí*.
Escape (*n.*), (from danger, &c.) *bacháo*; (from custody) *mafrúrí*.
Escape (*v.n.*), *bachná*; (to flee) *bhág jáná*, *farár honá*.
Especially, *khusúsán*.
Espionage, *jásúsí*.
Essence, *khulása*, *hír*.
Essential (indispensable), *zarúrí*.
Establish, *muqarrar karná*, *qáim karná*.
Estate (property), *milkiyat*, *milk*, 654.
Estimation, *ráe*, *hisáb*.
Etcetera, *wa-ghaira*.
Eternal, *abadí*.
Eternity, *abad*, *jáwidání*.
Etiquette, *see* "Deportment."
Evade, *ṭál dená*, *bálá batáná*, 184.
Evasion, *ṭál-maṭol*.
*An* Evasive answer—*gol jawáb*.
Even (level), *barábar*, *hamwár*.
Even now, *ab bhí*.
Even in that case, *taubhí*.
Evening, *shám*, *sánjh*.
Event (occurrence), *wuqúa*, *wáridát*.
Eventually (in the end), *ákhir men*, *ákhir kár*.
Ever, *kabhí*.
*For* Ever, *hamesha ke wáste*.
Everyday conversation (common parlance), *rozmarre kí bol-chál*, 509.
Evict, *be-dakhli karná*.
Eviction, *be-dakhlí*.
Evidence, *gawáhí*, *shahádat*; (circumstantial evidence) *wáqiát kí shahádat*.
Evident, *záhir*.
Evidently, *záhiran*.
Evil-doer, *badkár*.
Exactly, *ṭhík*—*bi-ainihi*.
Exactly alike, *eksán*.
Exaggeration, *mubálagha*.
Examination (proving), *jánch-partál*, *ázmáish*; (of a candidate) *imtihán*.
Examine, (prove) *jánchná*; (a candidate) *imtihán lená*; (money) *sahejná*.
Example, (illustration) *nazír*, *misál*; (pattern) *namúna*.
Exasperate, *chiṛáná*, *bhaṛkáná*.
Exceed (in quantity, &c.), *ziyáda honá*.
Exceedingly, *niháyat*—*az-hadd*.
Excel, *sabqat lejáná*.
Excellence, *umdagí*.
Excellent, *umda*, 388, 389.
Except (*prep.*), *ba-juz*, *chhoṛ*.
Examples.—Except this, *ba-juz iske*, *isko chhoṛ*.
Exception, *istisná*.
Excepted, *mustasná*.
Excess, *ziyádatí*.
Exchange, *adal-badal karná*.
Excise, *ábkárí*.
Excitement, *halchal*.
Exclaim, *bol uṭhná*.
Exclude, *khárij karná*, *mahrúm karná*.

Exclusion. This would be expressed by giving the verb *kháriј honá* a substantive sense, thus: This was the reason for your exclusion, *tumháre kháriј hone ká yih sabab thá.*
Excommunicate (from social intercourse), *huqqa páni band karná.*
Excuse, *uzr.*
Excusable, *mázúr.*
Execute (carry out), *bajá láná.*
Exempted, *mahfúz.*
Exercise, *riyázat*, 405.
Exertion, *daur-dhúp, koshish.*
Exhausted (as with fatigue, &c.), *apáhaj.*

*Note.*—In this word the stress is on the second syllable.

Exhibit (display), *dikhá dená.*
Exhibition, *numáish*; (display) *dikháwá.*
Exile, *jilá-watani.*
Existence, *hasti.*
Expanse (of land or water), *sath* (pron. *sateh*).
Expect, *tawaqqu rakhná.*
Expectation, *tawaqqu.*
Expedition (despatch), *shitábi.*
Expeditious, *jald-báz.*
Expeditiously, *shitábi se.*
Expenditure, *kharch.*
Expensive, *qimati.*
Experience, *tajriba.*
Experienced, *tajriba-kár.*
Experiment, *imtihán.*
Experimentally, *imtihánan.*
Expiate (atone for), *kafára dená.*
Expiration, *tamámi—inqizá.*
Expired (ended), *khatm—munqazi.*
Explain, *batláná, samjháná.*
Explanation, *tashríh*; (of one's conduct) *kaifiyat.*
Explicit, *saríh.*
Explicitly, *saríh taur par.*
Explode, *bhak se ur jáná*, 46.
Explosion, *chatákhá, dharáká.*
Exposure (laying bare), *chithár*; (of the person) *be-satri*; (of one's privacy) *be-pardagí.*
Extent (degree), *qadar*; *e.g.*, To some extent, *kisí qadar.*
Extenuating circumstances, *takhfif karnewálí súrat.*
Exterminate, *nest-nábúd karná.*
External, *báhiri, berúní—súri.*
Extinct, *mádúm.*
Extort (exact too much), *ziyáda-talabi karná.*
Extortion, *ziyáda-talabi.*
Extortioner, *ziyáda-talab.*
Extra, *fáltú.*
Extract (selection), *chumbak.*
Extraordinary (out of the common), *anúkhá.*
Extraordinary ability, *parle darje kí liyáqat*, 418.
Extravagance, *fazúl-kharchi.*
Extravagant, *fazúl-kharch.*
Extremely, *nipat, niháyat—az-hadd.*
*In* Extremities, *iztirár kí hálat men.*
*Driven to* Extremities, *ájiz*, 153.
Eye, *ánkh*; (of a needle) *náká.*
Eye-lash, *papní.*
Eye-lid, *palak.*
Eye-sight, *bínái, basárat*, 472.
Eye-sore, *khár ánkhon ká.*
Eye-witness, *gawáh-i-chashm-díd.*

Fable, *naql.*
Fabric, (building) *imárat*; (manufacture) *sákht.*

Fabricate, *banáná.*
Fabrication, *banáwaṭ.*
Face, *munh, chihra.*
*To* Face (confront), *sámhná karná.*
*To* Face in a particular way (as a house), *muháná honá.*

Example.—This house faces to the west, *is ghar ká pachhwán muháná hai.*

Facetious, *ṭhaṭṭhe báz—zaríf.*
Facilitate, *ásán karná.*
Facility, *ásání.*
Fact (reality), *haqíqat.*
Facts, *wáqiát;* (the real facts) *asliyat.*
Factory, *kár khána.*
Factotum, *harbábí.*
Faculty, *qúwat.*
Fade, (as a colour) *rang utarná;* (as a plant or flower) *kumhláná, murjháná.*
Faded (as a colour), *mánd, phíká* 292.
Fail, (not succeed) *ná kám honá, kámyáb nahin honá;* (as one's courage) *khatá hojáná;* (in business) *dewálá nikalná.*
Failing (coming short), *qásir, náqis.*
Failing (fault), *aib, nuqs.*
Failing of one's faculties, *qúwaton ká záil honá,* 406.
Failure, *ná-kámí.*
Faint (to swoon), *ghash áná.*
Fainting fit, *ghash, ghashí.*
Faint-hearted, *dil ká bodá.*
Fair, (market) *melá, háṭ;* (in complexion) *gorá.*
Fair (middling), *ausat darje ká.*
Faith, *ímán.*
Faithful (upright), *ímándár.*
Faithful (constant), *wafádár.*
Faithless (inconstant), *be-wafá.*
Faithlessness (inconstancy), *be-wafáí.*
Falcon, *báz.*
Fall, *girná, paṛná;* (fall foul of anyone) *kisí se ulajhná;* (fall out, quarrel) *bigaṛná,* 396, 560; (fall behind) *píchhe paṛná.*
Fallacious, *ghalat-kár.*
Fallacy, *ghaltí.*
Fallible, *sahw-pazír, qábil-i-khatá.*
Fallow (ground), *uftáda, bánjar.*
False, *jhúṭhá.*
Falsehood, *jhúṭh.*
False swearing (perjury), *darogh-halfí.*
Falsify, (give the lie to) *jhuṭláná;* (accounts, &c.) *banáná.*
Falter (waver), *ágá-píchhá karná.*
Fame, *shuhrat, námwarí.*
Familiar (not strange), *mánús,* 634.
*To be* Familiar to inferiors, *munh lagáná,* 633.
Family, *khándán, gharbár,* 198. *kumbá.*

*Note.*—For "Family relationships" see from 546 to 566.

Famine, *kál—qaht, qaht-sálí.*
Famished, to be, *bhúkhon marná.*
Famous (renowned), *námwar.*
Fanatic, fanatical, *muta'assib.*
Fancy, *khiyál, wahm;* (feel a fancy for) *jí lagná;* (take a fancy to) *jí lagáná.*
Far-distant (remote), *dúr-dast.*
Far-seeing (provident), *dúr-andesh, peshbín.*
Fare (passage-money) *bháṛá.*

Farm (lease), *ijára.*
Farmer (lessee), *ijáradár.*
Farmer (cultivator), *kisán, káshtkár,* 360.
Farrier, *sálotarí.*
Fascinate, *moh lená, farefta karná.*
Fascinated, *farefta.*
Fascinating, *dilrubá.*
Fascination, *dilrubái.*
Fashion (custom), *rasm;* (vogue) *charchá.*
Fashionable, *rasmí, mutábiq rasm ke.*
Fast, *n.* (religious) *roza;* (involuntary) *fáqa.*
Fasting, *fáqa-kashí.*
Fasten, *bándhná.*
Fastidious, *mirzá-mizáj.*
Fat, *moṭá—farbih.*
Fatal (deadly), *muhlik;* (wound) *kárí.*
Fated, doomed, *ajal-girifta.*
Father, *báp.*
Fatherland, *watan.*
Fatherly, *pidarána, pidarí.*
Fatigue, *mándagí.*
Fault, *qusúr, taqsír;* (defect) *ạib.*
Fault-finding, *ạib-gírí.*
Faulty (defective) *náqis.*
Faultless, *be-ạib.*
Favour (*n.*), *mihrbání, ri'ạyat.*
Favour (*v.a.*), *ri'ạyat karní.*
*Through another's* Favour, *badaulat, iqbál se.*
Favourable (propitious), *yáwar.*
Favourite, *manzúr-i-nazar, ạzíz.*
Fear, *ḍar, khauf.*
Fearful, *haulnák.*
Fearless, *be-bák.*
Fearlessly, *nidhaṛak.*
Fearlessness, *be-bákí.*
Feasible, to be, *ho sakná.*

Feast (entertainment), *ziyáfat.*
Feat, *achambhe ká kám, ạmal-i-ạjíb.*
*Distinguishing* Feature, *khás súrat, chihin.*
Fee (*n.*), *ujrat, mihnatána.*
Feeble, *kamzor, ná-táqat, nátawán.*
Feel, (touch) *chhúná;* (perceive) *mạlúm honá.*

Example.—I feel pain, *kuchh dard mạlúm hotá.*

Feel for (with the hand), *ṭaṭolná.*
*To* Feign, (dissemble) *bahána karná;* (affect ignorance of a thing or person), *anján banná,* 200.
Felicity, *khush-waqtí, sa'ạdatmandí.*
Fellow (one of a pair), *joṛá—juft.*
Fellowship, *rifáqat.*
Female, *mádín.*
Feminine (in grammar), *mu'annas.*
Fence (*n.*), *báṛ.*
Fermentation, *ubál—takhmír.*
Ferocious, (a dog, &c.) *kaṭkhaná;* (a bullock, &c.) *markhaná.*
Ferry, *guzára.*
Ferry-boat, *guzáre kí náo,* 631.
Fertile, *sansgar—jaiyid.*
Fertility, *sansgarí.*
Festival, *teohár, parab;* (Mahommedan) *íd.*
Festivities, *chahal-pahal, shádiyána.*
Fetters, (for prisoners) *beṛí;* (for animals) *páeband, pálahang.*
Fewness (paucity), *kamí, qillat.*
Fickle (inconstant), *mutalawwin, chanchal.*

Fiction, (romance) *kahání, dástán*; (invention) *banáwat*.
Fictitious (assumed), *farzí*.
*To* Fidget, *táná báná karná*, *chulbuláná*.
Fidelity, *ímándárí*; (constancy) *wafádárí*.
Field, *khet*.
Fierce, (a dog) *kaṭkhaná*; (a bullock) *markhaná*; (generally) *tund*.
Fig, *anjír*.
Fight (*v.a.*), *laṛná, laṛáí karná*; (*n.*) *laṛáí*.
Figure, *súrat, shakl*; (in arithmetic) *hindisa*.
File (implement), *retí*.
Fill, *bhardená*; (fill up a hollow) *páṭná*; (fill in a well, &c.) *anṭwáná*.
Film, *jhillí*.
Filth, *mail*—*ghalázat*.
Filthy, *ganda, ghalíz*.
Fin (of a fish), *par*.
Final, *ákhirí*; (conclusive) *qaṭ'í*.
Find, *páná*; (find out) *daryáft karná*.
Fine (not coarse), *mihín, bárík*.
Fine weather, *ásmán sáf honá*.
Fine (mulct), *jarimána*.
Finish (*v.a.*), *púrá karná, khatm karná*.
Fire (conflagration), *agwáí*.
Fire to break out, *ág lagná*.
Fire a gun, *bandúq chaláná*.
Fire-place, (native) *chúlhá*; (European) *átash-kháná*; (portable) *angeṭhí*.
Fireworks, *átash-bází*.
Fire-worshipper, *gabr*.
Firm (strong), *mazbút*—*ustuwár*, *mustahkim*.
Fishing-rod, *chhaṛ*.
First-class (*adj.*), *awwal qism*; (or *darje*) *ká*.
Fissure (cleft), *shigáf*, 345.
Fist, *muṭṭhí*.
*To* Fit, (as clothes) *ṭhík áná*; (fit into) *khapná*, 429.
*In a* Fitting manner, *jaisá ki cháhiye*.
Five senses, *hawáss-i-khamsa*, 622.
Fix, (a date, &c.) *muqarrar karná*; (to be fixed) *muqarrar honá, qarár páná*, 313.
Fix one's eyes on, *ṭakṭakí bándhná*, 636.
Flag, (large) *jhanḍá*; (small) *jhanḍí*.
Flame, *shola, lawaṛ*; (of a candle) *zabána*.
Flank, *pahlú*.
*To* Flap, *jhaṭás márná*.
Flare up (get angry), *jhunjhláná*.
Flash (of lightning), *chamak*.
Flashy (gaudy), *bhaṛkílá*.
Flat, *chapṭá*; (to flatten) *chapṭáná*.
Flatter, *khushámadí karná*.
Flattery, *khushámadí*.
Flavour (*n.*), *maza*—*mazáq*.
Flaw, *suqm, aib, nuqs*, 196.
Flay, *khál khainchná*.
Flee, *bhágná*—*farár honá*.
Fleet (*adj.*), *chust-chálák* (or only *chust*).
Fleshly, *jismání*; (sensual) *nafsání*.
Flick up (as a coin), *chuṭkí lagáná*, 146.
Flicker, *jhilmiláná*.
Flight (of a bird), *uṛán*; (from custody, &c.) *mafrúrí*.

Flighty, *achpalá, chanchal.*
Flimsy, *jhirjhirá.*
Flinch, *haṭná;* (not to flinch) *apne qarár par rahná.*
Flint, *chaqmaq.*
*To* Float, *tirná, bhasná;* (along with the stream) *bahná.*
Flock (of goats or sheep), *galla, rewaṛ;* (of birds) *jhunḍ, jhillaṛ.*
Flog, *chábuk márná—táziyána lagáná.*
Flood, *sailáb;* (in a river) *báṛh, tughyání.*
Floor, *zamín, farsh.*
Flour, *áṭá, maida;* (flour merchant) *parchúniya.*
Flourish, *lahlaháná;* (brandish) *ghumáná.*
Flow (*v.n.*), *bahná, jári honá.*
Flower-bed, *kiyári;* (garden) *chaman*, 497.
Fluency, *zabánáwarí.*
Fluent, *zabánáwar.*
Flurry, *haṛbaṛí.*
Flush with the ground, *zamíndoz.*
*To* Flush up, *chihre ká tamtamáná.*
*To* Flutter, *phaṛphaṛáná.*
*To* Fly, *uṛná;* (take to flight) *uṛánchhú hojáná*, 620.
Foal (colt), *bachherá—nákand.*
Foam, (*n.*) *jhág, kaf;* (of the sea) *phen.*
Fodder, *ghás, chára;* (for cattle) *sání.*
Foe, *dushman, bairí.*
Fog, *kúhrá, kuhásá.*
Foil (balk), *haráná.*
Fold (for sheep), *bheṛkháná, bheṛsálá.*
Fold up, *tah karná, lapeṭná.*
Follow, *pichhe ho lená, pichhe chalná;* (as a disciple) *pairawí karná*, 473.
Follower, (disciple) *shágird, muríd;* (imitator) *muqtadí.*
Folly, *bewuqúfí, himáqat*, 623.
*To be* Fond of, (a person) *cháhná;* (a thing) *kisí chíz ká shauq rakhná* (also *shauq honá*).

Example.—He is very fond of shooting, *usko shikár ká baṛá shauq hai.*

Food, *kháná — ghizá, khurák*, 623.
Fool, *ahmaq, múrakh*, 198; (make a fool of) *maskhara banáná.*
Foolish, *bewuqúf.*
Footpath, *pagḍanḍí, baṭiyá.*
Footprint, *pair ká nishán—naqsh-i-qadam.*
Footstep, *qadam.*
Fop, *bánkáchúr, chhailá.*
For (because), *kyúnki, is wáste ki, is liye ki.*
For certain, *ba-tahqíq*, 423.
Forbearance, *bardásht, tahammul.*
Forbearing, *mutahammil.*
Forbid, *mana karná.*
Forbidden, *mana.*
Force, (of current) *toṛ*, 69; (force of habit) *muqtazá-i-ádat.*
*By* Force, *zor se, ba-zor.*
Forceps, *chimṭá.*
Ford, *páyáb, gháṭ.*
Fordable, *páyáb.*
Foreboding, *andesha, khaṭká—khadsha.*
Forego (pass over or by), *darguzar karná*, 307.
Forehead, *máthá, peshání.*

Foreign, *begána, pardesí.*
Foreigner, *pardesí, ghair mulk ká ádmí,* 424.
Foremost, *pahlá, muqaddam;* (in a race) *mírí,* 649.
*In the* Forenoon, *do pahar se pahle.*
Foresight, *peshbíní.*
Forest, *jangal.*
Forethought (timely preparation), *peshbandí.*
*To* Forfeit one's right to a thing, *haqq játá rahná.*

Example.—I told him if he did this, he would forfeit his right to promotion, *main ne usse kahá ki agar yih kám karo, to tumhárá taraqqí ká haqq játá rahegá.*

Forgery, *jálsází.*
Forget, *bhúl jáná — farámosh karná.*
Forgetful (careless), *gháfil.*
Forgetfulness, *farámoshí.*
Forgive, *muáf karná.*
Forgiveness, *muáfí.*
Forlorn (friendless), *be-kas.*
Form, *súrat, shakl.*
Former, *aglá, sábiq.*
Formerly, *agle waqt men.*
Forsake, (a person) *chhor jáná;* (a thing) *chhor dená.*
Fort (fortress), *garh, qila.*
Fortitude, *istiqlál.*
Fortune, *nasíb;* (good fortune, luck) *khush-nasíbí;* (bad fortune, ill-luck) *bad-nasíbí.*
Forward (bold), *gustákh.*
Forwardness, *gustákhí.*
*To* Found, *bińá karná* (also to build).
Foundation, *neo, bunyád.*
*To be* Founded on fact, *haqíqat par mabni honá.*
Founder (originator), *báni.*
Founder (to sink), *dúb jáná — gharq honá.*
Fount, *chashma, mamba.*
Fountain, *fauwára.*
Fountain-head, *sar-i-chashma.*
Fox, *lomrí.*
Fraction (in arithmetic), *kasar.*
Fracture (in a building, &c.), *rakhna.*
Fragile (frail), *názuk, zaíf.*
Fragrance, *khushbúí, mahak.*
Fragrant, *khushbúdár.*
Frame (framework), *dhánchá.*
*Door* Frame, *chaukhat.*
Frank (open), *kusháda-dil.*
Fraud, *daghá.*
Fraudulent, *farebí.*
Freak, *wahm, lahar.*
Free, *ázád,* 623.
Freedom, *ázádagí.*
Freight, *naul, bhárá.*
*To* Frequent, *áyá jáyá karná.*
Frequently, *bár bár, bahut dafe, aksar.*
Freshness, *tázagí.*
*To* Fret, *kurhná.*
Fretful (peevish), *chirchirá.*
Fretfulness (peevishness), *chirchir'hat.*
Friction, *ragar.*
Friday, *jume ká roz, sukrbár.*
Friendly, *áshná-parast, dostána.*
Friendship, *dostí.*
Fright, *bhai, dahshat.*
Frightened, to be, *dar jáná.*
*To* Frighten, *daráná.*
Frightful, *daráwná, haibatnák.*
Fringe, *jhálar.*
*To* Frisk (skip), *kudakná.*
Frisky, *kudakkar, chulbulá.*
Frolicsome, *khilárí.*

Front (foremost place), *peshgáh, agáṛí.*
Frost, *pálá.*
Froth (foam), *phen, jhág, kaf.*
Frown, *bhauṉ ṭeṛhí karní.*
Frugal, *juzras.*
Frugality, *juzrasí.*
Fruit, *phal, mewa.*
Fruitful, *phaldár, baromand.*
Frustrate, *bátil karná.*
Fry, *talná, bhúnná.*
Frying-pan, *karáhí.*
Fuel, *índhan, sokhta.*
Fugitive, *farárí, bhagoṛá.*
Fulfil, *púrá karná, bar láná.*
Full, *bhará, bhar-púr, mạmúr;* (complete) *púrá.*
Fulness, *bharpúrí.*
Fun and frolic, *khel-kúd, khel-tamáshá.*
Function, *mansab, kám.*
Fundamental, *aslí, bunyádí, zarúrí.*
Fur, *pashm;* (made of) *pashmína.*
Furious, *ghazab-álúda.*
Fury, *ghazab, ghaiz.*
Furnace, *bhaṭṭhí, bháṛ.*
Furniture, *ghar ká asbáb.*
Furthermore, *ạláwa iske.*
Furtively, *chorí chorí.*
Futile, *lá-hásil, akárat.*
Future, *áyạnda;* (in future) *áyande meṉ.*

Gabble, *bak bak karná.*
Gadfly, *ḍáṉs.*
Gain, *nafạ, manfa'ạt.*
*To* Gain (acquire), *hásil karná, baham pahúncháná.*
Gait, *chál—raftár.*
Galled, *chhil gayá,* 620.
Gallant (brave), *diláwar, bahádur.*
Gallantry (bravery), *jawánmardí.*
Gallery, *chhajjá, bálá-khána.*
Gallop, (*n.*) *ḍánṭ-ḍapaṭ;* (*v.a.*) *rapṭáná.*
Gallows, *dár.*
Gamble, *júá khelná.*
Gambler, *júárí,* 192.
Gambling, *júá, hárjít.*
Gambols, *kaloleṉ.*
Game, (of chess, &c.) *bází;* (cricket, &c.) *khel,* 359.
Gang, *giroh.*
Gang-leader, *sarghana,* 370.
Gaol, *jel-khána.*
Gaoler, *dárogha.*
Gap, *chák, darár.*
Garb, *bhes, libás.*
Garden, (large) *bágh;* (small) *bághícha.*
Gargle (*v.a.*), *gargaráná.*
Garland, *málá;* (for weddings, &c.) *sihrá.*
Garlic, *lahsan.*
Garment, *kapṛá, jáma.*
Garnet, *támṛá.*
Garrulous, *bakwásí, fazúl-go.*
Gasp, *ulṭí sáṉs lená.*
Gate, *pháṭak.*
Gateway, *ḍeoṛhí* (native).
Gather, (collect) *binná, baṭorná;* (pick) *toṛná.*
Gather (together), *jamạ karná —faráham karná.*
Gaudy, *bhaṛkílá, rangílá.*
Gauge (*v.a.*), *nápná, paimáish karná.*
*To* Gaze on, *ṭakṭakí bándhn*, 636.
Gem, *ratan, jawáhir.*
Genealogy, *nasabnáma.*

Generally (for the most part), *aksar auqát, aksar.*
Generation, (race) *nasl*; (succession) *pusht, pírhí.*
Generous (liberal), *sakhí.*
Generosity, *sakháwat.*
Genial, (a person) *khush-taba*; (weather) *khush-gawár.*
Gentle, *halím, dhímá.*
Gentleness, *hilm, muláyamat.*
Gently! gently! *haule! haule!* (when anyone speaks too loud).
Genuine, *sachchá, pakká—khális.*
Germinate, *jamná.*
Gesticulate, *bháo batáná*, 184.
Gesture, *bháo—harakat.*
Get loose, *chhút jáná*; (get off, be acquitted) *chhút jáná*; (get away, escape) *bhág jáná*; (get out of the way) *hat jáná.*
Ghost (spectre), *bhút—ifrít.*
Gibberish, *barbaráí—wáhiyát.*
*To feel* Giddy, *sir ghúm jáná.*
Giddiness, *ghumrí.*
Gift, *bakhshish, inám*; (talent) *hunar.*
*To* Giggle, *khilkhiláná.*
Gills of a fish, *galphará*, 426.
Ginger, (undried) *adrak*; (dried) *sonth*, 598.
Girdle, *kamarband, patká.*
Gist, *asl matlab—khulása, hír.*
*To* Give in (be convinced), *qáil honá*; (give up) *háth utháná.*
*To* Give out (publish), *mashhúr karná.*
*To* Give way to, *kám farmáná.*

Example,—Do not give way to anger, *ghusse ko kám na farmáiye.*

Glad, *khush.*
Gladly, *ba-khushí tamám.*
Gladness, *khushí—masarrat.*
Glass, *shísha, kánch*; (mirror) *áína.*
Glimmer (*v.n.*), *jhilmiláná.*
Glisten, *chamakná* or *jhaljhaláná.*
Glitter (splendour), *chamak tamak*, or *jhalak*; (to glitter) *jhaljhaláná.*
Gloat over, *rijhná—názán honá.*
Gloom, *tíragí*; *dhumláí.*
Glorious (splendid), *raunaqdár.*
Glory (splendour), *raunaq—tajallí.*
*To* Glory in, *fakhr karná.*
Glossy, *chamakdár, chikná.*
Glove, *dastána.*
Glow (*n.*), *ánch, lapat.*
Glue, *saresh.*
Glutton, *bará kháú, kháú-bír.*
Gnarled (knotty), *gathílá, girehdár.*
Gnash the teeth, *dánt písná.*
Gnaw, *chabáná.*
Go, *jáná, chalná*; (along or away) *chalá jáná*; (go out—a candle, &c.) *bujh jáná*; (go off as a gun) *sar hojáná*; (go over, examine) *muláhaza karná*; go through, suffer) *jhelná*; (go for nothing) *akárat jáná*; (go without) *be—rahná.*
Goad (*v.a.*), *húl dená, khod dená.*
Goal, *manzil-maqsúd.*
Go-between, *darmiyání.*
Gold, *soná*; (made of) *sunahrá, sone ká—tiláí.*
Goldsmith, *sunár.*
Good (*adj.*), *achchhá, bhalá.*

These are occasionally used in a substantive sense.

Good (*n.*), *bhaláí, bihtarí;* (use of a thing) *kám—manfa'at*, 142, 143.
Good for nothing, *kuchh kám ká nahin, nikammá.*
Goods and chattels, *chíz-bast.*
Gorgeous, *bharkilá—raunaqdár.*
Gory, *khún-álúda, lahú-lahán.*
Gossip (*n.*), *gap-shap.*
Govern, *hukúmat karná.*
Government (the executive), *sarkár.*
*Belonging to* Government, *sarkárí.*
Governor, *hákim.*
Gout, *niqris.*
Grace (divine), *fazl, taufíq.*
Graceful, *sajílá—rána.*
Gracious, *mihrbán.*
Gradually, *rafta rafta.*
*To* Graft, *paiwand lagána.*
Grain, *anáj, ghalla.*
Grain merchant, *banjárá.*
Grammar (rules of), *qáida* or *qawáid.*
Granary, *ambár-khaná*, 463.
Grant, (bestow) *ináyat karná;* (a request) *qabúl karná.*
Grant, for the sake of argument, *máno, farz karo.*
Grape, *angúr.*
Grapple with, *kushtí karná.*
Grasp, *háth se pakarná, qabza karná.*
Grass, *ghás.*
Grasshopper, *tiddá.*
Grateful, *shukr-guzár, shákir.*
Gratify, (please) *khush karná;* (one's desires) *apná matlab púrá karná.*
Grating, *jálí.*
Gratitude, *shukr-guzárí—haqq-shinásí.*
Gratuitously, *muft, muft men.*
Gratuity, *bakhshish, inám.*
Grave (solemn), *sanjída-mizáj.*
Gravel, *kankarí—sangreza.*
Graze, *charná, chugná.*
Grease, (*n.*) *charbí,* (*v.a.*) *aungná.*
Greasy, *chikkat.*
Greedy, *chatorá.*
Greediness, *chatorpan.*
Green, *hará, sabz;* (light green) *dháni*, 484.
Greet, *salám karná.*
*Forms of* Greeting (general) *salám;* (Mahommedan) *salám alaikum;* (Hindu) *rám rám.*
Grey, (a horse) *sabz*, 232; (a cow) *khairí.*
Grief, *gham, ghamí, sog.*
Grievance, *báis ranj ká.*
Grieve, *afsos karná, kurhná.*
Grimaces (to make) *khís nikálná, munh banáná.*
Grin, *dánt nikálná.*
Grind, *písná.*
Gripes, *pechish.*
Grit, *patthrí, kirik.*
Groan, *karáhná.*
Groaning (*n.*), *karáhná.*
Groin, *janghásá.*
Gross, (heinous) *shadíd;* (obscene) *fuhsh.*
Grotesque, *báis hansí ká.*
Ground, *zamín;* (of complaint, &c.) *báis.*
Groundless, *be-bunyád.*
Group, *majma, jamá'at.*
Grow, *barhná;* (spring up) *ugná upajná.*
Growl, *ghurráná.*
Growth, *barháo* (of plants), *roídagí.*
*To* Grudge, *daregh karná.*

Grudgingly, *daregh se.*
Grumble (complain), *kurkuráná,* 403.
Grunt (*v.a.*), *kúnkhná.*
Guarantee (*v.a.*), *zámin honá, zimmedár honá.*
Guard (*v.a.*), *nigahbání karná, rakhwálí karná.*
Guardian (of a minor), *walí.*
Guardianship, *wiláyat.*
Guess (*v.a.*), *andáz karná, atkal karná.*
Guest, *mihmán, páhuná,* 608.
Guide (*v.a.*), *ráh batáná, rahnumáí karná.*
Guide (*n.*), *rahnumá.*
Guile, *riyá, makr.*
Guileless, *be-riyá.*
Guilt, *gunáh.*
Guiltless, *be-gunáh.*
Guilty, *gunahgár.*
Gulf, *khalíj.*
Gulp down, *ghúntná.*
Gum, *gond.*
Gums, *masorá.*
Gun, *bandúq.*
Gunpowder, *bárút.*
Gush out, *phút nikalná.*
Gust of wind, *jhoká, jhakorá.*
*With* Gusto, *raghbat se, shauq se.*
Gutter, *nábdán.*
Guttural, *halqí.*

Haberdasher, *bisátí.*
Habit (custom), *ádat, mámul,* 312, 313, 454, 455.
Habitable, *rahne ke qábil.*
Habitat, *rahne kí jagah.*
Habitation, *ghar, makán—maskan.*
Habitual, *mámúlí.*
Habitually, *hamesha, barábar.*
Habituate (oneself to), *ádat pakarná.*
Hackery, *chhakrá.*
Hades, *álam-i-arwáh.*
Haft (handle), *dasta, qabza.*
Hag, *churail.*
Haggle, *ragar jhagar machána.*
Hail (*v.n.*), *ole parná.*
Note. The plural form *ole* should always be used.
Hair, *bál;* (head of hair) *jhotá,* 442.
Hair's-breadth, *ek bál barábar.*
Hair-splitting, *mú-shigáfí.*
Hairy (shaggy), *jhabbúá.*
Hale and hearty, *tandurust, bhalá changá.*
Half, *ádhá—nisf;* (one-half) *ek ádh;* (half cooked) *ádh-pakká;* (half dead) *adh-múá.*
Half-caste, *mastísá.*
Half-heartedly, *be-dilí se,* 128.
Half-way, *bích ráste men;* (when he had gone half way) *jab ádhe ráste pahúnchá.*
Hall, *dálán.*
Halloo, *pukárná, hánk márná.*
Halo, *kundal, hála.*
Halt (*verb*), *thairná, maqám karná.*
Halter (*n.*), *bág-dor.*
Hammer (*n.*), *mártol;* (sledge-hammer) *hathorá.*
Hamper (*v.a.*), *atkáná.*
Hand, *háth;* (ready to one's hand) *sar-i-dast;* (to be hand and glove with) *se ittifáq rakhná.*
Handcuffs, *hath-karí.*
Handful, *muthí-bhar.*
*To be* Handicapped, *bár páná.*
Handicraft, *dastkárí, pesha.*

Handicraftsman (artificer), *kárígar.*
Handiwork (in a bad sense), *kársází.*
Handle (*n.*), *dasta, qabza*; (of an axe, hoe, &c.) *bainṭá*, 653.
*To* Handle, *múṭhná, chherná.*
Handmill, *chhakkí, jántá.*
Handsome, *khúbsúrat, sundar.*
Handwriting, *khatt.*
Hang (dangle), *laṭakná, hilgá rahná*, 212, 213.
Hanker after, *kisí chíz par lalcháná.*
Happen, *wuqú' men áná, ittifáq honá, án-parná.*
Happiness, *khushí, khushwaqtí, sa'ádatmandí.*
Happy, *khush, khush-hál, khushwaqt*; (happy go lucky) *lashṭam-pashṭam.*
Harangue, *taqrír.*
Harass (worry), *tang karná, halkán karná.*
Harbinger, *harkára, dauṛáhá.*
Harbour (*n.*), *bandar.*
Hard, *sakht, kaṛá*; (hard of hearing) *kam sunná*, 173.
Hardhearted, *sangdil, be-rahm.*
Hardihood, *dilerí*; (audacity) *be-bákí, ḍhiṭhái.*
Hardship, *sakhtí, taklíf, dukh*, 265.
Hare, *khargosh, lamhá.*
Harm (injury), *zarar*; (impropriety) *qabáhat*, 157.
Harmless, *ná-muzirr.*
Harness, *sáz.*
Harp, *barbat.*
Harrow (agricultural implement), *hengá.*
Harsh, *kaṛá mizáj—durusht.*
Harshness (severity), *sakhtí—khushúnat.*
Harum-scarum, *shutur-i-bemahár.*
Harvest, *fasl*; (spring) *rabí'*; (autumn) *kharíf.*
Hasp, *kunḍí, qulába.*
Haste, *jald bází, shitábí*; (hurry) *utáolepan.*
Hatch, *sewná.*
Hatchet, *kulháṛí.*
Hate, *adáwat rakhná—bughz rakhná.*
Hatred, *adáwat—bughz.*
Haughty, *maghrúr, ghamanḍí.*
Hauteur, *maghrúrí, ghamanḍ—ru'únat.*
*To* Have, *ke pás honá*; (to have to do a thing) *paṛná.*
Havoc, *kharábí, tabáhí*; (to make) *tabáh karná.*
Hawk, *báz, bahrí.*
Hazardous, *khatarnák.*
Haze, *dhundh*, 521.
Head (chief), *sardár.*
Headship, *sardárí.*
*From* Head to foot, *sir se leke páon tak.*
Headlong, *sir ke bhal*, 250.
Headstrong, *munh-zor, be-saláh.*
Heal (to cure), *achchhá karná—shifá dená*, 623.
Health, *tandurustí, sihhat*, 405, 172.
Healthy (in good health), *tandurust.*
Heap, *ḍher—ambár.*
Hear, *sunná*; (listen to) *kán dharke sunná*; (catch the sound of) *kán men paṛná*; (cause to hear) *sunáná—goshguzár karná*; (pretend not to hear) *kán men tel ḍálná.*

Hearing (of a case), *samá'at* 169.
Hearsay, *suní sunái*, 56.
Heart, *dil*, *khátir*.
Heart-broken, *dil-shikasta*; (with all one's heart) *dil-o-ján se*; (to one's heart's content) *khátir-khwáh*, 528.
Heartless (unfeeling), *be-dard*, *be-rahm*.
Heat, *garmí—harárat*; (burning) *jalan*; (pungency) *jhál*.
Heathen, *but-parast*.
Heathenism, *but-parastí*.
Heaven, *ásmán*, *bihisht*.
Heavenly, *ásmání*.
Heavy, *bhárí—girán*.
Hedge, *báṛ*.
*To* Heed (attend to), *mánná*, *khátir men láná*.
Heel, *eṛí*.
Height, *unchái*, *bulandí*.
Heinous, *sangín*.
Heir, *wáris*.
Hell, *jahannam*, *dozakh*.
Help (*n.*), *madad—i'ánat*; (*v.a.*) *madad karná*.
Helper, *madadgár*.
Helping hand, *dastgírí*, 149.
Helpless, *lá-chár*.
Helpless one, *bechára*.
Helplessness, *lá-chárí*.
Hem (of a garment), *goṭ—maghzí*.
*To* Hem, *turpáná*.
Herb, *paudhá*.
Herbage, *ghás-pát—nabátát*.
Herd (drove), *galla*.
Here and there, *idhar udhar*.
Hereabouts, *kahín idhar*.
Hereafter, *bád iske*.
Hereditary, *maurúsí*.
Heresy, *bidat*.
Heretic, *bidatí*.
Heritage, *mírás*.
Hermit, *gosha-gír*, *gosha-nishín*.
Hero, *bahádur*, *bír*.
Heroism, *bahádur*.
Hesitate (pause), *ta'ammul karná*.
Hesitation (pause), *ta'ammul*, 332.
*To* Hew, *kulhárí se káṭná*.
Heyday of youth, *unfuwán-i-shabáb*, 657.
Hiccough, *hichkí*.
Hidden (concealed), *poshída*, *chhipá*.
Hide (*v.n.*), *chhipjáná*; (*v.a.*) *chhipáná*.
*To be in* Hiding, *rúposh honá*, 165.
Higgledy-piggledy, *ulṭá pulṭá*, *ulaṭ pulaṭ*.
High, *únchá*, *buland*; (of high rank) *álíshán*.
Highhanded, *zabardast*.
Highhandedness, *zabardastí*.
Highway, *sháh-ráh*, *ráj-báṭ*.
Highway robber, *rah-zan*.
Highway robbery, *rahzaní*.
Hill, *pahár*, *parbat*.
Low hill, *ṭibbá*.
Hillock, *ṭílá*.
Hilly country, *kohistán*.
Hinder (obstruct), *aṭkáná*, *muzáhim honá*.
Hindrance (obstruction), *aṭkáo*, *muzáhamat*.
Hindmost, *pichhlá*; (in a race) *phisaḍḍí*, 650.
Hinge, *qabza*.
Hint (*n.*), *ishára—ímá*, 640.
Hip, *kúlá*, 641.
Hire (*v.a.*), *kiráe lená*; (*n.*) *kiráya*.

Hiss (as a snake), *phuphkárná.*
History, *tawáríkh, itihás.*
Hitch, *aṭak, rukáo.*
Hitherto, *abtak.*
Hoard, (*n.*) *ẕakhíra ;* (*v.a.*) *ẕakhíra karná, jama kar rakhná.*
Hoe (*n.*), *kudál*, 628.
Hold (*v.a.*) *pakṛe rahná*, 3 ; (hold in, restrain), *thamá dená.*
Holding (of land), *jot.*
Hole, *chhed, súrákh ;* (pit) *gaṛhá.*
Holiday, *táṭíl.*
Hollow (not solid), *polá, khokhlá*, 68.
Hollow (*n.*), *khol ;* (in the ground) *dabak—nasheb.*
Holy, *muqaddas.*
Homage, *taslímát ;* (to render) *taslímát bajá láná.*
Homicide, *mardum-kushí.*
Honest (upright), *kharú, diyánatdár*, 264.
Honey, *shahd.*
Honeycomb, *chhattá.*
Honour (reputation), *ịzzat—ábrú.*
*To* Honour, (a superior) *táẓím karná ;* (an inferior) *sarfaráz karná ;* (an equal) *ịzzat karná.*
Honourable, *mu'aẓẓiz.*
Hood (to a carriage), *chhatrí.*
Hoof, (of a horse) *sum ;* (of a bullock, &c.) *khur.*
Hook, *ánkṛí ;* (fish-hook), *bansí.*
Hope (*n.*), *ummed.*
Hopeful, *ummedwár.*
Hopeless, *ná-ummed.*
Horde, *giroh.*
Horn, *síng ;* (hunter's, &c.) *narsingá.*
Hornet, *bhaṛ.*
Horse, *ghoṛá.*

Hospital, *shifá-khána.*
Hospitality, *mihmándárí.*
Host, (entertainer) *mihmándár ;* (multitude) *bhíṛ—amboh.*
Hostile, *mukhálif.*
Hostility, *ạdáwat.*
Hot, *garm.*
Hot-tempered, *tund-mizáj.*
Hot wind, *lúh.*
Hour, *ghanṭá.*
Hour-glass, *ghaṛí ká shísha.*
House, *ghar, makán.*
House-searching, *khána-talúshí*, 206.
House-wife, *gharwálí.*
Hover, *thirakná, manḍláná.*
How? (in what way) *kyúṅkar? kistarah?* (in what condition) *kaisá?*
How many? *kaí? kitne?* (how much?) *kitná?*
Howl (lament), *kuhrám macháná—nála o-zárí karná.*
Hubbub, *shor wa shaghab.*
Huckster, *bisátí.*
Hug, *kaulí bhar lená, gale lagáná.*
Huge, *bahut baṛá, niháyat baṛá.*
Hullabaloo, *ghul-ghapára.*
Human, *insání.*
Humane, *rahm-dil.*
Humanity, *insániyat.*
Humble, *farotan, kháksár.*
Humid, *martúb.*
Humidity, *rutúbat.*
Humiliate, *khafíf karná.*
Humiliated, *khafíf*, 627.
Humiliation (being put to shame), *khiffat.*
Humility, *farotaní, kháksárí*, 237.
Hump (of a camel, &c.), *kub.*

Hundred, *sau*, *saikṛá*; (per cent.) *saikṛá*.
Hunger, *bhúkh*.
Hungry, *bhúkhá*.
Hurry, flurry, *haṛbaṛí*, 325, 326.
Hurt (*n.*), *choṭ*; (damage) *zarar*.
*To be* Hurt, *choṭ kháná* or *lagná*; (in one's feelings) *ranj honá*.
Hurtful (injurious), *muzirr*.
Husband, *khasam*—*shauhar*.
Hush! *chup!*
Hush-money, *muṇhbharí*.
Husk, *chhilká*.
Hustle (jostle), *dhakká dená*.
Hut (hovel), *jhompṛí*, *chhappar*.
Hyena, *lakaṛ-baghá*, *charkh*.
Hymn, *gít*, *bhajan*.
Hyperbole, *mubálagha*.
Hypocrisy, *riyákárí*.
Hypocrite, *riyákár*, *bagulá bhagat*.
Hyothesis, *farz*.
Hypothetical, *farzí*.

Ice, *barf*.
Idea, *khiyál*, *pindár*; (mental proposition) *tadbír*.
Identical, *wuhí*.
Identification, *pahchán* — *shinákht*.
Identify, *pahchánná* — *shinákht karná*.
Identity (being the same), *wuhí honá*; (used substantively.)
Idiom, *muháwara*.
Idiot, *báolá*, *págal*.
Idiotcy, *báolepan*.
Idle (lazy), *sust*.
Idleness (laziness), *sustí*.
Idler (skulker), *kám-chor*.
Idol, *but*, *múrat*, *múrtí*.
Idolater, *but-parast*.
Idolatry, *but-parastí*.

Ignoble, *pájí*—*kamína*.
Ignominious (disgraceful), *fazíhatí*.
Ignominy (disgrace), *fazíhat*.
Ignoramus, *hech-ma-dán*, 198.
Ignorance, *nádání* — *jahálat*; (of a particular fact) *lá-ilmí*.
Ignorant, *nádán*—*jáhil*.
Ignore, *anján banná* — *chashm-poshí karná*, 200.
Ill (unwell), *bímár*—*tabíat alíl*.
Ill-advised, *be-saláh*; (ill-behaved) *bad-chalan*; (ill-mannered) *be-ḍhang*; (ill-omened) *manhús*; (ill-tempered) *bad-mizáj*; (ill-gotten, *harám-hásil*.
Illegal, *khiláf-i-qánún*, *khiláf-qáida*.
Illegality, *be-zábtagí*, *khiláf-qánúní*.
*To be* Illegible, *paṛhá nahiṇ jáná*.
Illegitimate, *harámzáda*.
Illiberal (stingy), *tang-dast*, *kanjús*.
Illicit, *nájáiz*.
Illimitable (boundless), *be-hadd*, *be-páyán*.
Illiterate, *anpaṛhá*—*ná-khwánda*, *ummí*, 200, 510.
Illness, *bímárí*—*alálat*.
Illtreatment, *bad-sulúkí*, 563.
Illuminate (enlighten), *roshan-karná*—*munauwar karná*.
Illusion, *máyá*, *dhokhá*.
Illusive (delusive), *ghalat-kár*.
Illustrate, *tashríh karná*.
Illustration, *tashríh*, *ziman*.
Illustrious, *námwar*.
Image, *see* Idol.
Imaginary, *khiyálí*.

Imagination, *khiyál*; (the faculty) *mutakhaiyila.*
Imagine, *khiyál karná, tasauwur karná.*
Imbecile, *kam-aql.*
Imbecility, *kam-aqlí.*
Imbroglio, *uljherá—hais-bais.*
Imitate, *naql karná—tatabbu karná.*
Imitation, *tatabbu.*
Immaterial, *zarúrí nahin.*
Immature, *adhúrá, kachchá.*
Immaturity, *kachchepan, ná-bálighí.*
Immediately (at once), *abhí, ekdam—fauran.*
Immense, *niháyat bará.*
Imminent, *hone par, hone cháhtá.*
Immoderate, Immoderately, *be-andáza.*
Immodest, *be-hayá, be-sharm.*
Immoral, *bad-akhláq.*
Immorality, *bad-akhláqí.*
Immortal, *amar—ghair-fání.*
Immortality, *hamesha kí zindagí—baqá.*
Immunity, *muáfí, bacháo.*
Immutability, *be-tabdílí—be-taghaiyur.*
Impact, *sadma*, 631.
Impair, *bigárna, nuqsán pahúncháná.*
Impart, *dená, bakhshná.*
Impartial, *munsif, ádil, be-gharaz.*
Impartiality, *insáf.*
Impartially, *bilá rú-ri'áyat.*
Impassable (through natural obstacles), *aughat, qábil guzar ke nahin.*
Impatience, *be-sabrí.*
Impatient, *be-sabr.*
Impeach, *ilzám lagáná.*
Impede, *atkáná, rokná.*
Impediment, *atkáo—há,il*; (in speech) *lugnat*, 534.
Impel, *chaláná, hánkná.*
Imperceptible, *málúm nahin detá* (or *hotá.*)
Imperfect, *ná-tamám.*
Imperfection, *na-tamámí, kotáhí.*
Imperial, *bádsháhí.*
Imperil, *khatre men dálná.*
Imperious, *ammára.*
Imperishable, *be-zawál.*
Impertinence, *be-adabí.*
Impertinent, *be-adab.*
Impetuosity, *tezí*; (of a current) *tezraví.*
Impetuous, *tez*; (rapid) *tezrav.*
Impetus, *tahrík.*
Implement, *hathyár, auzár.*
Implicate, *uljháná, pech men dálná.*
Implicitly, *be-uzr.*
Implore, *minnat karná, girgiráná.*
Imply, *isháre se batláná.*
Import (*v.a.*), *mál báhar se* (or *ghair mulk se*) *láná.*
Importance, *qadar, giráni—waqat.*
Importunate, *minnatí, mutaqází.*
Importune, *píchhá lená—bajidd honá.*
Impose, *lagáná*; (impose upon) *chhal dená.*
Impossible, *ghair-mumkin, an-honá.*
Impotent, *za'íf, ná-tawán.*
Impracticable (out of the question), *muta'azzir.*
Imprecation, *bad-du'á, lánat, kosá.*
Impress (on the mind), *dil nishín karná.*

Impression (of a seal, &c.) *naqsh*; (effect) *asar*.
Imprinted (on the memory) *zihn-nishín*.
Imprison, *qaid karná*.
Improbable, *khiláf-i-qaiyás*.
Impromptu, extempore (*adv.*), *zabán-i-hál se—filbadíha*.
Improper, *ná-munásib*, *be-já*.
Impropriety, *ná-sháistagi*; (harm) *qabáhat*, 157.
Improve, (become better) *taraqqí karná*; (make better) *aur achchhá karná*.
Improvement, *bihtarí*, *taraqqí*.
Improvident, *kotah-andesh*.
Imprudence, *be-tamízí*.
Imprudent, *be-tamíz*.
Impudence, *gustákhí*, *be-adabí*.
*With* Impunity, *baghair sazá mile húe*.
Impure, *nápák*, *najis*; (as blood) *fásid*.
Impurity, *nápákí*, *najásat*.
Imputation, *tuhmat*.
Inaccessible, *be-lagáo*.
Inaction, *kuchh nahin karná*.
Inadequate, *kifáyat nahin kartá*; *ná-káfí*.
Inadmissible, *qábil manzúrí ke nahin*.
Inadvertence, *bhúl—sahv*.
Inanimate (without life), *beján*, 182.
Inapplicable, *ghair-muta'alliq*.
Inattention, *kam-tawajjuhí*.
Inattentive, *kam-tawajjuh*.
Incantation, *jantar-mantar*.
Incapable, *ná-qábil—ná-rasá*.
Incapacity, *ná-rasái*, 416.
In case, *dar súrate ki*.
Incautious, *be-ihtiyát*.
Incautiously, *be-ihtiyátí se*.
Incendiarism (arson), *átashzaní*.
Incense (*n.*), *lobán*.
Incentive, *targhíb*.
Incessantly, *be chhúṭe se*, *har dam—be-waqfa*.
Incident, *wáridát*, 201.
Incision, *chheh*; (to make an) *chheh dená*, 183.
Incite, *uksáná*, *ubhárná—tahrík karná*.
Inclination, *shauq*, *raghbat—mail*.
Include, *shámil karná*.
Income, *ámdaní*.
Incomparable, *be-misál*, *be-nazír*.
Incompetent, *ná-qábil*.
Incomplete, *ná-tamám*.
Incomprehensible, *samajh se báhar*.
Inconceivable, *be-qaiyás*.
Incongruity, *ná muwáfaqat*.
Inconsiderate, *be-liház*, *be-fikr*.
Inconvenience, (*n.*) *taklíf*, *harj*; (*v.a.*) *taklíf dená*.
Incorrect, *ghalat*, *ná-durust*.
Incorrigible, *ná-isláh-pazír*.
Increase (*n.*), *baṛháo*, *baṛhtí—afzáish*.
Increase (*v.n.*), *baṛhná*, *ziyáda honá*.
Increase (*v.a.*), *baṛháná*, *ziyáda karná*.
Incredible, *qábil i'tibár ke nahin*.
Incumbent on, *wájib*, *farz*, *lázim*.

*Example.*—It was incumbent on you to report the matter, *tumko lázim* (or *tumpar wájib* or *farz*) *thá ki isbát kí rapoṭ kar dete*, 501.

Incurable, *be-dawá*, *lá-iláj*.
Indecency, *ná sháistagí*.
Indecent, *ná sháista*.

Indeed, *wáqi men*; (in fact, as a case in point) *chunánchi*.
Indefinite (vague), *muhmil*.
Indelible, *nahin miṭne ká*.
Indelibly impressed, *naqsh-kal-hajar*.
Independence, *ázádagí*; (wanting nothing) *be-niyází*.
Independent (not dependent), *be-niyáz*, 380.
Index, *fihrist*; (to character, &c.) *namúd*.
Indication, *namúd*, *ishára*; (trace) *patá*, *lim*.
Indifference, *be-parwáí*.
Indigenous, *desí*.
Indigent, *muhtáj*.
Indigestible, *saqíl*.
Indigestion, *bad-hazmí*, 224,
Indignity, *tahattuk*, *be-izzatí*.
Indigo, *níl*; (colour of indigo) *nílá*.
Indiscreet, *be-tamíz*.
Indiscretion, *be tamízí*.
Indiscriminately, *be-imtiyází se*.
Indispensable, *zarúrí*.
Individual, (*adj*.) *fard*; (*n*.) *shakhs*.
Indolent, *sust—káhil-mizáj*.
Induce to do a thing, *targhíb deke karáná*.
Indulge (give way to), *kám farmáná*.
Industrious, *mihnatí*.
Ineffectual, *be-asar*.
Inevitable, *lá-buddí*.
Infamous (character), *bahut hí badnám*.
Infancy, *bachpan—tufúliyat*.
Infatuated, *farefta*.
Infatuation, *fareftagí*.
Infectious, *muta'addí*.
Infer, *qaiyás karná*.
Inference, *qaiyás*.
Inferior, *níchá*; (subordinate) *má-taht*; (in rank) *kam-rutba*.
Inferiority, *pastí*.
Infirm, *za'íf*, *kamzor*, 545.
Inflammation, *sozish*.
Influence, *asar*; (personal) *dabáo*.
Influential (powerful), *qábú-yáfta*, *zordár*.
Inform, *khabar dená*, *ittilá karná*.
Information, *khabar*, *ittilá*.
Informer, *mukhbir*; (secret information), *mukhbirí*.
Infringe, *torná*.
Infuse, *bhigoná*.
Ingenious, *hikmatí*.
Ingenuity, *hikmat*.
Ingenuous, *bholá*, *sáda*, *be-riyá*.
Ingratitude, *ná-shukrí*, *namak-harámí*.
Ingredient, *juz*.
Ingredients, *ajzá*, 496.
Inhabit, *basná*, *rahná—sukúnat karná*.
Inhabitant, *rahnewálá — báshinda*.
Inhabited, *ábád*.
Inherit, *mírás men páná*, *wáris honá*.
Inheritance, *mírás*.
Inhuman, *qasáí*, *sangdil*.
Inhumanity, *be-rahmí*.
Iniquity, (injustice) *be-insáfí*; (wickedness) *sharárat*.
Initial, *pahlá—ibtidáí*.
Initiative, to take the, *pahal karná*, *shurú' karná*.
Injection, to give an, *pichkárí dená*.
Injunction, *táhíd—taqaiyud*.

Injure, *zarar pahúncháná, nuqsán pahúncháná.*
Injury, *zarar, nuqsán—mazarrat,* 100, 101.
Injustice, *be-insáfí ;* (wrong) *andher.*
Ink, *siyáhí—roshnáí.*
Inkstand, *dawát.*
Innate, *zátí, jibillí.*
Inner, *andarlí,* 95.
Innocence, (of childhood) *másúmiyat ;* (of a crime) *be-qusúrí.*
Inopportune, *be-mauqa.*
Inquire, *púchhná.*
Inquiry (judicial), *tahqíqát.*
Inquisitive, *rázjo, khojí.*
Inquisitiveness, *ráz-joí,* 443.
Insane, *báolá ;* (or *báorá*) — *majnún.*
Insanity, *bauráí—majnúní.*
Insect, *kírá.*
Insects, *kíre makaure.*
Insects in general, *hasharát-ul-arz.*
Insensible, *be-hosh, be-sudh.*
Insert (in a book, &c.), *darj karná.*
Inside, *bhítar, andar.*
Insight, *basírat ;* (one who has it) *mubassir.*
Insignificant, *adná sá—se—*or *sí.*
Insincere, *dú-rangá, riyákár.*
Insinuate, *isháre se kahná.*
Insipid, *be-namak, be-maza, phíká.*
Insist, *tákíd karná, israr karná.*
Insoluble, *lá-hall, hall nahin hone ká.*
Inspect, *dekh lená, muláhaza karná.*
Inspiration, *ilhám, wahí.*
Instalment, *qist.*
Instance, (example) *nazír ;* (occasion) *waqt, dafa.*
*For* Instance, *chunánchi, maslan.*
Instant (moment), *dam, lahza.*
*The 1st* Intsant, *máh-hál ki pahlí táríkh.*
Instantaneous (instantaneously), *ek án kí án men, bát kí bát men.*
Instead of this (in exchange for), *iske badle* (or *iwaz*)—*bajáe iske.*
Instead of (doing) this, *bar-aks iske, ba-jáe iske.*
Instigate, *uskáná, sikhláná.*
Instigation, *sikháo—ighwá.*
Instigator, *sikhlánewálá—báni-i-fasád.*
Instil (into the mind), *zihn-nishín karná.*
Instinct, *aql, hosh.*
Instinctively, (*khwáh-ma-khwáh.*
Institute (*v.a.*), *barpá karná, qáim rakhná.*
Instruct, *sikhláná, parháná, tálím karná.*
Instruction, *tálím.*
Instructor, *ustád.*
Instrument, *ála, hathyár, auzár ;* (agent) *wasíla.*
Instrumental, *madadgár—mu'ín.*
*Through his* Instrumentality, *uske wasíle se.*
Insubordinate, *ná-farmán.*
Insufficient, *kam.*
Insult (*v.a.*), *be-izzatí karná* (or *be-izzat* )
Insult (*n.*), *be-izzatí—tahattuk.*
Insulting (as language), *tahattukámez.*
Insurance, *bíma.*
Insured, *bímá-shuda.*
Insurrection, *bagháwat, balwá.*

Intact, *jon ká ton, jaise ká taisá.*
Intellect, *aql.*
Intellectual, *aqlmand.*
Intelligence (tidings), *khabar.*
Intelligent, *samajhdár.*
Intemperate, *bad-parhez.*
Intemperance, *bad-parhezí.*
Intend, *iráda karná.*
Intention, *iráda.*
Intense, *sakht, shadíd.*
Intently, *ghaur se.*
Intercede, *shifá'at karná.*
Intercession, *shifá'at.*
Intercept, *rokná.*
Intercourse, *ámad-raft ;* (social) *suhbat.*
Interest (usury), *byáj, súd;* (personat) *gharaz.*
Interesting, *pur-lutf, pur-kaifiyat.*
Interfere, *háth ḍálná, dakhl dená,* 197.
Interference, *dast-andází,*
Interior (n.), *bhítar.*
Interment, *dafan-kafan.*
Interminable, *be-intihá, be-gháyat.*
Internal, *bhítarí—andarúní, bátiní.*
Interpret, *tarjuma karná.*
Interpretation, *tarjuma.*
Interpreter, *tarjumán, dobháshiyá.*
Interrupt, (in speaking) *bát káṭná;* (otherwise) *bhánjí dená.*
Interval (of time), *arsa ;* (of space) *fásila.*
Intervene, *bích men áná* or *parná ;* (as an obstruction) *háil honá,* 187, 188.
Interview (n.), *muláqát, bheṭ.*
Intestate (property), *lá-wárisí.*
Intestines, *antṛiyán.*

Intimacy, *irtibát, rabt-zabt,* 369.
Intimidate, *daráná.*
Intolerable, *bardásht se báhar.*
Intoxicate, *matwálá karná.*
Intrepid, *jánbáz.*
Intrepidity, *jánbází.*
Intricate, *pechdár.*
Intrigue, *ánt-sánt, bandish.*
Intrinsic, *aslí, zátí.*
Introduce, (originate) *barpá karná,* 138, *járí karná ;* (mention) *darmiyán láná.*
Intrude, *ghusná—mudákhalat karná.*
Intrusion, *mudákhalat-bejá.*
Inundated, *gharqí.*
Inundation, *áhlá—sailáb, gharqí.*
Invaluable, *amol—be-bahá.*
Invariably, *barábar.*
Invasion, *yúrish.*
Invent, *íjád karná.*
Inventor, *mújid.*
Inventory, *táliqá.*
Investigate, *tahqíqát karná.*
Investigation, *tahqíqat—taftísh.*
Invisible, *gháib—ná-padíd.*
Invitation, *buláhaṭ, nyotá—dáwat.*
Invoice, *bíjak, chálán.*
Involuntary, *be-ikhtiyár.*
Involuntarily, *be-ikhtiyárí se.*
Irksome, *thakáú, ná-gawár.*
Iron, *lohá ;* (made of iron) *áhaní.*
Irony, *hajo.*
Irrational, *ná-máqúl.*
Irregular, *be-qáida ;* (an act) *khiláf-qáida.*
Irrelevant, *ghair muta'alliq.*
Irreligious, *be-dín.*
Irremediable, *be-dawá.*
Irresistible (not to be stopped), *lá-tadáruk.*

Irresolute, *mutaraddid*; (to be irresolute) *ágá píchhá karná.*
Irresolution, *taraddud.*
Irrigate, *sínchná.*
Irrigation, *áb-páshí*, 189.
Irritability, *be-dimághí.*
Irritable, *tunuk-mizáj.*
Irritate, *chherná.*
Island, *jazíra*, *ṭápú.*
Issue (*v.n.*), *nikalná*, *jári* (or *sádir*) *honá.*
Issue (*v.a.*), *járí karná.*
Issue (*n.*), *natíja.*
Isthmus, *kháknáe.*
Itch (*n.*), *khuilí*; (*v.n.*), *khujláná*; (also, *v.a.*, to scratch).
Item (entry), *raqam*, 106, 456.
Itinerate, *idhar udhar phirná.*
Ivory, *háthí-dánt*; (of ivory) *ájí*, *háthí dánt ká.*

Jackfruit, *kaṭhal.*
Jackal, *gídar.*
Jaded, *thaká-mánda.*
Jagged, *dandánadár.*
Jail, *qaid-khána*, *jel-khána.*
Jam (*n.*), *murabbá.*
Jangling (wrangling), *khaṭpaṭ.*
Jar (*n.*), (large) *maṭká*; (small) *maṭkí*; (for pickles, &c.) *bhoiyám.*
Jar (*v.n.*), *kharkharáná*, *burá lagná.*
Jarring (sound), *kharkharáhaṭ.*
Jaundice, *yarqán.*
Jaw, *jabṛá*; (the jaws) *kallá.*
Jealous, *ghairat-kash*, *rashkí*,
Jealousy, *ghairat*, *rashk*, 495, 624.
Jeer, *ṭhaṭṭhá márná.*
Jeering, *ṭána-zaní.*
Jeopardy, *khatra.*
Jeopardize, *khatre men ḍálná.*
Jerk, (*v.a.*) *jhaṭak dená*; (*n.*) *jhaṭká*; (two persons trying to get possession of a thing) *jhaṭkam-jhaṭká.*
Jessamine, *yásmín*, *ráebel.*
Jestingly (in jest), *ṭhaṭṭhe se*, 238.
Jew, *yahúdí.*
Jewel, *jawáhir*, *gahná.*
Jeweller, *jauharí.*
Jingle, *jhanjhanáná*, *ṭhanṭhanáná.*
Job, *kám.*
Jocular, *ṭhaṭhebáz.*
Join, (*v.a.*) *joṛná*; (*v.n.*) *juṛná*, *milná*; (go along with) *sáth ho lena*; (as a broken bone) *juṭná*, *saṭná.*
Joined, *paiwasta*, *juṛá húá.*
Joint, *joṛ*; (of a bamboo, &c.) *por.*
Joke, *khillí*; (to make jokes) *mazákhen karná.*
Jolting (of a vehicle), *hachkolá*, 122.
Jostle, *dhakká dená.*
Jot (*iota*), *zarrá*, *ek zarrá.*
Journey, *safar*; (very short) *khep.*
Joy, *khushí—masarrat.*
Joyful, *bahut khush—masrúr.*
Joyfully, *khushí khushí.*
Judge, *hákim.*
*To* Judge, *tajwíz karná.*
Judgment, *tajwíz*, *faisala*; (opinion) *dánist*; (discrimination) *tamíz.*
Judicious, *bá-tamíz*; (an act) *máqúl.*
Juggler, *jádúgar.*
Juice, *ras—araq.*
Juicy, *rasílá.*

Jumble, (*v.a.*) *garbar karná*; (*n.*) *gadmad*.
Jump, *kúdná*, *phándná—jast karná*, 624.
Jump over, *tap-jáná*, *phánd jáná*.
Junction, *jor—paiwand*; (of two forces or streams) *miláo*.
Junior, *chhotá*.
Jurisdiction, (powers) *ikhtiyár*; (realm) *qalamrau*.
Just, *ádil*, *munsif*; (as a sentence) *wájib*, *wájibí*.
Justice, *insáf*.
Justifiable, *jáiz*, *rawá*.
Justify (one's conduct), *wajh batláná*.
Justification (valid reason), *wajh-káfí*.
Juvenile (as clothes, shoes, &c.) *bachkáná*, 205.

Keen (as an edge), *tez*; (acute) *sakht*, *shadíd*.
Keep, *rakhná*; (guard) *nigahbání karná*; (one's word) *nibáhná*.
Keeper (guardian), *nigahbán*, *rakhwálá*.
Keepsake, *yádgár*, *nishání*.
Kernel, *guthlí*.
Key, *chábí*, *tálí*.
Kick (as a horse), *látmárná*; (as a man) *thokar márná*.
Kid, *halwán*.
Kidnap, *churá lejáná*.
Kidney, *gurda*.
Kill, *márdálná*, *ján se márná*, *qatl karná*.
Kiln, *pajáwa*, *bhathí*.
Kind, (sort) *qism*, *nau*; (all kinds) *anwá'-o-aqsám*, 497; (various kinds) *tarah ba tarah*.
Kind (*adj.*), *mihrbán*; (kind-hearted) *rahmdil*.
Kindle (*v.a.*), *sulgáná*, *jaláná*.
Kindly, *mihrbání se*, *mihrbání kí ráh se*.
Kindred, *bhái-band—birádarí*.
King, *bádsháh*, *rájá*.
Kingdom, *bádsháhat*.
Kingly, *bádsháhána*, *sháhána*.
Kiss (*n.*), *chúmá*, *bosa*.
Kiss (*v.a.*) *chúmná*, *bosa dená* or *lená*.
Kitchen, *báwarchí-khána*.
Kite (bird), *chíl*; (paper kite) *patang*.
Knack, *salíqa*, *dhab*.
Knapsack, *jholí*.
Knave, *aiyár*, *daghábáz*, 111, 184.
Knavery, *daghábází*.
Knead, *gúndhná*.
Knee, *ghutná*, *theoná*, 636.
Kneecap, *chapní*.
Kneel, *ghutne tekná*.
Knife, *chhurí*; (pocket knife) *chakkú*; (pen knife) *qalam-tarásh*.
Knit, *binná*.
Knock (blow), *chot*, *chapet—zarb*.
Knock (*v.a.*), *márná*; (knock down) *márke giráдená*; (knock off, as another's hat) *patak dená*.
Knot, *girah*, *gánth*; (knotty) *girehdár*.
Know, *jánná*, *málúm honá*, *wáqif honá*.
Knowing (sharp), *hoshyár*, *siyáná*.
Knowledge, *ilm*, *dánish*; (special) *waqfiyat*.
Known, *málúm*; (known as) *márúf*.

Knuckle, *unglí kí gánṭh.*

Label *chiṭ, paṭá.*
Laborious, *mihnatí*; (arduous) *sakht, dushwár.*
Labour, *mihnat.*
Labourer, *mazdúr, qulí.*
Labyrinth, *warta.*
Lace, *goṭá, jálí.*
Lacerate, *pháṛná.*
Lack (be lacking in), *be-bahra honá.*
*To be* Lacking (short), *báqí honá* or *rahná.*
Lad, *laṛká, chhokṛá, launḍá.*
Ladder, *síṛhí.*
Lade, *ládná.*
Laden, *ladá húá*; (with debt) *zerbár.*
Ladle, *ḍoí.*
Lady, *sáhiba, bíbí.*
Lady's (in contradistinction to a man's), *bibiyána,* 205.
Lag, *ḍhílá chalná.*
Lair (of a wild beast), *baiṭhak, mánd.*
Lake, *jhíl, táláb.*
Lamb, *bheṛí ká bachcha.*
Lame, *langṛá*; (to go lame) *lang karná.*
Lament (grieve), *afsos karná*; (audibly) *nála karná.*
Lamentable (sad), *afsos kí bát—jáe-afsos.*
Lamentation, *kuhrám, nála-o-zárí.*
Lamp (native kind with oil and wick), *chirágh.*
Lampas, *tálú, tárú.*
Lampoon, *hajo.*
Lance, *bhálá, barchhí—neza.*
Lancer, *ballam-bardár.*
Lancet, *nashtar.*

Land, *zamín*; (country) *sar zamín, mulk, des.*
*To* Land (from a boat), *utarná*; (*v.a.*) *utárná.*
*By* Land, *khushkí kí ráh se.*
Landholder (landlord), *zamíndár.*
Landtax (from each ryot), *lagán*; (Government revenue) *málguzárí.*
Landmark (boundary), *menḍ, ḍaul, ḍánḍá.*
Landslip, *zamín ká upar se khasak jáná.*
Lane, *galí, galiyárá—kúcha.*
Language, *bolí, zabán*; (words spoken) *kalám*; words written) *ibárat.*
Languid, *sust, mánda.*
Languor, *sustí, mándagí.*
Lap (*n.*), *god, godí.*
Lapidary, *sang-tarásh.*
Lapse, (of time) *muddat*; (error) *bhúl, khatá.*
Larceny, *chorí.*
Large, *baṛá*; (larger) *aur baṛá*; (largest) *sab se baṛá.*
Lash, *koṛá*; (to lash) *koṛá márná.*
Lassitude, *see* Languor.
Last (*adj.*), *pichhlá, ákhirí.*
Last resource, *háre darje kí ṭadbír,* 419.
Last (to continue), *rahná, nibhná,* 633.
Lasting, *qáim—páedár.*
Late, *der*; (to be late) *derí honá* or *lagná*; (of late) *ájkal, chand roz se*; (the late) *marhúm.*
*Quite* Lately, *thoṛe roz kí bát, hál men.*

Latent (dormant) *chhipá — makhfí.*
Lathe, *kharád, kharrát.*
Latitude (freedom, scope), *wasạt.*
Latter (last-mentioned), *jiská pichhlá mazkúr húá.*
Lattice, *jáfarí.*
Laudable, *hamída, sitúda.*
Laugh, (*v.n.*) *hansná*; (to burst out laughing) *khilkhilá uṭhná*; (to laugh loudly) *qahqaha márná.*
Laughable, *maqám hansí ká.*
Laughing (or merry) face, *hansmukh—khanda-peshání.*
Laughing-stock, *maskhara*; (to make one) *maskhara banáná.*
Lavish, (*v.a.*) *uṛáná*; (bestow largely) *kasrat se dená.*
Lavish (*adj.*), *musrif, uṛáú*; (liberal), *faiyáz.*
Law (in general), *qáida-qánún*; (of nature) *khilqat ká qáida*, 470.
Lawful, *jáiz, rawá.*
Lawless, *be-qáida.*
Lawsuit, *muqaddama.*
Lawyer (pleader), *vakíl*; (attorney) *mukhtár.*
Lax, *ḍhílá.*
Lay down, *níche rakhná*; (as a carpet) *bichháná*; (lay by) *bachá rakhná*; (lay aside) *alag rakhná*; (lay to heart) *khátir men láná.*
Layer, *parat—tah*; (of masonry) *raddá.*
Lazy, *sust*; (indolent) *káhil-mizáj.*
Lead (metal), *sísá.*
Lead, (conduct) *le-chalná*; (guide) *rasta batláná.*
Lead astray, *bahkáná.*
Leader, (guide) *ráh batánewálá—rahnumá*; (master) *peshwá.*
Leadership, *peshwáí.*
Leaf, (of a tree) *pattá*; (of a book) *waraq.*
League (compact), *sázish, bandish.*
Leak, (*v.n.*) *chúná*; (spring a leak) *súrákh khul jáná.*
Lean, (forwards) *jhukná*; (lean on) *ṭekná.*
Lean (*adj.*), *dublá—lághar.*
Leap (*v.n.*), *kúdná, phándná—jast karná.*
Learn, *síkhná, ilm hásil karná*; (to hear) *sunne men áná.*
Learning (*n.*), *ilmiyat, ilm.*
Lease (of a house), *kiráya*; (of a farm) *ijára.*
*To* Lease, *kiráe dená*; (take on lease) *kiráe lená.*
Least, *sab se chhoṭá—kamtarín.*
Leather, *chamṛá.*
Leave (*n.*), *chhuṭṭí, rukhsat*; (permission), *ijázat, parwánagí.*
*To give* Leave to go, *rukhsat dená*; (to take leave) *rukhsat lená.*
*Having* Leave to go, *rukhsat hokar.*
*To* Leave (depart), *chalá jáná*; (leave out, omit) *chhoṛná*; (leave off) *báz áná*; (abandon) *chhoṛ-jáná.*
Leaven, *khamír.*
Lecture, *dars*; (to deliver one) *dars sunáná.*
*Giving* Lectures (lecturing), *ṭadrís.*
Leech, *jonk*, 616.

Left (opposite to right), *báyán* (inflected *báen* and *báín*).
*To be* Left (remaining), *rahjáná, báqí rahná.*
Left-handed, *báenhathá*, 415.
Leg, *táng;* (of a table or chair) *páya;* (calf of leg) *pindlí.*
Legacy, *wirsa*, 564.
Legal, (pertaining to the law) *qánúní;* (lawful) *jáiz.*
Legality (lawfulness), *jawáziyat.*
Legend, *riwáyat.*
Legible, *parhá já saktá.*
Legitimate, *jáiz, rawá.*
Leisure, *fursat—farághat.*
Lemon, *nimbú* or *nembú.*
Lend, (money) *qarz dená;* (a book, &c.) *udhár dená—áriyatan dená.*
Length, *lambáí—túl.*
Lengthen (*v.a.*), *lambá karná.*
*Lay it* Lengthways, *lambá karke rakho.*
*He lay at full* Length, *lambá hoke pará thá.*
Lenient (as a sentence), *halká.*
Leniency, *rahm—muláyamat.*
Leper, *korhí.*
Leprosy, *korh kí bímárí.*
Less, *kam, ghát.*
*To* Lessen, *kam karná.*
Lessee, (of a house) *kiráyadár;* (of a farm) *ijáradár.*
Lesson, *sabaq.*
Lest, *aisá na ho ki—mabáda.*
Let (allow), *dená, e.g.* let him come, *usko áne do;* let him go *usko jáne do.*
*To* Let go (loose hold of), *chhor-dená;* (let down as a blind) *níche girá dená;* (let know) *khabar dená.*
Letter, *chitthí, khatt;* (of the alphabet) *harf.*
Levée, *darbár.*
Level, *barábar, battá-dhál—ham-wár.*
Lever (to raise water), *dhenklí.*
Levity, *ochhepan.*
Levy (a tax), *utháná.*
Liable to, the affix *pazír* after the thing signified, *e.g.* liable to decay, *zawál-pazír.*
Liar, *jhúthá, jhúth bolnewálá, labár.*
Libel (defame), *badnám karná;* (*n.*) *buhtán.*
Liberal (generous), *sakhí, faiyáz.*
Liberality, *sakháwat, faiyází.*
Liberate, *chhor dená, khalás dená.*
Liberty, *ázádagí;* (liberation) *makhlasí.*
Library, *kutub-khána.*
License, *pattá;* (diploma) *sanad.*
Licentious, *luchchá;* (licentiousness) *luchchámí.*
Lick, *chátná.*
Lid, *dhakná;* (of a saucepan, &c.) *dhakní.*
Lie, (*n.*) *jhúth;* (lie down) *letná;* (lying down) *pará húá.* First he lay on his back, then on his face, and then on his side, *Pahle chit pará thá, tab aundhá pará thá, phir karwat se pará thá.*
*To* Lie in wait for anyone, *kisí kí ghát men lagná.*
Life, *ján, jí, zindagí.*
Lifetime, *umr;* (all one's life) *umr-bhar* (pron. *umar, umar-bhar*).
Lift, *utháná.*
Ligament, *asab.*

Light, *roshní, chándná, ujálá,* 26; (to come to light) *zuhúr men áná.*
Light of the sun, *jalwa,* 293.
Light (*adj.*), *halká—subuk.*
*To* Light, (as a fire) *sulgáná, jaláná*; (a candle) *bálná.*
*To* Lighten, *halká karná*; (flash) *chamakná.*
Lightness, *halkápan, halkái.*
Lightning, *bijlí*; (flash of) *bijlí kí chamak,* 629, 630.
Like (*v.a.*), *pasand karná, pasand honá.*
Like (similar), *muwáfiq, mánind —misl.*

Note.—This last word is used as in English, *before* the noun of resemblance: *e.g.*, hailstones like eggs were falling, *ole misl andon ke parte the.*

Likelihood, *ummed.*

Note.—This word is commonly used for "likelihood," whether the thing spoken of be welcome or unwelcome.

Likeness, *shabáhat, mushábahat.*
Likewise, *bhí—níz.*
Liking (fondness), *shauq, raghbat.*
Lilac (the colour), *túsí,* 484.
Lime, *chúná*; (the fruit) *nimbú* or *nembú.*
Limit, *hadd, síwána.*
Limited, *mahdúd.*
Limits (confines), *sar-hadd.*
*To* Limp, *lang karná, langráná.*
Limpid, *shaffáf, nithrá.*
Line, (drawn on paper, &c.) *lakír*; (of writing) *satar.*
Line (cord), *dor, dorí.*
Linen, *katán.*
Linguist, *zabán-dán.*
Lining, *astar* or *ástar.*
Link, *karí.*
Lion, *singh, sher-i-babar.*
Lip, *honth—lab.*
Liquorice, *mulhattí.*
List, *fihrist.*
Listen, *sunná.*
Literal, *harf-ba-harf.*
Litter, (rubbish) *kúrá*; (brood) *jhol.*
Little, *chhotá*; (small quantity) *thorá, thorá sá, zarra, zarra sá.*
Live, (exist) *jíná*; (dwell) *rahná,* 245; (get along) *guzrán karná.*
Livelihood, *rozgár—ma'ásh.*
Lively (vivacious), *zinda-dil.*
Liver, *kaleja.*
Livery, *wardí.*
Living (alive), *jítá—zinda.*
Lizard, *chhipkalí.*
Load, *bojh, bhár—bár.*
Loaf, *rotí.*
Loan, (of money) *qarza*; (of other things) *udhár.*
Loathe, *nafrat karná.*
Local, *maqámí.*
Lock, (*n.*) *tálá, qufl*; (*v.a.*) *tálá lagáná, qufl karná*; (lock of a gun) *chámp*; (of hair) *zulf.*
Locust, *tiddi.*
*To* Lodge, (stay at) *thairná*; (give a lodging to) *thairá rakhná,* 367.
Lodge with ... *ke yahán mihmán honá.*
Lofty, *únchá, buland.*
Logic, *mantiq.*
Loins, *kamar.*
Loiter, *der lagáná.*

Loneliness, *tan-tanhái;* (lonely) *tan-tanhá.*
Long. (*adj.*), *lambá—daráz.*
*So* Long as I have you, *tumháre hote;* (as you have me) *mere hote.*
*No* Longer, *aur,* or *áge ko,* followed by *nahin.*
Long for, *tarasná—ká mushtáq honá.*
Longing (*n.*), *chát—ishtiyáq.*
Longlived, *umar-daráz.*
Look, (*v.a.*) *dekhná, nigáh karná;* (look for) *talásh karná, ḍhúnḍhná;* (to look well) *achchhá* or *khushnumá málúm honá;* (to look bad) *burá* or *badnumá málúm honá.*
Looking for, (in search of) *mutalúshí;* (looked for, expected) *mutasawwir,* 132, 133.
Loom, *ráchh.*
Loop, *phánsí.*
Loop-hole, *raini.*
Loose, *ḍhílá;* (to get loose) *chhúṭ jáná.*
Loosen, *ḍhílá karná.*
Lord, *khudáwand, kháwind.*
Lose, (*v.a.*) *kho dená;* (be lost) *kho jáná, játá rahná.*
Lose (in a game), *hár jáná.*
Loss, *nuqsán, zarar,* 102.
Lot, (a quantity) *bahut, bahut sá;* (fortune) *nasíb.*
*To fall to one's* Lot, *paṛná, ittifáq honá.*
*To cast* Lots, *chiṭṭhí ḍálná—qura ḍálná.*
Loud (as a voice), *baṛá, buland.*
Loudly, *zor se.*
Lout, *dabang.*
Love, *piyár, muhabbat;* (sexual) *ishq.*
*To* Love, *piyár karná, muhabbat rakhná;* (a thing) *dost rakhná.*
*To be in* Love, *áshiq honá, loṭpoṭ honá.*
*To fall in* Love, *lág lagná.*
Loveliness, *mahbúbí.*
Lovely, *dil-rubá, dil-fareb.*
Lover, *cháhnewálá — dildár, áshiq.*
Low (*adj.*), *nichá—past,* 373.
Low-born, *páji, kam-asl, kamína.*
Low spirits, *afsurdagí.*
Loyal, *namak-halál, khair-khwáh.*
Loyalty, *namak-halálí, khair-khwáhí,* 489.
Lucid, *saríh.*
Lucidity, *saráhat.*
Luck, *khush-nasíbí,* 147, 148.
Lucky, *khush-nasíb.*
Lucrative, *súdmand.*
Ludicrous, *báis hansí ká.*
Luggage, *asbáb, chíz-bast.*
Lukewarm, *gunguná, shír-garm.*
Lull (*n.*), *niwá—waqfa.*
Luminous, *roshan, núrání.*
Lump, (swelling) *sújan, waram;* (payment in a lump) *ek-musht, bil-muqta.*
Lunatic, *págal—majnún.*
Lungs, *phephre,* 519.
*To* Lure, *phuslána, tama dikhláná.*
*To* Lurk, *dabak baiṭhná* or *rahná.*
Luscious, *míṭhá, lazíz.*
Lusciousness, *miṭhás, lazzat.*
Lust, *shahwat.*
Lustful, *shahwatí.*
Lustre, *chamkáhaṭ—tajallí.*
Lusty, *cháq-chauband, mazbút.*
Luxurious, *aiyásh.*
Luxury, *aiyáshí.*
Lynx, *siyáh-gosh.*

Machination, *sázish, bandish.*
Machine, *jantar, kal*; (machinery) *kal-kánṭá.*
Mad, *págal, díwána;* (madman) the same with *ádmí* added.
Made-up story, *banáwaṭ.*
Maggot, *kíṛá.*
Magic, *jádú, jádúgarí — tilismát.*
Magician, *jádúgar—afsún-gar.*
Magnet, *chumbak—miqnátis.*
Magnificent, *álíshán, bahut hí ụmda.*
Magnify, *baṛá karná, baṛáí karná.*
Magnifying-glass, *k͟hurd-bín.*
Maid, (maiden) *kunwárí, laṛkí;* (servant) *laundí.*
Mail, *wiláyatí ḍák.*
Maim, (wound) *g͟háil karná, zak͟hmí karná;* (make lame) *langṛá karná.*
Main (principal), *sadar, baṛá.*
Mainly (mostly), *beshtar, aksar.*
Maintain, *pálná, parwarish karná.*
Maintenance, *parwarish—k͟hurposh.*
Maize (Indian corn), *bhuṭṭa, makaí.*
Make, *banáná;* (a mistake, &c.) *karná;* (make away with, kill) *k͟hapáná;* (make off, decamp) *chal dená;* (make out, state) *záhir karná;* (make out, understand) *samajh men áná;* (make over to) *sompná, hawála karná.*
Maker, *banánewálá;* (Creator) *k͟háliq.*
Malady, *bímárí, maraz.*
Male, *nar, nariná.*

Malediction (curse) *kosá, baddụá, lạ́nat.*
Malefactor, *badkár.*
Malevolent, *badk͟hwáh.*
Malformation, *ṭeṛháí — k͟hamídagí.*
Malice, *kína, bug͟hz;* (malicious) *kínawar.*
Malignant, *k͟habís;* (malignity) *k͟habásat.*
Mallet, *mek͟hchú, mogrí.*
Maltreat, *bad-sulúkí karná.*
Maltreatment, *bad-sulúkí.*
Man, (distinguished from woman) *mard;* (human being) *ádmí.*
Pertaining to Men (as clothes, &c.), *mardána.*
Manage (control), *sambhálná* 36, 37.
Manager (agent), *gumáshta, sarbaráhkár.*
Mane, *aiyál, yál,* 300.
Mange, *k͟hujlí.*
Manger, *charní.*
Mankind, *baní-ádam.*
Manner, (behaviour) *waza;* (way of doing things) *taur, tarah, taríqa.*
Manners (in general), *chál-ḍhál,* 201.
Mansion, *hawelí.*
Manslaughter, *mardum-kushí.*
Manufactory, *kár-k͟hána.*
Manufacture, *dastkárí, sák͟htagí.*
Manure, *k͟hát, k͟hád.*
Manuscript, *tahrírát.*
Many, *bahútere, bahut;* (as many as) *jitne ... itne ...;* (twice as many) *doguná, dúchand.*
Map, *naqsha.*
Marble, *sang-i-marmar.*
March (*v.n.*), *kúch karná.*

Mare, *ghoṛí.*
Margin, *kinára;* (of a page) *háshiya.*
Marine, (*adj.*) *bahrí;* (nautical) *jahází.*
Mark, (*n.*) *nishán, dágh;* (*v.a.*) *nishán karná, dágh dená.*
Market, *bázár.*
Marriage, *byáh, shádí;* (Mahommedan) *nikáh,* 627, 636.
Married, *byáhtá;* (married woman) *shádí-wálí, khasam-wálí.*
Marrow, *gúdá, maghz.*
Marry, *byáhná, shádí karná.*
Marsh, *daldal.*
Martial, *lashkarí, jangí.*
Martyr, *shahíd;* (martyrdom) *shahádat.*
Marvellous, *ajíb, ajab.*
Masculine (in grammar), *muzakkar.*
Mask, *haddo.*
Mason, *ráj mistrí—mimár.*
Massacre, *qatl-i-ámm.*
Mast, *mastúl.*
Master, *málik, áqá;* (master a subject) *máhir ho jáná.*
Mat, *boriyá;* (door-mat) *ghulámgardish;* (matting) *chaṭáí.*
Match, (lucifer) *diyá-saláí;* (equal) *joṛ ká, ṭakkar ká.*
Material (substance), *mádda;* (essential) *zarúrí.*
Materials, *asbáb, sámán.*
Maternal, *mádarí.*
Mathematics, *ilm-i-riyází.*
*To* Matter, *muzáyaqa honá, e.g.* what does it matter? *kyá muzáyaqa?*
*No* Matter, *kuchh parwá nahín.*
*As a* Matter of fact, *dar asl, haqíqat men.*
Matter (affair), *bát.*
*In the* Matter of your promotion, *tumhárí taraqqí ke báre men.*
*What is the* Matter? *kyá húá?*
Matter (pus), *píb—rím.*
Mattress, *gadelá, toshak.*
Mature, *pakká;* (of mature age) *siyáná, báligh;* (*fem.*) *báligha.*
Maxim, *maqúla, kaháwat.*
*It* May be so, *sháyad ki báshad, ho to ho.*
*Be that as it* May (anyhow), *har kuchh ho, par.*
Meal, (flour) *áṭá;* (a repast) *kháná.*
Mean, (low) *pájí, kamína;* (stingy) *thuṛ-dilá.*
*What does this* Mean? *iske máne kyá hain? iská matlab kyá hai?*
Meaning, *mání, matlab.*
*What is* Meant by ... ? ... *kis se murád?*
Meanness, *pájípaná—kamínagí.*
Means (pecuniary), *gunjáish, dastgáh,* 174, 175.
*By* Means of, *wasíle se, zaríe se.*
Meanwhile, *is darmiyán men.*
Measure (*n.*), *náp—paimáish.*
*To* Measure, *nápná—paimáish karná.*
Meat, *gosht.*
Medal, *taghma.*
Meddle, *dakhl dená, háth ḍálná.*
Meddling (*n.*), *dastandází.*
Mediate, *bích-bicháo karná,* 261.
Mediator, *darmiyání,* 330, *bichwání.*
Medicine, *dawá;* (science of) *tabábat.*
Mediocre, *ausatí.*
Mediocrity, *ausat.*
Medium (of communication, &c.) *wásita, wasíla.*

*The happy* Medium, *andáza wájib.*
Meek, *gharíb—halím.*
Meet, *milná, muláqát honá, do-chár honá.*
Meeting, *muláqát, bheṭ;* (gathering) *jalsa,* 532, 543.
Melancholy (*n.*), *saudá.*
Melancholic, *saudáí.*
Melodious (as a bird or a singer), *khush ilhán.*
Melody, *khush-ilhání, sarod.*
Melon, *kharbúza;* (water melon) *tarbúz.*
Melt (*v.n.*), *galná;* (dissolve) *ghulná.*
Melted, dissolved, *galá húá, ghulá húá—gudáz.*
Member (of the body), *ụzv;* (of a society) *sharík.*
Memorable, *yád rakhne ke qábil.*
Memorandum, *yád-dásht.*
Memory, *yád;* (the faculty) *háfiza.*
*To commit to* Memory, *hifz karná.*
Mend (*v.a.*), *marammat karná.*
Mental, *dilí.*
Mention (*n.*), *zikr, mazkúr, tazkira.*
Mention (*v.a.*), *zikr karná, mazkúr karná.*
Mentioned (aforementioned), *mazkúr;* (polite term) *mausúf.*
Mercantile, *saudágarí.*
*From* Mercenary motives, *ujrat ke lálach se.*
Merchandise, (traffic) *tijárat;* (goods) *saudágarí mál.*
Merchant, *saudágar, baipárí.*
Merciful, *rahím, dayál.*
Mercury, *pára.*
Mercy, *rahm, rahmat.*
Mere (sheer), *mahz, nirá,* 510.
Merely, *nirá, sirf, mahz,* 511.
Merit, *liyáqat, sazáwárí.*
*To* Merit, *sazáwár honá, láiq honá.*
Merry, *khushdil—khanda-peshání.*
Mesh, *khána,* 432.
Mess (confusion), *gaṛbaṛí—abtarí.*
Message, *paiyám, sandesá.*
Messenger, *qásid.*
Messmate, *hánḍíwál—ham-niwála.*
Metal, *dhát;* (of metal) *dhátí.*
Metaphor, *tashbíh—istiạ́ra.*
Metaphorical, *majází.*
Metaphorically, *majázan.*
Meteor, *shiháb-i-sáqib,* or only *shiháb.*
Method, *ḍhab, taríqa;* (system) *bandobast;* (want of) *be-ạnwání.*
Microscope, *khurd-bín.*
Midday, *do pahar din.*
Middle, *bích;* (in the middle) *bích meṉ.*
Middle-aged, *adheṛ;* (of middle height) *ausat-qadd.*
Midnight, *ádhí rát.*
Might (power), *zor, bal.*
Mighty, *zoráwar, balwant—qudrat-wálá.*
Mild, *narm-mizáj, halím, dhímá.*
Mildew (smut), *lenḍhá, gerúí.*
Mile, *míl, ádh-kos.*
Military, *lashkarí.*
Milk, *dúdh.*
Milky Way, *kahkashán.*
Mill, *jántá, ásiyá,* 467; (water-mill) *pan-chakkí.*
Millet, *joár.*

Millstone, *chakkí*.
Mimic (*v.a.*), *swáng láná, naql karná.*
Mimic (actor), *swángí, naqqál*; (actress) *naqqálin.*
Mimicry (acting), *swáng, taqlíd*, 271.
Minaret, *mínár.*
Mind (*n.*), *khátir, zihn, jí*; (to bear in mind) *khiyál rahná*, 409; (he doesn't mind in the least) *wuh bilkull parwá nahin kartá*; (mind what I tell you) *merá kahná yád rakho.*
Mine (*n.*), *khán.*
Mineral (*n.*), *dhát—jamád.*
Minor, *kam-umr, ná-báligh, chhotá.*
Minority (immaturity), *chhutpan, kam-umrí.*
Minstrel, *bhát—mutrib.*
Mint, (herb) *podína*; (for coinage) *taksál.*
Minute (*n.*), *lamha, lahza.*
Minute (tiny), *niháyat chhotá.*
Minutely (in detail), *tafsílwár—min-wa-an.*
Miracle, *muájiza.*
Miraculous (as an escape), *ajíbtar, ajab.*
Mirror, *áína, darpan.*
Mirth, *hansá-hansí, chahal-pahal.*
Miscarriage of justice, *haqq-talafí, be-insáfí*, 381, 383.
Miscellaneous, *mutafarriq*; (fem.) *mutafarriqa.*
Miscellany (odds and ends), *mutafarriqát.*
Mischief, *nuqsán, zarar.*
*The* Mischief of it is that, *ghazab yih hai ki*, 155.
Mischief-maker, *khalal-andáz, fasádí.*
Mischief-making, *khalal-andází.*
Mischievous, *muzirr, ziyánkár.*
Mischievousness, *ziyánkárí.*
Misconception, *ghalat-fahmí, ultí-samajh.*
Misconduct, *bad-chalní.*
Miser, *kanjús, bakhíl.*
Misery, *pareshání, tang-hálí.*
Misgiving, *khatká, andesha—khadsha*, 364.
Miss (the mark), *khatá kar jáná, chúkná*, 48, 50.
*To be* Missing, *játá rahná, gum honá.*
Mist, *kohar, kuhásá.*
Mistake (*n.*), *bhúl, ghaltí.*
Mistrust (*v.a.*), *e'tibár nahin karná.*
Mistrust (*n.*), *bad-gumání, bad-e'tiqádí.*
Mistrustful, *bad-gumán, bad-e'tiqád.*
Misunderstand, *ultá samajhná, ghalat samajhná.*
Misunderstanding (between friends), *phút, ikhtiláf.*
Mix, *miláná*; (mix with, associate) *milná julná, ikhtilát karná*, 561.
Mixture, *milauní, ámezish.*
Moan (*v.n.*), *karáhná.*
Moaning (*n.*), *karáhná.*
Moat, *khandaq, kháí.*
Mock, *thatthá márná.*
Model, *namúna.*
Moderate, *miyána, motadil.*
Moderately (in moderation), *andáze se*; (equably) *e'tidál se.*
Moderation (in conduct), *miyána-raví.*
Modern, *jadíd, hálí.*
Modest, *hayádár, sharmgín.*
Modify, *tarmím karná.*

Moist, *gílá, tar, namín*, 347.
Moisture, *gíláí, rutúbat, namnákí.*
Molasses, *guṛ*, 614.
Molest, *chheṛná—ta'arruz karná.*
Molestation, *chheṛ-chháṛ—ta'arruz.*
Monday, *pír ká roz, sombár.*
Money, *rúpiya—zar.*
Money-changer, *sarráf.*
Mongrel, *do-nasla—doghla.*
Monkey, *bandar*, 515.
Monotonous, *be-maza, phíká.*
Month, *mahíná—máh.*
Monthly (*adv.*), *har mahíne—máh-ba-máh.*
Monthly wages, *máhwárí*; (monthly return) *máskabár.*
Mood, *mizáj.*
Moon, *chánd—máhtáb.*
Moonstone, *gau-dantá.*
Moral, *nekchalan*; (of a story) *hásil*, 515.
Moral courage, *yárá*, 482.
Morality, (morals) *akhláq*; (of conduct) *nek-chalní.*
More, *aur, ziyáda.*
Moreover, *siwá iske, aláwa iske.*
Morning, *fajr, subh, bhor.*

Pronounce the first two as *fajar* and *subeh*, the *e* very short.

*As soon as it is* Morning, *fajar hote* or *subeh hote.*
Morose, *tursh-rú.*
Mortal, *fání, faná-pazír*; (a wound) *kárí*, 310.
Mortality, *faná*, 309, 629.
Mortar (cement), *gach.*
Mortgage (*n.*), *rihn, girau.*
Mortgage (*v.a.*), *rihn rakhná, girwí rakhná.*
Mortgaged, *girwí.*
Moss-agate, *sijrí.*
Moth, *parwána*; (small) *kapṛe ká kíṛá.*
Mother, *má*; (village term) *mahtárí.*
Mother-in-law, *sás—khush-dáman.*
Motion, *hiláo—harakat*; (shaking) *takán*, 122.
Motionless, *be-harakat.*
Motive, *gharaz, niyat*, 158.
Motto, *kaháwat, maqúla.*
Mould (for casting), *sánchá.*
Mouldiness, *phaphundí*, 348.
Mouldy, *phaphundí lagí húí.*
Moult (as birds), *kuríz karná, dasokhá jháṛná.*
Mount (a horse), *sawár ho jáná, píṭh lagná.*
Mountain, *paháṛ, parbat.*
*To* Mourn (for a deceased relative), *mátam karná.*
Mouse, *chúhiyá.*
Moustache, *múchh.*
Mouth, *munh*; (from his own mouth) *uskí zabání.*
Mouthful, *nawála.*
Move (*v.n.*), *hilná — harakat karná.*
Move (cause to move), *hiláná*, (out of the way), *sarká dená.*
Movement, *chaláwá—harakat.*
Much, *bahut*; (how much?) *kitná?* (so much) *itná.*
Much of a muchness, *kuchh ekhí sí kaifiyat.*
Mud, *kíchaṛ*, 70, *kádá.*
Muddy (water), *gadlá*, 448.
Mule, *khachchar.*
Multiply (in arithmetic), *zarb karná*, 523.
Multitude, *bhíṛ—amboh.*

Murder, (*n.*) *qatl*; (*v.a.*) *qatl karná.*
Murderer, *khúní.*
Murmur (grumble), *kuṛkuṛáná.*
Muscle, *paṭṭhá.*
Music, *músiqí*; (musician) *músíqí-dán.*
Must, *cháhiye*; *e.g.* you must go, *tumko jáná cháhiye.*
Mustard, *ráí*; (the plant) *sarsoṉ.*
Muster, (*n.*) *ginti*; (*v.a.*) *gintí karná.*
*The great* Mutiny, *ghadar* (lit. treachery, perfidy).
Mutual, *ápasí—báhamí.*
Mutually, *ápas meṉ — ba-ham-dígar.*
Muzzle (for cattle), *chhíká.*
Myrtle, *ás*, 656.
Mystery, mysterious, *bhed kí bát, ujúba.*

Nail, (of finger) *nákhun*; (iron) *kíl, pareg.*
Naked, *nangá*; (stark naked) *nang-dhaṛang, nangá-i-mádar-zád.*
Nakedness, *nangepan, barahnagí.*
Name, *nám*; (named, by name) *nám*, after the name.
Nap (short sleep), *jhapkí.*
Nape (of neck), *guddí.*
Narcotic, *nínd-áwar.*
Narrate, *bayán karná, kah-sunáná.*
Narrative, *qissa, bayán.*
Narrow, *tang, saket*; (too narrow) *kam-arz.*
Narrowness, *tangí.*
Nasty, *mailá—najis.*
Nastiness, *mail—najásat.*
Nation, *qaum.*
Nationality, *qaumiyat.*
Native, *desí*; (person) *rahnewálá —báshinda.*
Native land, *watan, zádbúm, janam-bhúm.*
Natural, *tabíí, zátí*; (as a colour, not artificial) *qudratí*, 339, 340.
Nature (true nature, or essence), *máhiyat.*
Nature, (constitution) *tabíat, sarisht*; (temperament) *mizáj.*
Nature (creation), *khilqat.*
*To feel* Nausea, *jí matláná.*
Nausea, *jí kí matláí.*
Nave (of a wheel), *náh.* See "Wheel."
Navigable, *qábil guzar kishtí ke.*
Near, *pás, nazdík, qaríb*; (close to) *muttasil.*
Nearly, (almost) *qaríb*; (as nearly as possible) *qaríb qaríb.*
Neat, *suthrá, khushnumá.*
Neatness, *suthráí, khúbí.*
Necessary, *zarúr, lázim*; (requisite) *darkár, cháhiye.*

Note.—The single word *cháhiye* corresponds to both *zarúr hai* and *darkár hai.*

*Very* Necessary (important), *zarúrí.*
Necessaries, *zarúriyát*, 231.
Necessity, *zarúrat*; (in times of necessity or emergency) *zarúrat ke waqt.*
Neck, *gardan*; (throat) *galá.*
Necklace, *kanṭhá, málá, hár.*
*To be in* Need, *muhtáj honá* (*i.e.* the needer of), *hájat honá* (*i.e.* the want of the thing to be).

Examples.—I am in need of a house, *maiṉ ghar ká muhtáj húṉ, mujhko ghar kí hájat hai.*

Needful. See "Necessary."
Needle, *súí*; (needlework) *súí ká kám.*
Needy (necessitous), *kangál, muhtáj.*
Neglect (negligence), *ghaflat—tasáhul.*
*To* Neglect (be negligent), *ghaflat karná.*
Negligent (neglectful), *gháfil.*
Negotiation, *muámala.*
*To* Neigh, *hinhináná.*
Neighbour, *parosí, hamsáya.*
Neighbourhood, *pás-paros*, 62.
Neither this nor that, *na yih na wuh.*
Nemesis, *shámat*, 276.
Nephew, (brother's son) *bhatíjá*; (sister's son) *bhánjá.*
Nerve, *paṭṭhá—ạsab.*
Nervous (timid), *dil ká bodá.*
Nest, *ghonslá.*
Net, *jál.*
Never, *kabhí nahin, hargiz nahin.*
Nevertheless, *taubhí, tispar bhí—táham.*
New, *nayá, táza*; (fresh, unused) *korá, ṭaṭká.*
News, *khabar*; (good news) *basharat, khush-khabarí.*
Newspaper, *akhbár*; (the editor) *murattib.*
Next, *dúsrá.*
Niche, *táq.*
Nick of time, *ạin waqt men.*
Nickname, *ụrfí nám.*
Niece, (brother's daughter) *bhatíji*; (sister's daughter) *bhánjí.*
Night, *rát—shab.*
Night and day, *rát-din.*
Nightly, *rát rát.*
Nimble (agile), *chust-chálák, phurtílá.*
Noble (in birth or rank), *sharíf, najíb.*
Nobleman, *amír.*
Noble-minded, *ạlí-himmat.*
Nobody, *koí nahin*; (a nobody) *ná-kas.*
*To consider as* Nobody, *náchíz samajhná.*
Noise, *ghul, shor-ghul*; (racket) *údham.*
*To make a* Noise, *ghul macháná* or *karná.*
Noiselessly, *be-áwáz.*
Noisy (clamorous), *ghaugháí.*
Nolens volens, *khwáh-makhwáh.*
Nominal, *nám ká, námí, sirf kahne ko.*
None, *kuchh nahin.*
Non-existence, *ạdam, nestí.*
Nonsense, *wáhiyát, behúdagí.*
Noon (noonday), *do pahar din.*
Noose, *phánsí.*
*In its* Normal *condition, ba-dastúr.*
North, *uttar—shimál.*
Northern, *shimálí.*
Northward, *uttar kí taraf.*
Nose, *nák.*
Nosegay, *gul-dasta.*
Nostril, *nathná.*
Notable (notorious), *mashhúr.*
Note (letter), *chiṭṭhí—ruqạ.*
Note, (to notice) *dekhná*; (note down) *likh rakhná.*
Nothing, *kuchh nahin.*
Notice (notification), *ishtihár.*
*To give* Notice (public), *ishtihár karná.*
*To* Notice (attend to), *dhyán karná, liház karná.*
Notion (idea), *khiyál, pindár.*

Notwithstanding, *bá-wujúde ki, harchand.*
Nourish, *pálná, parwarish karná.*
Nourishment. See "Food."
Now, *ab, abhí, isíwaqt;* (just now) *bilfel.*
Now-a-days, *áj-kal.*
Now and then, *kabhí kabhí.*
Nowhere, *kahín nahin.*
Nowise (in no wise), *kisí tarah se nahin.*
Null and void (a dead letter), *kal-adam.*
*To be* Numbed, *thithir lagná.*
Number, *adad;* (the whole number) *tidád.*
Number (a good many), *bahut.*
Numberless, *be-shumár.*
Numerous, *bahut—kasrat se.*
Nurse, (wet-nurse) *dái;* (dry-nurse) *khilái;* (sick-nurse) *tímárdár.*
*Sick*-Nursing, *tímárdárí.*
Nutmeg, *jáephal.*

Oar, *dánd;* (oarsman) *dándí.*
Oats, *jai.*
Oath, *qasam;* (judicial) *halaf.*
Obedience, *farmánbardárí—itá'at,* 622, 625.
Obedient, *farmánbardár, tábidár.*
Obey, *mánná, hukm sunná.*
Object (intention), *gharaz, murád.*
Object (*v.a.*), *uzr karná, uzr honá, e.g.* I object, *mujhko uzr hai* (pron. *uzar*).
Objection, *uzr—etiraz;* (take objection to) *etiráz karná.*
Objector, *motariz.*
Obligation, (favour) *ihsán;* (under one) *mamnún.*
Obligatory, *zarúr, wájib, farz.*
Oblige, (favour) *mihrbání karná;* (compel) *majbúr karná.*
Obliged, (compelled) *majbúr;* (much obliged) *mamnún.*
Oblique, *tirchhá;* (obliquely) *tirchhái se.*
Obliterate, *mitáná, mitá dená.*
Oblong, *kitábí.*
Obscene, *fuhsh.*
Obscenity, *fuhsh.*
Obscure, (vague) *muhmil;* (a person) *gumnám.*
Obscurity, (darkness) *táríkí;* (privacy) *gumnámi.*
Obsequious, *tábidár, mutí.*
Obsequiousness (implicit obedience), *mutába'at.*
Observe, (notice) *dekhná;* (keep) *mánná.*
Observance, *mánná.*
Observation, *muláhaza;* (to come under) *dekhne men áná;* (to avoid) *nazar bacháná.*
Obstacle, *atak—háil, amar-máni.*
Obstinacy, *gariyári—tamarrud.*
Obstinate, *gariyár—mutamarrid,* 252.
Obstruct, *atkáná, háil honá;* (hinder) *muzáhim honá.*
Obstruction, (wilful) *muzáhamat;* (natural) see "Obstacle."
Obtain, *páná, hásil karná.*
*To be* Obtainable, *milná—muyassar honá.*
Obviate—Your coming obviates the necessity of my going, *tumháre áne se mere jáne kí zarúrat ab nahin rahí.*
Obvious, *záhir.*
Occasion (on one occasion), *ek waqt, ek martabe.*

*Had* Occasion to go there, *wahán jáne ká ittifáq húá*, 39.
Occasionally, *kabhí kabhí—báẓí auqát.*
Occupation, *kám-dhandá, pesha;* (something to do) *mashghala*, 214, 549.
Occupied, to be, *lagná—mashghúl honá.*
Occur, *honá—wáqi* (or *sarzad*) *honá;* (suggest itself to one) *sújhná.*
Occurrence, *wuqúa, wáridát*, 425.
Odd, (strange) *ta'ajjub kí bát;* (not even) *phuṭkar.*
Odious, *nafratí—makrúh.*
Odour, *bú, bás;* (pleasant) *mahak.*
Of course, *albatta, aur kyá?*
Off (off from), *par se;* (be off out of this) *saṭak jáo yahán se.*
Offal, *ojh—fuzla.*
Offence, *qusúr, gunáh;* (in law) *jurm.*
Offend (displease), *ranjída karná.*
Offended, *nákhush, ranjída.*
Offensive (as a smell), *badbúdár.*
Offer (to do a thing), *taiyár honá, kahná.*
Offer (proposal), *bát, kahná.*
Office, *mansab, uhda;* (office-room) *daftar, daftar-kháná*, 457.
Officer (native) *uhdadár.*
Official (adj.) *sarkárí.*
Offspring, *aulád.*
Often, *aksar;* (repeatedly) *bár bár.*
Ogre (bugbear), *hauwá.*
Oil, (sweet) *míṭhá tel;* (mustard) *karwá tel;* (castor) *renḍí ká tel.*
Oil-merchant, *telí.*
Ointment, *roghan.*
Old, (a man) *búṛhá;* (a woman) *buṛhiyá;* (an article) *puráná.*

Note.—The first two are applicable also to animals.

Old age, *buṛhápá—pírí.*
Omen, *fál;* (good omen) *fál nek;* (ill omen) *fál bad.*
Omission, *bhúl.*
Omit, *chhoṛná — faroguzásht karná*, 236.
Omitted (left out), *chhúṭá húá—faroguzásht.*
Omnipotent, *qádir-i-mutlaq.*
Omniscience, *hamadání.*
Omniscient, *hamadán.*
Once, *ek bár, ek dafe, ek martabe.*
Once on a time, *agle waqt men, sábiq zamáne men.*
*At* Once, *abhí, jhaṭpaṭ—fauran.*
One by one, *ek ek karke;* (one and a half) *ḍeṛh;* (one and a quarter) *sawá.*
One-eyed, *káná*, 615, 618.
Onion, *piyáz.*
Only, *khálí, sirf—faqat.*
Open, (*adj.*) *khulá;* (*v.a.*) *kholná;* (*v.n.*) *khul jáná.*
Openly, *khulá-khulí, barmalá*, 440.
Opening, (opportunity) *ráh, mauqa;* (in a rock, mountain, &c.) *shigáf, darár.*
Operate, (perform an operation) *amal karná;* (take effect) *tásír karná, asar honá.*
Operation (surgical, &c.), *amal.*
Opinion, *ráe, samajh, dánist.*
Opium, *afyún, afím.*
Opponent, *mukhálif;* (rival) *haríf.*

Opportune, opportunely, *bar waqt, waqt par.*
Opportunity, *mauqa, ausar*, 39, 218, 580.
Oppose, *mukhálif honá, muzáhim honá; muqábala karná.*
Opposite, *sámne, rúbarú;* (exactly opposite) *ámne sámne.*
Opposite (contrary), *bar khiláf, bar aks, birudh.*
Opposition, *mukhálafat, muzáhamat;* (spiteful) *zidd*, 221.
Oppress, *zulm karná—dast-darází karná.*
Oppressed (down-trodden), *mazlúm.*
Oppression, *zulm—dastdarází.*
Oppressor, *zálim.*
Option (choice), *ikhtiyár, marzí.*
Oral, *zabání.*
Orange, *nárangí, náranjí.*
Oration, *taqrír.*
Ordeal, *imtihán, ázmáish.*
Order, (command) *hukm;* (*v.a.*) *hukm dená* or *karná;* (method) *tartíb, dhab;* (in regular order) *tartíb se;* (put in order) *durust karná;* (in order that) *táki.*
Orderly (*n.*), *chaprásí, piyáda.*
Ordinary, (usual) *mámúlí;* (common) *ámm qism ká.*
Organic, *zátí, aslí.*
Oriental, *sharqí.*
Origin, *asl, jar, múl.*
Original, *pahlá;* (in the original, not a copy) *bajinsihi.*
Originally, *pahle men, ibtidá men.*
Ornament (for the person), *zewar, gahná.*
Ornamentation, *árástagí.*
Orphan, *yatím.*
Ostensible, *záhirí;* (ostensibly) *záhir men, ba-záhir*, 437.
Ostentation, *dikháwá, numáish.*
Other, *aur, dúsrá—dígar, ghair.*
*The* Other side, (of a river) *uspár;* (of a town, &c.) *parlí taraf.*
Otherwise, *kuchh aur tarah se;* (if not) *nahin to—warna.*
Out, *báhar;* (out of one's mind) *be-khud;* (out of place) *be-mauqa;* (out of season) *be-mausim;* (out of sight) *gháib;* (out of the way) *ghair-házir;* (out of the question) *ná-mumkin, muta'azzir.*
Outbreak (of sickness), *phail jáná bímárí ká.*
Outcast, *khárijí.*
Outcome, *natíja, hásil.*
Outcry, *shor-ghul, rúká-raulá.*
Outer, *báhirí, báharlí*, 95.
Outlet, *nikás*, 156.
Outline, *khákú.*
Outlive, *jánbar honá.*
Outlook (prospect), *pesh-nazar.*
Outrage, *andher, ghazab.*
Outside, *báhar;* (on the outside) *báharlí taraf.*
Outskirts, *sarhadd.*
Outstrip (surpass), *sabqat lejáná, píchhe dálná*, 337, 338, 499.
Outwardly, *záhir men.*
Outwards, *báhar kí taraf.*
Oven, *tandúr.*
Over, *úpar;* (over against) *ámne sámne.*
*To be* Over (remaining), *bachá* or *báqí honá* or *rahná.*
Over and over again, *bár bár.*
Overawe, *dabá rakhná— ... ká rob háwí honá.*

Overflow, *chaṛhke bahná*; (as a vessel) *chhalakná—labrez honá.*
Overhanging bank, *ḍháng*, 342.
Overhear, *kán men̲ paṛná.*
Overlooking, (commanding) *musharraf* or *mushrif*; (ignoring, *n.*) *chashm-poshí.*
Overpower (vanquish), *g̲h̲álib-áná*; (subdue) *dabáná, bas men̲ láná.*
Overrun, *dháwá karná.*
Overshadow (overspread), *chháná, chhá rahná—sáya karná.*
Oversight, *bhúl, g̲h̲altí.*
Overtake, *já lená*, 66.
Overthrow, *girá dená.*
Overturn, *ulaṭ dená.*
Overwhelmed, *ḍúbá húá—g̲h̲arq húá.*
Owe, *dharáná*, ... *ke zimme honá.*
Owing to (because of), *azbaski*, 407, 631.

Note.—This word is only used as the opening word in a sentence; it answers to our words "being" and "having" in such sentences as, "Being of a timid disposition," "Having no other resource," &c.

Own (*adj.*), *apná, nijká, e.g.* this is my own, *yih mere nijká hai.*
Owner, *málik.*
Ox, *bail.*

Pace, *qadam*; (paces, way of going) *raftár.*
Pacify, *ṭhanḍá karná—iskát karná.*
Pack (clothes, &c.), *sandúq men̲ band karná.*
Packet, (small, of medicine) *puṛiyá*; (parcel) *bidrí.*
Pad (for an elephant), *gaddí.*
Padlock, *tálá.*
Page (of a book), *safha.*
Pail, *báltí.*
Pain, *dard, dukh*; (of mind) *ranj, ranjish*, 596.
Painful, *sak̲h̲t*; (trying, distressing) *sháqq*, 152.
To take Pains, *mihnat karná—zahmat uṭháná.*
Painstaking, *mihnatí.*
Paint, (*n.*) *rang*; (*v.a.*) *rang dená* or *lagáná*; (a picture) *taswír khainchná.*
Painter, *rang-sáz*; (artist) *musawwir.*
Pair (*n.*), *joṛá—juft.*
Palace, *daulat-k̲h̲ána, qasar.*
Palate, *tálú.*
Pale, *zard, pílá*; (faded) *phíká*, 292.
Palm, (of the hand) *hathelí*; (tree) *táṛ.*
Palpitate, *phaṛakná, dhaṛakná.*
Palpitation, *k̲h̲afaqán.*
Palsy, *jholá—fálij*; (afflicted with) *jhole ká márá húá—maflúj.*
Pan (large earthen), *nánd.*
Pane of glass, *áína.*
Panic-stricken, *bad-hawáss.*
Pant, *hámphná.*
Pantry, *boṭal-k̲h̲ána.*
Paper, *kág̲h̲az*; (papers) *kág̲h̲azát*; (blotting) *siyáhí ká kág̲h̲az.*
Parable, *tamsíl.*
Parade (for drill), *qawáid.*
Paradise, *bihisht—jannat.*
Paragraph, *fiqra.*
Paramour, *áshná.*
Parapet, *fasíl.*
Parcel (such as comes by post), *bidrí.*

Parch (bake), *bhúnná.*
Parched, (grain) *chabená;* (ground) *ṭhokrí zamín.*
Parcher of grain, *bharbhúnjá.*
Pardon (*n.*), *muáfí—maghfirat.*
Pardon (forgive), *muáf karná.*
Pare (peel), *chhílná.*
Parentage, *waldiyat.*
Parents, *má báp—wálidain.*
Parrot, *totá.*
Parry (a blow with),...*par rokná.*
Part, (portion) *hissa, juz;* (piece) *ṭukṛá.*
*To take* Part in, *sharík honá.*
Part, (*v.n.*) *judá honá;* (*v.a.*) *judá karná.*
Partake, *hissa-dár honá, sharík honá.*
Partial, *tarafdár;* (in part only) *juzví.*
Partiality, *tarafdárí.*
Partially, *kuchh hisse se.*
Particle, *ṭukṛá—purza, parcha;* (smallest particle) *daqíqa.*
Particular (*adj.*), *kháss;* (every particular) *har tafsíl.*
Particularly (more particularly), *khusúsan, khásskar.*
Partisan, *tarafdár—jánibdár.*
Partner (associate), *sájhí, sharík.*
Partnership, *sájhá, sharákat.*
Partridge, *títar.*
Party, (set, clique) *thok—firqa,* 357; (to a suit) *faríq;* (both parties) *faríqain.*
Pass, (between mountains) *gháṭí;* (bad state of things) *naubat,* 219, 220.
Pass the time, *waqt káṭná, auqát basar karná.*
Passage (passing through), *guzar,* 226, 296.
Pass over (overlook), *darguzar karná.*
Passenger, *musáfir.*
Passion (fury), *ghazab—ghaiz.*
Passionate, *tund-mizáj, ghussawar.*
Past (over and gone), *gayá-guzrá;* (the past year) *pichhlá sál—sál-guzashta.*
Paste, *leí;* (to paste in) *wasl karná.*
Pasturage, *charáí.*
Pat (*v.a.*, a horse) *thapkí dená.*
Patch, (*n.*) *thiglí, paiwand;* (*v.a.*) *thiglí* or *paiwand lagáná.*
Path, (footpath) *pagḍanḍí, baṭiyá;* (garden path) *ravish.*
Patience, *sabr—sabúrí*
Patient, *sábir, burdbár;* (sick person) *bímár,* 251, 623.
Patriot, *watan dost.*
Patriotism, *watan-dostí,* 489.
Pattern (model), *namúna.*
Pauper, *kangál, muflis.*
Pause, (hesitation) *ta'ammul;* (brief cessation) *waqfa.*
Pavement (side walk), *kharanjá.*
Paw (of a tiger, &c.), *panja.*
Pay (wages), *talab, tankhwáh.*
Pay (as a debt), *adá karná, bhar dená.*
Paymaster, *bakhshí.*
Payment, *adáí.*
Pea, *maṭar.*
Peace, (amity) *sulh, áshtí;* (repose) *chain, árám;* (of mind) *itmínán, khátir-jamaí.*
Peaceable, *sulh-khwáh.*
Peace-maker, *sulh-karnewálá.*
Peach, *áṛú.*
Peacock, *mor.*
Peak (summit), *choṭí, shikhar*

Peal (of thunder), *kaṛak.*
Pear, *náshpátí.*
Pearl, *motí.*
Peasant, *ganwár—dihqán.*
Pebble, *kankarí—sangreza.*
Peck (as birds), *ṭhongá márná.*
Peculiar, *kháss*, 358.
Peculiarity, *khássiyat, khusúsiyat*, 358.
Pedlar, *bákaswálá, bisátí.*
Pedigree, *hasab-o-nasab.*
Peel, (*n.*) *chhilká*; (*v.a.*) *chhilká utárná.*
Peep, *jhánkná*; (peeping, *n.*) *jhánká-jhánkí.*
Peg, *khúnṭí*; (tent-peg) *mekh.*
Pelican, *hawásil.*
Pellet, *ghulelá, golí.*
Pen, *qalam.*
Penalty, *sazá—táwán.*
Penetrate (pierce), *ghusná, chhub-jáná*
Penetration (sagacity), *firásat, tez-fahmí.*
Penitence, *pachhtáwá, tauba—nadámat.*
Penitent, *pashemán, táib.*
Penknife, *qalam-tarásh.*
Pension, *pinshin—wazífa.*
People, *log*; (nation) *qaum.*
Pepper, (black) *gol-mirch*; (red) *lál-mirch.*
Per, (each) *píchhe, fí*; (per thousand) *hazár píchhe, fí hazár.*
Perceive, *dekhná, málúm karná, táṛ jáná*, 203, 204.
Per cent., *saikṛá*; (percentage) *fí-sadí.*
Perception, *samajh—fahmíd.*
Perfect, *kámil*; (complete) *tamám.*
Perfection, *kamáliyat.*
Perfidy (treachery), *ghadar, khiyánat.*
Perform, *adá karná, kar dikháná, bajá láná*, 129.
Perfume (*n.*), *khushbúí, mahak*, 599.
Perfunctorily, *sahl-angárí se*, 127.
Perhaps, *sháyad.*
Peril, *khatra.*
Perilous, *khatarnák.*
Period, *arsa, muddat*; (fixed term) *mí'ád.*
Periodically (from time to time), *waqtan-fa-waqtan.*
Perish, (die) *marná, halák honá*; (go bad) *kharáb hojáná.*
Perjure (oneself), *jhúṭhí qasam kháná—darogh-halfí karná.*
Perjury, *darogh-halfí.*
Permanent, (lasting) *qáim, dáimí*; (an appointment) *mustaqil.*
Permission, *ijázat—parwánagí*, 155, 638.
Permit (allow), *dená, ijázat dená.*
Perpetrate, *irtikáb karná.*
Perpetrator, *murtakib*, 162.
Perpetually, *hamesha, sadá.*
Perpetuity, *dawám, hameshagí.*
Perplex (drive wild), *hairán karná, pareshán karná.*
Perplexed (distracted), *hairán, pareshán.*
Perplexity, *janjál, pareshání.*
Perquisite, *haqq.*
Persecute, *satáná, tang karná.*
Persevere, *sábit-qadam rahná, darpai rahná.*
Perseverance, *sábit-qadamí, istiqlál.*
Person, *shakhs, ádmí.*

*Persona grata*, *manzúr-i-nazar*.
Perspiration, *pasíná*.
Perspire, *pasíná nikalná*.
Persuade, *manáná*, *targhíb dená*.
Pest, *fitna*, *wabál*.
Pestilence, *marí*, *wabá*.
Petal, *pankhṛí*, 628.
Petition, *darkhwást*, *arzí*.
Petticoat, *sáya*, *lahngá*.
Pewter, *jastá*.
Phial, *shísha*.
Philosopher, *hakím*.
Philosophy, *hikmat*.
Phrase, phraseology, *istiláh*.
Physic, *dawá*.
Physician, *hakím*, *tabíb*, *baid*, 623.
Pick, (pluck) *toṛná*; (pick up, gather) *binná*.
Pickaxe, *gaintí*.
Pickles, *áchár*.
Picture, *taswír*.
Picturesque, *khushnumá*.
Piebald, *ablaq*.
Piece (fragment), *ṭukṛá*—*purza*.
Pierce, (*v.a.*) *chhedná*; (penetrate) *ghusná*, *chubhná*.
Pig, *súar*; (young pig) *ghenṭá*.
Pigeon, *kabútar*.
Pig-headedness, *khar-dimághí*.
Pile (heap), *ḍher*—*toda*.
Pilgrim, *játrí*.
Pilgrimage, *játrá*—*ziyárat*; (to Mecca) *hajj*, 613.
Pill, *golí*.
Pillage (*v.a.*), *lúṭ lená*—*ghárat karná*.
Pillar, *khambá*, *sutún*.
Pillow, *takiya*; (pillow-case) *takiye ká ghiláf*.
Pilot, *arkáṭí*—*mu'allim*.
Pincers, *chimṭá*; (blacksmith's) *saṇrsí*.
Pinch, *noch lená*, *chuṭkí bhar lená*.
Pine (fir), *chíṛ ká darakht*.
Pine-apple, *ananás*.
Pink, *gulábí rang*.
Pious, *khudá-parast*—*muttaqí*.
Pit, *gaṛhá*.
Pitch, *rál*—*qír*.
Pitcher, *ghaṛá*.
Piteous (pitiable), *dard-angez*.
Pith, *gúdá*; (essence, gist) *khulása*, *hír*.
Pitted (with small-pox) *chechakrú*.
Pity, *rahm*, *tars*; (a great pity) *baṛe afsos kí bát*.
*To* Pity, *rahm karná*, *tars kháná*.
Pivot, *chúl*.
Placard, *ishtihárnáma*.
Place, *jagah*, *mauqa*; (of residence) *maqám*.
*Proper* (*allotted*) Place, *ṭhikáná*.
Plague (pestilence), *marí*, *wabá*.
Plague, (to worry) *maghz cháṭná*; (worry to death) *ján khá jáná*, 281.
Plain, (unaffected) *bholá*, *sáda*; (level expanse) *maidán*.
Plaint (in a civil suit) *dáwá*.
Plaintiff, *muddaí*.
Plait (*v.a.*), *gúndhná*.
Plan, (scheme) *tadbír*, *tajwíz*; (sketch) *naqsha*.
Plane (carpenter's), *randá*.
Planet, *saiyára*.
Plank, *takhta*.
Plant, (*n.*) *paudhá*, *peṛ*; (*v.a.*) *lagáná*.
Plaster (for walls) *puchárá*; (for a wound) *marham*.
Plaster (smear), *lípná*, *potná*, *thopná*.

Plastic (easily led or influenced), *mom kí nák.*
Plate, *básan, bartan.*
Plausible (specious), *záhirdár.*
Play, (v.n.) *khelná;* (an instrument) *bajáná.*
Play (pastime), *khel, bází.*
Plaything, *khilauná.*
Plea (contention), *hujjat, bahs,* (pron. *baihs*).
Plead (judicially), *hujjat* or *bahs karná.*
Pleader, *vakíl.*
Pleasant (agreeable), *dil-pasand—khushóyanda.*
Please (v.a.), *khush karná, rází karná.*
Please (be pleasing to), *pasand áná, bháná.*
Pleased (gratified), *khush—mahzúz.*
Pleasing (giving pleasure), *dil-pasand, dilpazír.*
Pleasure, *khushí—hazz;* (frivolity) *khel-tamásha.*
Pledge, *rihn, girau.*
Pledged (an article), *girwí.*
Plentiful, *bahut, kasrat se.*
Plenty, *bahutáyat, kasrat.*
Plot (of ground), *qita,* 628.
Plot (intrigue), *sázish, bandish.*
Plot (conspire), *sázish karná.*
Plough, (n.) *hal;* (v.a.) *hal jotná,* 628.
Ploughboy (or man), *háli.*
Pluck, (courage) *himmat;* (pluck up) *ukhárná.*
Plucky (courageous), *himmati, himmat-wálá.*
Plug, *ḍát, ḍaṭṭá, ṭhekí.*
Plum, *álúcha.*
Plumage, *bál-o-par.*

Plummet, *sáhaulí.*
Plunder, (n.) *lúṭ—ghárat;* (v.a.) *lúṭ lená—ghárat karná.*
Pocket, *jeb.*
Pod, *phalí, chhímí.*
Poem, *qasída;* (amatory) *ghazal.*
Poet, *sháir.*
Poetry, *shir, sháirí.*
Point, (end) *nok;* (of a spear) *ání;* (of an arrow) *gánsí;* (of a story) *hásil,* 513, 514, 515.
Point of view, *pahlú, etibár.*

Examples.—From whatever point of view you look at it, *Jis pahlú se dekho.* From the religious point of view, *Díndárí ke etibár se,* 301.

Point out, (explain) *batlá dená;* (an object) *dikhlá dená,* also *nishán dená,* e.g. I pointed out the house to the policeman, *pulíswále ko main ne ghar ká nishán diyá.*
Pointed (sharp), *nokdár, nokílá.*
Poison, *zahr, máhur;* (v.a.) *zahr khiláná.*
Poisonous, *zahrílá, zahrdár.*
Poke, (prod) *khod dená;* (in the ground with the point of a stick, &c.) *kurelná.*
Polish (v.a.), *saiqal karná, chamak dená.*
Polite, *mu'addab—bá-waza.*
Politeness, *milansárí, khush-akhláqí.*
Pollute, *mailá karná, nápák karná.*
Pollution, *álúdagí;* (defilement) *chhút—laus.*
Pomegranate, *anár.*
Pommel (of a saddle), *harná.*

Pommel (beat severely), *dhaul-chhakkaṛ karná — zad-o-kob karná.*
Pomp, *dhúm-dhám, shán-o-shaukat.*
Pond, *táláb, pokhar.*
Pony, *ṭaṭṭú.*
Poor, *gharíb—miskín*; (the poor fellow) *bechára.*
Population, *ábádí.*
Populous, *ábád—mámúr.*
Porch, *usárá.*
Porcupine, *sáhí, sáhil.*
Pore (or pores) of the skin, *masám.*
Port (harbour), *bandar.*
Portion, *hissa, bánṭ* or *bánṭ-chonṭ.*
Portmanteau, *peṭí.*
Pose as (pretend to be), ... *ká bhagal bharná.*
Position (situation), *jagah, maqám.*
Possess, *rakhná*; (in possession of) ... *ke pás.*
Possession, *qabza*, 124, 125; (in the possession of one's senses) *hosh-hawáss kí durustí men*, 229.
Possessions, *mál-milkiyat.*
Possessor, *málik*; (holder) *qábiz*, 124, 125.
Possible, *mumkin*; (possibility) *imkán.*
Post (for letters), *ḍák*; (postage) *ḍák ká mahsúl.*
Postpone, *multawí rakhná.*
Postscript, *tatimma.*
Pot, *bartan*; (cooking-pot) *hánḍí.*
Potato, *álú.*
Potter, *kumhár.*
Pottery, *básan-bartan waghaira.*
Poultry, *murghí-batak.*
Pounce on, *jhapaṭná*, 256.
Pound, (weight) *ádh-ser*; (for cattle) *kájí-haus.*
Pour, *ḍálná* or *ḍhálná*; (pour out) *unḍelná.*
Poverty, *muflisí, kangálpan.*
Powder (gunpowder), *bárút.*
Power, (authority) *ikhtiyár*; (to do a thing) *maqdúr, majál, táqat*; (strength) *zor, qúwat, bal.*
*To be in another's* Power, *kisí ke bas men honá.*
Powerful, *zoráwar*; (influential) *qábú-yáfta, zordár.*
Practice, (doing) *amal*; (habit) *ádat*; (constant practice of a thing) *mashsháqí.*
*To* Practise (with a view to proficiency), *mashq karná.*
Praise (*n.*), *táríf—sitáish*; (to praise) *táríf karná*, 282.
Praiseworthy, *tárífí*; (is praiseworthy) *táríf ke láiq hai.*
Prance, *lambiyán karná.*
Pray, *duá mángná*; (say prayers) *namáz paṛhná.*
Prayer, *duá*; (formal) *namáz.*
Preach, *wáz karná*; (preaching) *wáz, manádí.*
Preacher, *wáiz.*
Precaution, *peshbandí*; (against something) *tadáruk.*
*To take the* Precaution of, &c. *ihtiyátan koí kám karná.*
Precede, (go on ahead) *agáṛí* or *áge chalná*; (in time) *áge* or *peshtar honá.*
Precedent (*n.*), *nazír, misál.*
Precious, *qímatí, besh-qímat*, (exquisite) *nafís.*
Precipice, *ḍháng.*
Predict, *áge se kahná.*

Preface (*n.*), *díbácha.*
Prefer, *ziyáda pasand karná, bihtar jánná*; (to place above in one's estimation)...*par tarjíh dená.*
*To be* Preferable *to...par tarjíh rakhná.*
Preference, *tarjíh.*
Pregnant, *dopastá, hámila.*
Prepare, *taiyár karná.*
Preparation, *taiyárí.*
Prescribe (medically), *nuskha batláná*; or simply *batláná* with the particular thing prescribed).
Prescription, *nuskha.*
Presence, *huzúr* or *huzúrí*; (in the presence of) *ke sámne,... ke rú-ba-rú.*
Present, (not absent) *maujúd, házir*; (not past) *hál* or *hál ká, e.g.* in the present month, *hál ke mahíne men*; (for the present, just now) *bilfel*; (at the present time) *in dinon.*
Present, (gift) *hadya*; (reward) *inám.*
Presently, *abhí.*
Preserve (take care of), *hifázat se rakhná.*
Preservation (safe-keeping), *hifázat, muháfazat.*
Preside (at a meeting), *mír-majlis honá.*
Presidency (Indian term), *iháta.*
President (chairman), *mír-majlis.*
Press (*v.a.*), *dábná*; (press down) *dabáná.*
*To be very* Pressing, *píchhá lená —isrár karná.*
Pressing (persistent), *bajidd, musirr.*

Pressure, *dabáo*; (of business) *kám* (or *kár*) *kí kasrat.*
Presumption (inference), *qaiyás.*
Pretence, *baháná—híla.*
Pretend, *bahána karná*; (make oneself out to be) *apne taín ... batláná* or *záhir karná.*
Pretext, *baháná—híla*, 541.
Pretty, (a person) *khúbsúrat*; (a thing) *khushnumá.*
Prevalent, *járí, phailá húá.*
Prevaricate, *bát banáná, bálú batáná.*
Prevarication, *bát-banání—sukhan sází.*
Prevent, *rokná*; (restrain) *báz rakhná.*
Prevented (by valid cause), *mázúr*, 279.
Prevention (checking), *insidád*, 132.
Prey, *shikár.*
Price, *dám, qímat*; (price-current) *bháo, nirkh.*
Prick (puncture, *v.a.*), *chubhoná, chubho dená*; prick up one's ears) *kán khare honá.*
Prickly-heat, *ghamaurí.*
Pride, *ghamand, maghrúrí*; (pride oneself on) *náz karná.*
Priest, *imám, káhin.*
Prime, (best quality) *awwal qism ká*; (of life) *ain-jawání—shabáb.*
Prince, *sháhzáda*; (princess) *sháhzádí.*
Principal, (chief) *awwal, sadar, sardár*; (capital) *púnjí, asl.*
Principle (of a thing), *usúl*; (same in the plural).
Print, (*v.a.*) *chhápná*; (to be printed) *chhapná.*

Printing office, *chhápá-khána.*
Prison, *qaid-khána, jel-khána.*
Prisoner, *qaidí.*
Private (as property), *kháss—khánagí.*
*In* Private, *niråle meṉ—khalwat meṉ.*
Privately, *nirálemeṉ—khufyatan.*
Privy, *páekhána—jáe-zarúr.*
Prize, (reward) *inạm*; (in a game) *bází.*
*To* Prize (make much of), *ghanímat jánná,* 218.
Prize (value highly), *ạzíz jánná.*
Probability, *ihtimál*; (in all probability) *ghálíban.*
Probable, *ghálib*; (most probable) *aghlab.*
*It is* Probable that, *ghálib hai ki*; (most probably) *aghlab hai ki.*
Probably, *sháyad.*
Probation, *imtihán*; (to appoint on) *imtihánan muqarrar karná.*
Problem, *masla.*
Proceedings, (judicial) *kár-rawáí*; (goings-on) *harakateṉ.*
*Written* Proceedings, *rúedád.*
Process, *ạmal*; (judicial) *hukm-náma.*
Procession (marriage), *barát.*
Proclaim, *manádí karná, ishtihár karná.*
Proclamation, *manádí, ishtihár,* 610.
Procrastinate, *áj-kal karná—imroz-fardá karná,* 199.
Procrastination, *ṭál-maṭol—tákhír.*
Procurable, *miltá, mil saktá—muyassar,* 90, 91.
*To be* Procurable, *milná—muyassar honá,* 93.
Procure (*v.a.*), *mangwáná, baham pahúncháná.*
Produce (*v.a.*), *nikálná, báhar láná*; (bring forward) *pesh karná.*
Produce (of land, &c.), *paidáwárí.*
Productive (fertile), *upajáú, sansgar*; (as trees) *phaldár.*
Profanation, *be-hurmatí.*
Profane (in language), *kufr baknewálá.*
Profess, *iqrár karná*; (make a loud profession of) ... *ká dam bharná.*
Profession (occupation), *pesha.*
Professional, *pesha-war* (stress on last syllable).
Professor, *mudarris.*
Proficiency, *mahárat*; (expertness) *mashsháqí.*
Proficient, *máhir*; (expert) *mashsháq.*
Profit, *nafạ—manfạ'ạt*; (*v.a.*) *nafạ uṭháná, fáida uṭháná.*
Profitable, *fáidamand, súdmand,* 159.
Profitless, *be-fáida, lá-hásil.*
Profligacy, *aubáshí.*
Profligate (*n.*), *aubásh, rind.*
Progress, (*n.*) *taraqqí*; (*v.n.*) *taraqqí karná, peshraft honá.*
Prohibit, *manạ karná.*
Prohibited, *manạ.*
Prohibition, *mumániạt.*
Project (*n.*), *tadbír, mansúba.*
Prolong, *aur lambá karná, aur baṛháná.*
Promise, (*n.*) *wạda*; (*v.a.*) *wạda karná.*
*Breaking of a* Promise, *wạda-shikaní.*
*To fulfil a* Promise, *wạda púrá karná.*

Promote (give promotion to), *taraqqí dená*.
Promoter (starter of a business), *barpá karnewálá*, 140.
Promotion, *taraqqí*, 408, 538.
Prompt (*adj.*), *chálák, jald*.
Promptly, *be-ta'ammul*; (aptly) *barjasta*, 242.
Prong (of a fork, &c.), *phánk*.
Pronounce, *talaffuz karná*; (I can't pronounce this word) *is lafz ká talaffuz mujhko nahín átá*.
Pronunciation, *talaffuz*.
Proof, *dalíl, subút*.
Prop, *ṭek, ṭekan, chánṛ*.
Propagate, *phailáná, bo chalná*.
Propensity, *mailán*.
Proper, *munásib, ba-já*; (correct) *ṭhík, durust*.
Properly, *achchhí tarah se, munásib taur par*.
Property, *mál, milkiyat*.
Prophecy, (foretelling) *peshíngoí*; (office of a prophet) *nubúwat*.
Prophesy, *peshíngoí karná, áge se batláná*.
Prophet, *nabí, paighambar*.
Propitious, *yáwar*.
Proportion, *hissa*; (extent) *qadar*, e.g. In proportion to your efforts will be your success, *jisqadar koshish karoge, usí qadar tumhárí kámyábí hogí*, 538, 539.
Proprietor, *málik*.
Prose, *nasar*.
Prosecution, *pairaví*, 474.
Prosecutor, *muddaí*.
Prospect (front-view), *pesh-nazar*.
Prosperity, *iqbálmandí — tálimandí*.
Prosperous, *tálimand, iqbálmand*.
Prostitute, *kasbí, chhinál*.
Protect, *bacháná, himáyat karná*.
Protection, *bacháo*; (safe keeping) *hifázat*, 188.
Protector, *bachánewálá—hámí*.
Protégé, *riáyatí*.
Protruding, *niklá húá*.
Protuberance, *ubhár*.
Proud, *ghamanḍí, maghrúr*.
Prove, *sábit karná*; (to show clearly) *sáf záhir karná*.
Proved, (by evidence) *sábit*; (by experience) *mujarrab*.
Proverb, *masal, kaháwat*.
Proverbial, *zarb-ul-masal*.
Provide, *taiyár karná, maujúd rakhná*.
Provided that, *ba sharte ki*.
Providence, *khudá*.
Providentially, *khudá ke fazl se*.
Province, *súba*.
Provisions, *rasad, kháne ká sámán*.
Provocation, *chheṛ-chháṛ*.
Provoke, *chiṛáná, bhaṛkáná*.
Prudence, *ihtiyát*; (foresight) *peshbíní*.
Prudent, *hoshyár*.
Public, *ámm*.
Publicly (openly), *barmalá — aláníya*, 440.
Publish, (a book) *sháya karná*; (a matter) *záhir karná*.
Pucker (*v.n.*), *jhol paṛjáná*.
Pull, *khainchná*; (pull down) *girá dená*; (pull up) *ukháṛná*, 536.
Pulp, *gúdá*.
Pulse, *nabz*.
Pulverize, *búk ḍálná*.
Pump (*n.*), *bambá*.
Punch (the implement), *chheoní*.

Pungency, *jhál.*
Pungent, *tez, jháldár.*
Punish, *sazá dená.*
Punishment, *sazá.*
Pupil, *shágird;* (of the eye) *putlí.*
Purchase, *mol lená, kharídná.*
Purchaser, *kharídár.*
Pure, *pák, sáf;* (as gold, &c.) *khális, khará.*
Purely (simply, merely), *sirf, mahz.*
Purify, *sáf karná;* (purification) *safáí.*
Purity, *pákízagí, safáí.*
Purple, *bainganí, údá—kákrezí.*
Purpose, (*n.*) *gharaz, matlab;* (intention) *iráda.*
Purposely, *ján bújhke—dída-o-dánista.*
Purr, *khur khur karná,* 202.
Purse, (common kind) *baṭúá, basni;* (better kind) *hamiyání.*
Pursue, *píchhá karná, píchhe lagná* or *daurná.*
Pursuit (chase), *raged—ta'áqub.*
Push, *dhakká dená, ḍhakelná;* (to push by steady pressure) *ṭhelná.*
Put, *rakhná, dharná;* (put away) *rakh dená;* (put down) *níche rakhná, rakh dená;* (put off, defer) *multawí rakhná;* (put on, as clothes) *pahinná, oṛhná;* (put out, extinguish) *bujhá-dená;* (put to, a horse) *jotná;* (put up a person) *ṭhairá rakhná;* (put up at) *ṭhairná;* (put a stop to) *band kar rakhná;* (put up with, endure) *gawárá karná,* 153.
Putrid, *saṛá húá.*
Puzzled, to be, *dubdhe men honá.*
Quack (doctor), *jálí hakím.*
Quadruped, *chárpáya.*
Quail, *baṭer;* (small kind) *lawá.*
Qualified (eligible), *láiq, qábil.*
Quality, (of good quality) *achchhí qism ká;* (of bad quality) *burí qism ká, náqis.*
Quantity, (a small quantity) *thoṛá;* (a large quantity) *ḍher, bahut.*
Quarrel, *jhagṛá, qaziya.*
Quarrelsome, *jhagṛálú, takrárí,* 62.
Quarry, *khán.*
Quarter, *páo;* (a quarter) *páo hissa* or *chauthái hissa;* (three quarters of an hour) *paun ghanṭá;* (one and three quarters) *paune do* (*i.e.* a quarter less one and a quarter less two. Note that for the first three quarters the word is *paun,* and for all others *paune*); (one and a quarter, two and a quarter) *sawá ek, sawá do.*
*To give* Quarter to an enemy, *amán dená.*
Quarter (in a town), *muhalla.*
Quarterly (three monthly), *si-máhí.*
Quash, *radd karná.*
Quay, *ghát.*
Queen, *malika, rání.*
Queer, *jáe-ta'ajjub, ta'ajjub kí bát.*
Quell, *dabáná, malmeṭ karná.*
Quench, *bujháná.*
Quest, *talásh.*
Question, *suwál;* (questioning, *n.*) *istifsár.*
*Out of the* Question, *dar kinár.*
*To* Question (call in question), *kalám karná,* e.g. I do not question it, *ismen main kalám nahin kartá.*

Questionable, *mushtabih.*
Quick, *jald, chálák;* (expeditious) *jald-báz.*
Quickly, *jaldí se, phurtí se.*
Quickness, *phurtí—shitábí;* (of apprehension) *zúd-fahmí.*
Quicksilver, *párá.*
Quiet (an animal), *g͟haríb.*
*To keep* Quiet, *áwáz nahín karná.*
Quietly (gently), *haule haule.*
Quietness (repose), *ráhat, chain.*
Quill pen, *par ká qalam.*
Quilt, *razáí.*
Quince, *bihí.*
Quire (of paper), *dista.*
Quit (vacate), *k͟hálí karná, nikal jáná.*
Quite, *bilkull;* (altogether) *sar-ásar.*
Quiver, *tarkash.*
Quotation, *iqtibás.*
Quote, *darpesh láná.*

Rabble, *razíl log;* (a rabble) *razílon ká g͟hol.*
Race, *daur;* (horse-race) *ghur-daur.*
Race, (family) *k͟hándán;* (nation) *qaum.*
Racecourse, *ghur-daur ká maidán.*
Rack, (torture) *shikanja;* (to apply it) *shikanje men khainchná.*
Radish, *múlí.*
Raft, *berá.*
Rags, *chithre, latte.*
Rage, *g͟hazab—taish;* (as an epidemic) ... *ká zor honá,* 120.
Ragged (a person), *chithre pahne húe.*
Raid, *dháwá—turktází.*
Railroad, *rel kí sarak.*
Rain, *menh, bárish;* (the rains) *barsát.*
Rain (*v.n.*), *pání parná, menh barasná;* (cats and dogs) *músle dhár barasná,* 371.
Rainbow, *dhanuk—qaus-i-quzah.*
Raise, *uthána;* (prices) *barháná.*
Raisin, *kishmish.*
Rake (profligate), *aubásh, rind.*
Ram, *mendhá.*
Ramble (wander), *phirná,* also *hándná.*
Rank (*n.*), *rutba, darja;* (of inferior rank) *kam-rutba.*
Rankle (as a thorn), *khatakná.*
Ransack, *chhán márná, jhár lená.*
Ransom, *fidiyá;* I gave a thousand rupees for his ransom, *hazár rupai uske fidiye men diye.*
Rap (at a door), *khatkhatáná.*
Rapid (as a stream), *tezrav,* 631.
Rapidity, (velocity) *tezraví;* (expeditiousness) *shitábí.*
Rare, (scarce) *kamyáb;* (strange, uncommon) *nirálá,* or *nirálí qism ká;* (choice) *tuhfa.*
Rarely (seldom), *kam, thorá.*
Rarity, *nudrat;* (quite an exceptional thing) *nudrat kí bát.*
Rascal, *badzát, harámzáda.*
Rascality, *badzátí, harámzádagí.*
Rash, *be-ta'ammul.*
Rashness, *be-ta'ammulí.*
Rat, *chúhá.*
Rat-trap, *chúhá dám.*
Rate (of calculation), *hisáb;* (bazar rate) *nirk͟h, bháo;* (at any rate, at all costs) *ba-har hál, ba-har súrat.*

Rather (than that), *isse pahle, isse bihtar;* (somewhat) *kisí qadar, thoṛá bahut.*
Rational (reasonable), *máqúl.*
Rationally, *máqúl taur par.*
Rations (for soldiers), *rasad.*
Rattle, *kharkharáná.*
Rattling, *kharkharáhaṭ.*
Ravage (*v.a.*), *páemál karná.*
Ravages, *páemálí.*
Rave, *barbaráná.*
Raving, *barbaráí.*
Ravine, *nálá.*
Raw, *kachchá.*
Ray (of light), *kiran.*
Rays (of light), *partau.*
Razor, *ustura.*
Reach, *pahúnchná;* (attain or come up, to) *lagná.*
Read, *paṛhná.*
Reading and writing, *likhá-paṛhá,* 83.
Ready, *taiyár.*
Readiness, *taiyárí.*
Ready money (in hand), *naqdí.*
Real (genuine), *sachchá—haqíqí,*
*The* Real facts of a case, *asliyat, asl máhiyat,* 441.
Reality, *haqíqat;* (in reality) *haqíqat men, dar asl.*
Realization (of a debt), *wusúl.*
Really, *haqíqat men, dar asl.*
Realm, *mamlukat, mulk.*
Reap, *káṭná—dirau karná;* (reap benefit from) *fáida uṭháná.*
Rear, (in the rear) *pichháṛí men;* (to bring up) *pálná, parwarish karná;* (as a horse) *síkh-pá honá,* 304.
Reason, *sabab, wajh* (pron. *wajeh,* the *e* very short); (intellect) *aql.*
*It stands to* Reason that, *qaiyás cháhtá ki,* 231.
*Contrary to* Reason, *khiláf-i-qaiyás,* 592.
Reasonable, (just) *wájib;* (sensible) *máqúl.*
Reasonableness, (propriety) *wájibiyat;* (good sense) *máqúliyat.*
Rebel against,... *se phir jáná,* 625.
Rebut, *kí tardid karná.*
Receipt, (for money) *rasíd;* (coming to hand) *wusúl.*
Receive, *páná.*
Recent, *áj kal ká, hál ká;* (fresh, new) *nayá, táza.*
Recently, *hál men.*
Recite (repeat from memory), *paṛhná.*
Reckon, (count) *ginná,* (compute) *hisáb karná.*
Reckoning, (counting) *gintí;* (calculation) *hisáb.*
Reclaim, *sudhárná—isláh karná,* 511.
Reclaimed, *sudhará húá—isláh-pazír,* 262.
Recline, *leṭná, paṛná.*
Recognise, *pahchánná—shinákht karná.*
Recognition, *pahchán—shinákht.*
Recoil (as a gun), *píchhá karná.*
Recollect, *yád karná* or *honá.*
Recommend, *kí sifárish karná.*
Recommendation, *sifárish.*
Reconcile (two persons), . . . *ká mel karáná.*
Reconciliation, *mel-miláp.*
Record (of a case in court), *misl;* (to record) *likh dená* or *rakhná.*
*To have* Recourse to for help, . . . *ke pás iltijá lejáná,* 623.

Recover (a lost thing), *phir páná*, or in the neuter form, *mil jáná*—*dastyáb hojáná*.

Recover, (from sickness) *achchhá hojáná*, *árám hojáná*; (from a faint) *phir ifáqe meṉ áná*.

Note that *ifáqa* answers exactly to our phrase, "coming round again."

Recovery, (of lost property) *dastyábí*; (from sickness) *shifá*. 451.

Rectify, *durust karna*, 411.

Red, *lál*—*surkh*. Redness, *lálí*—*surkhí*.

Redeemer, *naját denewálá*, *munjí*.

Redress, *badlá*, *taláfí*; (of grievances) *dád-rasí*.

*To* Redress grievances, *dád ko pahúnchná*.

Reduce, *kam karná*, *ghaṭáná*; (to writing) *qalamband karná*.

Reduction, *ghaṭáo*.

Reed, *sarkanḍá*.

Reed-grass, *sirkí*, *senṭhá*.

Reel (stagger), *laṛkhaṛáná*.

Refer (allude) to, *zikr karná*—*tazkira karná*.

Refer to (cite as authority), . . . *ká hawála dená*, 382.

Reference, (allusion) *zikr*; (citing as authority) *hawála*.

*What does this* Refer to? *yih kisse murád?*

Refinement (of manners), *tahzíb*.

Reflect, *sochná*—*ta'ammul karná*.

Reflection, (thought) *soch*—*ta'ammul*; (shadow) *ạks*, *parchháiṉ*.

Reform, &c. *See* Reclaim, &c.

Refractory, *magrá*—*mutamarrid*, 252.

Refrain from, *háth uṭháná*, *báz-áná*.

Refresh, *táza karná*, *táza-dam karná*.

Refuge, *panáh*; (take refuge with) *ke pás panáh lená*; (place of refuge) *maljá*.

Refund (a refund), *zar-i-wápasí*.

Refusal, *inkár*.

Refuse, *inkár karná*; (rubbish) *fuzla*, *jhúṭhá*.

Refute, *jhuṭál dená*, *bátil karná*.

Refutation, *ibtál*.

Regard, *dhyán karná* or *rakhná*, *liház karná*.

Regard for, *liház*; (for a person's wishes, &c.) *pás*.

*With* Regard to ... *kí nisbat*.

Regeneration, *nayá janam*—*naupaidáish*.

Regiment, *palṭan*.

Region, *diyár*.

Register, *kitáb*; (shop-books) *khátá-bahí*.

Regret, *pachhtáwá*, *afsos*, *ta'assuf*.

Regular, (according to rule) *báqáịda*; (in good order) *batartíb*.

Regulations, *qáịda-qánún*.

Reign, (*n.*) *ráj*, *julúsí*; (to reign) *saltanat karná*.

Reins, *bág*, *rás*.

Reject, *ná-pasand karná*, *ná-manzúr karná*.

Rejection, *ná-pasandí*, *ná-manzúrí*.

Rejoice, (*v.n.*) *khushí karná*; (*v.a.*) *khush karná*.

Rejoiced, *bahut khush*—*mahzúz*.

Relate, *kah sunáná*, *bayán karná*.

Relation, *nátedár*, *rishtadár*; (relations) *bháíband*.

Relationship, *rishtadárí*, *qarábat*.

Relax, *dhílá karná, narm karná.*
Release, *chhoṛ dená, khalás dená.*
Relent, *muláim honá, tars khána.*
Relevant, *muta'alliq.*
Reliance, *bharosá, ásrá—takiya.*
Relief (from pain), *ṭhanḍak, árám.*
Relieve one's mind, *apná jí ṭhanḍá karná.*
Relieved (rid of), *subuk-dosh*, 343.
Religion, *mazhab—dín.*
Religious, *díndár.* Religiousness, *díndárí.*
Relinquish ... *se háth uṭháná, ... se dastbardár honá.*
Reluctance, *daregh.*
Reluctant, to be, *jí haṭ jáná, daregh karná.*
Rely on ... *par bharosá rakhná— ... par eṭimád rakhná.*
Remain, (stay on) *rah jáná;* (be left) *báqí rahná.*
Remainder, *bachtí—baqaiya.*
*The* Remaining ones, *báqí-mánda.*
Remark (*n.*), *zikr—tazkira.*
Remark (*v.a.*), *kahná, zikr karná.*
Remarkable, *qábil liház ke;* (man) *anúkhá.*
Remedy, *iláj, dawá.*
Remember, *yád karná* or *rakhná.*
Remembrance, *yád.*
Remind, *yád diláná.*
Reminder, *yád-dihí;* (urgent) *tákíd.*
Remiss, *ghafil.*
Remissness, *ghaflat—tasáhul.*
Remit, (send) *bhej dená;* (let off) *muáf karná.*
Remonstrance, *samjháná* (the verb used in a substantive sense).
Remonstrate, *samjháná.*
Remorse, *pachhtáwá, ta'assuf.*
Remote, *bahut dúr—dúr-dast*, 620.
Remove, (take away) *lejáná;* (put out of the way) *dúr karná.*
Remunerate, *ujrat dená.*
Remuneration, *ujrat*, 331, 332, *mihnatána.*
Renew (as a lease, &c.), *nayá ... lená.*
Renounce ... *se háth dhoná.*
Renown, *námwarí, shuhrat.*
Renowned, *námwar, mashhúr.*
Rent, (of a house) *kiráya;* (for land) *lagán.*
Renunciation, *tark.*
Repair (*v.a.*), *marammat karná.*
Repairs, *marammat;* (in need of repair) *marammat-talab*, 536.
Repeat, *phir kahná—mukarrar kahná.*
*To* Repeat over and over again, *mukarrar sikarrar kahná.*
Repel, *haṭá dená, dafa karná.*
Repent, *pachhtáná, tauba karná.*
Repentance, *pachhtáwá, tauba.*
Reply, (*n.*) *jawáb;* (*v.a.*) *jawáb dená.*
Report, (official) *kaifiyat;* (rumour) *khabar;* (of a gun) *áwáz;* (of a cannon) *shalak.*
Represent, (state) *batláná; guzárish karná;* (appear for another) ... *kí taraf honá.*
Representation, *guzárish, arz.*
Representative, *mukhtár.*
Reprimand, *tambíh karná;* (*n.*) *tambíh—sarzanish.*
Reproaches, *uláhná.*
Reproof, *malámat, tambíh.*
Reprove, *malámat karná.*
Repudiate, *mukar kar jáná, ... ká inkár karná.*

Repugnance, *bezárí, nafrat.*
Repugnant (contrary) to, ... *se baíd.*
Repulsive, *nafratí—makrúh.*
Reputation, *nám, neknámí—ábrú;* (of good) *neknám;* (of bad) *badnám.*
Request, (*n.*) *darkhwást, arz;* (*v.a.*) *darkhwást karná—iltimás karná.*
Require (to need), ... *ko cháhiye,* ... *ko darkár honá.*
Required (requisite), *cháhiye, darkár.*
Requite, *badlá dená.*
Requital, *badlá;* (of a wrong) *mukáfát.*
Rescue (*v.a.*), *bachháná, chhuraná.*
Rescue (*n.*), *chhutkárá, naját.*
Resemblance, *mushábahat, shabáhat.*
Resemble, ... *kí mánind honá—ke mushábih honá.*
Resent, *burá mánná.*
Resentment, *kína, bughz.*
Reside, *rahná—sukúnat karná.*
Residence (residing), *sukúnat, qaiyám.*
Resident, *rahnewálá—báshinda.*
Residue, *bachtí—baqaiya.*
Resign (an office), *istifá dená.*
Resin, *dhúná, rál.*
Resist, *muqábala karná, muzáhim honá.*
Resistance, *muqábala, muzáhamat.*
Resolute, *sábit-qadam, mustaqill.*
Resolution (resolve), *iráda-musammam.*
Resource, *tadbír.*
Resourceless, *be-tadbír.*
*Last* Resource (forlorn hope), *háre darje kí tadbír,* 419.

Respect, (*n.*) *adab;* (consideration) *liház.*
*In one* Respect, *ek khusús men.*
*To* Respect (a person), ... *ká liház rakhná;* (his wishes) ... *ká pás karná.*
Respectable, *motabar.*
Respectful, *mu'addab.*
Respite, *muhlat.*
Responsible, *zimmedár* or *zimmewár,* 109.
Responsibility, *zimmedárí, jawábdihí.*
Rest (*n.*), *árám—istiráhat.*
*To* Rest, (take rest) *sustáná, árám karná;* (rest on) *tikná.*
Restless, *be-chain;* (troubled in mind) *be-qarár, muztarib.*
Restlessness, *be-chainí;* (trouble of mind) *be-qarárí, be-árámí.*
Restore, (give back) *pher dená,* (reinstate, &c.) *ba-hál karná.*
Restrain, *thámná, báz rakhná.*
Restrict, *munhasar karná, mahdúd karná.*
Result, *natíja, hásil, phal.*
Resume (work, &c.), *phir karne lagná.*
Resurrection, *qiyámat.*
Retain, *rakhná.*
Retaliate, *badlá dená, paltá dená.*
Retaliation, *badlá, paltá—mukáfát,* 573.
Retentive (memory, to have), *khúb yád karná,* or *rakhná.*
Reticence, *khámoshí.*
Reticent, *khámosh.*
Retinue, *jilau.*
Retire (from service), *naukarí chhor dená—khidmat se alag hojáná,* 395.

Retreat (as an army), *haṭ jáná—pas-pá honá.*
Retrial, *sání tajwíz.*
Retribution, *badlá, ịwaz—muká-fát.*
Return (*v.n.*), *lauṭná, wápas áná, phir áná.*
*On his* Return, *uske lauṭne par.*
Return (give back), *wápas dená, pher dená.*
Reveal, *záhir kar dená—fásh karná.*
Revelation (disclosure), the verb *záhir ho jáná* used substantively—also *isrár.*
Revenge, *intiqám;* (to take one's) *intiqám lená,* 440.
Revenue, *mál-guzárí.*
Reverence (*v.a.*), ... *kítázím karná.*
Revile, *gáliyándená, lạn-tạn karná.*
Revive (*v.n.*), *dam men dam áná, dobára jíná.*
Revolt, *ghadr, baghávat.*
Revolution, *gardish;* (upsetting of a government) *bisát ká ulaṭ jáná* (*lit.* overturning of a chess-board).
Revolver, *pisṭól.*
Reward, *ajr* (pron. *ajar*); (gift) *bakhshish, inám.*
Rib, *paslí;* (the ribs) *pánjar.*
Ribbon, *fíta.*
Rice, (growing) *dhán;* (husked) *chánwal* (boiled) *bhát.*
Rich, *daulatmand, máldár.*
Rick (stack), *kúb.*
Ricochet, *ṭappe khá khá kar chalá jáná,* 493.
Rid of (relieved of), *subuk-dosh.*
Riddle (puzzle), *pahelí, mu'ammá.*
Ride, *sawár honá.*
Ridge (of a house), *banḍeri.*
Ridicule (*n.*), *hansí—tamaskhur.*
Ridicule (*v.a.*), *hansí men ḍálná, ṭhaṭṭhe men uṛáná.*
Rifle, *bandúq* or *rafl bandúq.*
Right, (lawful) *jáiz, rawá;* (correct) *ṭhík, durust;* (not left) *dahná.*
Right (title), *haqq, haqqiyat.*
*To be in the* Right, *haqq par honá.*
Rightful (owner), *haqqdár,* 386.
*The term does not* Rightly apply to him (or it), ... *uspar sádiq nahin átá.*
Righteous, *rástbáz.*
Righteousness, *rástbází.*
Rigid, *kaṛá, sakht.*
Rigidity, *kaṛápan, sakhtí.*
Rim, *kinára;* (of a coin) *báṛ.*
Rind, *chhilká.*
Ring, (finger) *angúṭhí;* (curtain, &c.) *kaṛí.*
Ring (a bell), *ghanṭá bajáná.*
Ringleader, *sarghana,* 370.
Ringlet, *kákul, zulf.*
Rinse, (the mouth) *kullí karná;* (a vessel) *khangálná.*
Riot, *balwá, hangáma,* 75.
Rip, *chírná, chák karná.*
Ripe, *pakká.*
Ripen, *pakná.*
Ripples (on water), *chhoṭí chhoṭí laharen.*
Rise, (*v.n.*) *uṭhná;* (a rise in prices, &c.) *baṛhão,* 328.
Risk, *khatra, jokhim.*
Risky, *jokhimí.*
Rite, *sunnat.*
Rival, *haríf,* 335, 449.
Rivalry, *harífí, hiská.*
River, *naddí, daryá* or *daryáo.*
Road, *rasta* or *rástá, ráh, báṭ.*

Roam, *phirná.*
Roan (colour), *chíná*, 232.
Roar (as a tiger), *garajná.*
Roast (*v.a.*), *kabáb karná.*
Rob, *lúṭ lená.*
Robber, *ḍákú—rahzan*, 76.
Robbery, *ḍakaití—rahzaní.*
Robe, *khilat.*
Rock (*n.*), *chaṭán.*
Rocket, *hawáí.*
Rock-salt, *kálá nimak.*
Rod, *chhaṛí.*
Rogue, *aiyár, daghábáz*, 111.
Roll, (*v.n.*) *loṭná*; (roll about) *loṭ-poṭ karná.*
Roller (garden-roller), *belan.*
Roof, *chhat*; (thatched) *chhappar.*
Roofing (putting on a roof), *chháoní*, 522.
Room, (in a native's house) *koṭhrí*; (in a bungalow) *kamara*; (space) *jagah—gunjáish.*
Roomy, *kusháda.*
Root, *jaṛ*; (to take root) *jaṛ pakaṛná.*
Rope, (thick) *rassá*; (smaller) *rassí.*
Rose (flower), *guláb.*
Rot (*v.n.*), *saṛ jáná.*
Rotten, *saṛiyal, saṛá húá.*
*By* Rote, *zabání—az bar.*
Rough, (not smooth) *khurkhurá*; (as ground) *únchá nichá, úbaṛ khábaṛ*; (in manner) *sakht.*
Rough-handling (ill-usage), *tashaddud.*
Round (in shape), *gol*; (round about) *ás-pás.*
*To go one's* Rounds, *gasht phirná.*
Rouse up (*v.a.*), *jagáná.*
Rout (*v.a.*), *shikast dená.*
Route, *rástá, ráh.*
Routine, *dastúr, mámúl.*
Row, (line) *saff*; (disturbance) *hallá-ghulá.*
Row (a boat), *kheoná.*
Royal (regal), *sháhí, bádsháhí.*
Rub, *malná, málish karná*; (rub out) *miṭá-dená.*
Rubbish, *kúṛá.*
Ruby, *lál, chunní.*
Rudder, *patwár.*
Rude, *be-adab.*
Rudeness, *be-adabí.*
Rug, *kammal*; (for the floor) *ghálícha.*
Rugged, *bíhaṛ, úbaṛ-khábaṛ.*
Ruin (*n.*), *kharábí, tabáhí.*
Ruins, *khanḍar.*
Rule (sway), *amaldárí, hukúmat.*
*As a* Rule, *aksar.*
Rules, *qawáid.*
Ruler, *hákim.*
Rummage, *chhán márná.*
Rumour, *afwáh*; (Hindi) *sungar.*
Rump, *chútaṛ.*
Rumple (crumple), *dal-masal karná.*
Run, *dauṛná*; (run away) *bhágná*; (run off with) *le-bhágná*; (run short) *kam ho jáná*; (run out) *kharch ho jáná.*
Runner, *dauṛnewálá.*
Running water, *bahtá pání.*
Running down (speaking ill of, *n.*), *mazammat*, 280.
Ruse (stratagem), *híla-bahána.*
Rush (*v.n.*), *jhapaṭke* (or *lapakke*) *dauṛná.*
Rush out upon ... *par ṭúṭná.*
Rust, *zang, morcha.*
Rusty, *zang-álúda.*
Rut (wheel-mark), *pahiye kí lík.*

Ruthlessly, *be-rahmí se.*

Sabre, *talwár—shamsher.*
Sack, (*n.*) *borá*; (for carrying on bullocks, &c.) *gon*, 597.
*To* Sack (a town), *lúṭ lená—ghárat karná.*
Sacred (holy), *muqaddas.*
Sacrifice, (*n.*) *qurbání*; (to offer one) *qurbání guzránná* or *charháná.*
Sacrifice (give up something for the sake of another), *tasadduq karná, qurbán karná.*
Sad, *udás—malúl.*
Sadness, *udásí—malál.*
Saddle, (*n.*) *zín*; (*v.a.*) *zín bándhná* or *kasná.*
Safe, Safely, in Safety, *salámat.*
Safe and sound, *sahíh-wa-sálim.*
Safe (for meat), *ḍolí.*
Safety, *salamatí*, 378.
*For* Safety's sake / *To be on the* Safe side } *ihtiyátan, ba-taur ihtiyát ke*, 87, 88.
Saffron, *zạfarán*, 628, *kesar.*
Sagacious, *siyáná, hoshyár.*
Sagacity, *hoshyárí—firásat.*
Sago, *ságú.*
Sail (*n.*), *pál—bádbán.*
Sailor, *jahází, malláh.*
Saint, (Hindu) *sádhú*; (Mahommedan) *walí, pír.*
Sake, *khátir, wáste, liye.*
Salary, *tankhwáh.*
Sale, *bikrí.*
Sallow, *sánwlá—zard.*
Sally (from a fort, &c.), *khurúj.*
Salt, *nimak.*
Salt-cellar, *nimakdán.*
Salt, (as meat) *namkín*; (as the sea) *shor.*
Saltness (brackishness), *shoriyat.*
Saltpetre, *shora.*
Salutary, *mufíd.*
Salute, (*n.*) *salám*; (*v.a.*) *salám karná.*
Salvation, *naját.*
*The* Same, *wuhí*; (as it was originally, as I left it, &c.) *jaise ká taisá, jon ka ton*; (it comes to the same thing) *ek hí bát hai.*
Sample, *namúna.*
Sanction, (*n.*) *manzúrí*; (*v.a.*) *manzúr karná.*
Sanctioned, *manzúr húá.*
Sand, (in Upper India) *ret*; (in Bengal) *bálú.*
Sandy, *retílá.*
Sane, *sahíh-ul-ạql, aql ká durust.*
*For* Sanitary purposes, *safáí ke liye.*
Sanitation, *safáí.*
Sap (juice), *ras—ạraq*, 183.
Sapphire, *nílam.*
Sarcasm, *án-tán kí báten—tạnamihná.*
Satire, *hajo.*
Satisfaction, (that everything is right) *dil-jamạí, itmínán*; (of a master with his servant) *khushnúdí.*
Satisfied (contented), *rází—khushnúd.*
Satisfy (to please), *rází karná, khush karná.*
Saturday, *saníchar—shamba.*
Savage, (wild) *janglí—wahshí*; (fierce) *tund-mizáj.*
Saucer, *pirich.*
Saucy, *shokh, gustákh.*
Sauciness, *shokhí, gustákhí.*

Save, (*v.a.*) *bacháná;* (in the religious sense) *naját dená.*
Savings, *pas-andáz ká rúpiya, bachat ká rúpiya.*
Savoury, *mazedár.*
Saw, (tool) *árá;* (small) *árí.*
Sawdust, *buráda.*
Say, *bolná, kahná;* (that is to say) *yáni.*
*You don't* Say so! *sach kaho!*
Scab, *khurand, khúṭhí.*
Scabbard, *káṭhí, miyán.*
Scaffolding, *páṛ, machán.*
Scale (of a fish), *sihrá.*
Scales, (for weighing) *tarázú, palle;* (small) *nikti.*
Scar, *zakhm* (or *gháo*) *ká dágh.*
Scarce, *kamyáb, thoṛá.*
Scarcity, *mahangí, kamyábí.*
Scare (to frighten), *ḍaráná.*
Scatter, *bikherná, chhitráná;* (an enemy) *tittar bittar karná.*
Scattered about, *bikhare húe, khinḍe húe.*
Scavenger, *bhangí—khák-rob.*
Scene (spectacle), *tamáshá.*
Scent, *bú, bás.*
Sceptic, *shakkí ádmí.*
Schedule, *fard, fihrist.*
Scheme, *tadbír, mansúba.*
Schism, *bidaṭ, phúṭ.*
Scholar, *shágird, tálib-ilm.*
School, (primary) *maktab;* (better class) *madrasa.*
Science, *bidyá, ilm.*
Scientific, *ilmí.*
Scissors, *quinchí.*
Scoff, *istihzá karná, ṭhaṭṭhá karná.*
Scold (*v.a.*), *ḍánṭná, dhamkáná.*
Scorch, (*v.a.*) *jhulsáná;* (his hair got scorched) *uske bál jhulas gae.*
Score (*n.*), *koṛí.*
Scorn (contempt), *hiqárat.*
Scorpion, *bichchhú.*
Scoundrel, *badma'ásh.*
Scour, *mánjná,* 461.
Scout (*n.*), *jásús.*
Scowl (to frown), *bhaun ṭeṛhí karná.*
Scramble (for pice, &c.), *chhíná-chhání karná.*
Scrap, *ṭukṛá;* (of paper, &c.) *parcha.*
Scrape (*v.a.*), *chhílná.*
Scratch, (as a cat) *noch lená;* (an itchy place) *khujláná.*
Scratch (skin-wound), *kharásh.*
Scream, *chilláná—chíkh márná,* 620.
Screen, *ṭaṭṭí, jhámp;* (curtain) *parda.*
Screw (*n.*), *pench.*
Screwdriver, *penchkash.*
"Screw loose somewhere," "something wrong," *futúr,* 194, 195.
Scrub (*v.a.*), *mánjná.*
Scruple (*n.*), *shubha, ta'ammul.*
Scrutinize, *khúb jánchná.*
Scrutiny, *jánch-partál.*
Scum, (on boiling liquid) *gáj;* (on stagnant water) *káí.*
Scurf, *rúsí.*
Sea, *samundar—daryáe-shor.*
Seal, *muhar;* (to seal) *muhar lagáná.*
Sealing-wax, *láh, chapṛá.*
Seam (*n.*), *síwan, joṛ.*
*To* Search for, *ḍhúnḍhná, talásh karná.*
*In* Search of, *ká mutaláshí,—ká khojí.*
Searching (for a thing), *talásh;* (of a thing) *taláshí;* (of a house) *khána-taláshí;* (of the

person) *badan kí taláshí.* The verb used with these phrases is *lená*, 208.
Season, *mausim;* (to season) *baghárná, masálah dená.*
Seasonable, seasonably, *waqt par, bar waqt.*
Seasoned (old), *anwásá.*
Seat, (place of sitting) *baiṭhne kí jagah, baiṭhak;* (if cushioned) *gaddí.* See "Chair" and "Stool."
Seat (cause to sit), *baiṭhá dená, biṭhlá dená.*
Second, (*adj.*) *dúsrá—sání;* (a second time) *phir, dobára.*
Secondhand, *istęmálí, bartá húá,* 535.
Secrecy, *chhipáo, poshídagí.*
Secret, (*n.*) *bhed, ráz;* (*adj.*) *poshída, makhfí.*
*In the* Secret, *rázdár, hamráz.*
Secretary, *kátib.*
Secrete, *chhipáná—poshída rakhná.*
Secretly, *chorí chhipe—bálá bálá;* (privately) *khufyatan.*
Section, *fasl.*
Secular matters, *dunyádárí kí báteṉ.*
Secure, (safe) *mahfúz;* (*v.a.*) *mahfúz rakhná.*
Security, (safety) *hifázat, salámatí;* (for a debt, &c.) *zamánat—kafálat.*
Sediment, *gád, talchhaṭ*, 448.
Sedition, *dangá-fasád.*
Seduce, *bahkáná, warghaláná.*
Seduction, *phusláo* or *phusláhaṭ.*
See, *dekhná.*
Seeing that (whereas), *chúnki.*
Seed, *bij.*
*To* Seek redress, *chára-joí karná;* (seek to win) *dil-joí karná*, 444, 443.
*To* Seem, *málúm honá.*
Seemingly, *dekhne meṉ.*
*To be* Seen (visible), *dikháí dená, nazar áná.*
Seize, *pakaṛná, ... par qabza karná.*
Seizure, (capture) *giriftárí;* (falling ill) the verb *bímár paṛná* used substantively.
Seldom, *kam, thoṛá.*
Select (*v.a.*), *chunná, chhánṭná.*
Self, *áp, khud;* (one's own self) *áp hí áp, khud.*
Self-deception, *nafs ká makar.*
*Belonging to* oneself, *nijká—zátí.*
*N.B.*—*Zát* and *nafs* both mean "self," the man's essence.
Self-defence, *apná bacháo.*
Self-denial, *nafs-kushí.*
Self-evident, *badíhí, záhir*, 309, 485.
Selfish, *khud-gharaz.*
Selfishness, *khud-gharazí.*
Selfwill, *khudsarí.*
Selfwilled, *khudsar.*
Sell, *bechná—farokht karná;* (*v.n.*) *bikná.*
Send, *bhejná;* (send for a thing) *mangwáná;* (for a person) *bulwáná;* (send word) *kahlá bhejná.*
Senior, *baṛá.*
Seniority, *baṛáí.*
Sensation, *sudh—hiss;* (without sensation) *be-sudh—be-hiss.*
Sense, (intelligence) *aql, samajh;* (in one sense) *ek hisáb se.*
Senseless, (unconscious) *be-hosh;* (unmeaning) *be-máṇí, behúda.*

Sensible, *samajhdár, máqúl-pasand* (word or act) *máqúl*.
Sensual, *nafs-parast;* (pleasures, &c.) *nafsání*.
Sensuality, *nafs-parastí, nafsániyat*.
Sentence, (in a book) *jumla;* (of a court) *hukm*.
Sentry, *pahrawálá*.
Separate, (*adj*.) *judá, alag;* (distinct or apart) *aláhida*.
Separate, (*v.a*.) *judá karná*.
Separately (one by one), *ek ek karke, judá judá*.
Separation, *judái—mufáraqat;* (severance, split) *tafriqa*.
Series, *silsila*.
Serious (important), *bhárí—sangín*.
Servant, *naukar, chákar—mulázim*.
Servants (collectively) *naukar-chákar*.
Serve, *naukarí karná, khidmat karná*.
Service, *naukarí, khidmat*.
Serviceable, to be, *kám áná, kám ká honá*.
Servile, *ghulám-mizáj, pájí-mizáj*.
Servilely, *ghulám kí tarah*.
Servility, *ghulám-mizájí*.
Set (party, clique), *thok—firqa*.
Set, (as the sun, &c.) *ḍúbná—ghurúb honá;* (set aside) *ek taraf karná;* (set about) *shurú karná;* (set aside) *bar taraf karná;* (set going) *járí karná;* (set out) *rawána honá*.
Settle (decide), *tai karná, faisal karná*, 71, 72, 96.
Settlement, (decision) *faisala;* (colony) *mámúra*.

Several, (some) *kai ek;* (a good many) *bahut*.
Severe, *sakht—shadíd;* (Hindí) *kaṭhin*.
Severity, *sakhtí—shiddat*.
Sew, *siná, siláí karná*.
Sewer, *sanḍás, badar-rau;* (main sewer) *ganda-nálá*.
Sex, *jins*.
Shabby, *bahut puráná—kasíf*.
Shade, Shadow, *sáya, chhánw*.
Shady, *sáyadár*.
Shafts (of a carriage), *phaṛ*.
Shaggy, *jhabbúá*.
Shake, (*v.n*.) *hilná;* (*v.a*.) *hiláná*.
Shaking (of a carriage, &c.), *takán*.
Shallow (water), *chhichhlá*.
Shallowness, *chhichhláí*, 430, 431.
Sham, (counterfeit, *adj*.) *jhúṭá, jálí;* (*n*.) *banáwaṭ, jál*.
Sham, (*v.a*.) *bahána karná*.
Shamming, (*n*.) *bahána*.
Shame, (*n*.) *sharm—hayá*.
Shameful, (provided it does not precede the noun qualified) *sharm kí bát*.
Shameless, *be-sharm—behayá*.
Shape, *súrat, shakl, ḍaul*.
Share, (*n*.) *hissa, bánṭá;* (*v.a*.) *bánṭná, hissa karná*.
Sharp, *tez;* (pointed) *nokdár, nokílá;* (sharp practice) *thaṭhera-badláí*.
Sharpen, *tez karná, dhár banáná*.
Shatter, *chakná chúr karná*.
Shave, *dáṛhí* (or *dáṛhí múchh*) *banáná;* (the head) *múṇḍná*, 637.
Sheaf, *púlá*.
Shear (*v.a*.), *katarná*.

Shears, *katarní.*
Sheath, *káṭhí, miyán.*
Sheathe, *miyán meṉ karná,* or *miyán karná.*
Shed, (*n.*) *chhappar;* (*v.a.*) *baháná.*
Shedding of blood, *khúnrezí.*
Sheep, (collectively) *bheṛ;* (ewe) *bheṛí.*
Sheep-fold, *bheṛ-kháná.*
Sheer, *nirá, mahz.*
Sheer off (slink away), *katráná.*
Sheet, *chádar;* (a sheet of water) *ek sath* (pron. *sateh*) *páni ká.*
Shelf, *takhta, táq.*
Shell, *sípí, síp—sadaf.*
Shelter, (*n.*) *áṛ, oṭ;* (under shelter of) ... *kí áṛ meṉ* ... *kí oṭ meṉ.*
Shelving, *ḍháldár* or *ḍhálú.*
Shepherd, *gaṛariyá—chaupán.*
Shew, *dikhláná;* (indicate) *batláná.*
Shield, *ḍhál—sipar.*
Shift (be displaced), *khasak jáná,* 234.
Shimmer, *tirmiráná.*
Shine, *chamakná;* (as the sun and moon) *roshan honá—jalwagar honá.*
Shining (bright), *chamakdár.*
Ship, *jaház.*
Shirk (or evade) a question, *lapeṭ-sapeṭ se kahná.*
Shirt, *qamís.*
Shiver, *kámpná.*
Shock, *sadma.*
Shoe, *jútá* or *jútí;* (of a horse) *nál.*
Shoemaker, *mochí.*
Shoot (with a bullet), *golí márná;* (birds) *márná.*
Shoot up (as a plant), *phabakná.*
Shooting, (sport) *shikár;* (to go out shooting) *shikár khelná.*
Shop, *dúkán.*
Shopkeeper, *dúkándár.*
Shore, *kinára.*
Short, *chhoṭá;* (shortsighted) *kotáh-bín.*
Shortly, *jald, thoṛe dinoṉ meṉ.*
Shortsightedness, *kotáh-bíní, kotah-andeshí.*
Shot, *chharrá.*
Shoulder, *kanḍhá* or *kándhá;* (the shoulders, top of the back) *monḍhá.*

*N.B.*—The top of the shoulder only is called *kandhá,* or *kándhá.*

Shout, *hánk, pukár;* (shout out to) *hánk márná, pukárná,* 145.
Shove, *dhakká dená, ṭhelná.*
Shovel, *bel;* (small) *belcha.*
Show, (display) *dikháwá;* (spectacle) *tamáshá.* See "Shew."
Shower, (of rain) *jhaṛí;* (of drizzling rain) *jhúsí.*
Shrewd, *siyáná—tezfahm.*
Shriek (*v.a.*), *chilláná—chíkh márná.*
Shrieks, *chilláhaṭ—chíkheṉ.*
Shrill, *tez.*
Shrine, *tírth, mazár.*
Shrink, *haṭná;* (from an undertaking) *dil churáná;* (as clothes) *sukaṛ jáná.*
Shrub, *peṛ, jháṛ.*
Shudder, *haṛhaṛáná.*
Shuffle (prevaricate), *lapeṭ sapeṭ karná.*
Shun ... *se dúr bhágná—gurez karná.*

Shut, (*v.a.*) *band karná*; (folding doors) *bherná*; (shut in, enclose) *bherná*; (shut up shop) *dúkán barháná*.
Shy (bashful), *mahjúb, munh-chor.*
Shy (as a horse), *bidak jáná*, 61, 234.
Sick, *bímár*; (to be sick of a thing) ... *se uktáná.*
Sickle, *darántí*, 464.
Sickness, *bímárí—maraz.*
Side, *taraf, baghal*; (of the body) *kokh*, 492; (of a road) *kinára*; (lie on the side) *karwaṭ se parná*, 22, 23.
*On this* Side (of a river), *ispár*; (of a town, &c.) *warlí taraf.*
*On that* Side (of a river), *uspár*; (of a town, &c.) *parlí taraf.*
Side with anyone, *kisí ká sáth dená.*
Side by side, *hamdosh.*
Siege, *muhásara*; (lay siege to) *gher lená.*
Sieve, *chhalní.*
Sift, *chhánná.*
Sigh (*v.n.*), *áh bharná, sáns bharná.*
Sight, (vision) *bínáí, basárat*, 471, 631; (sight of) *nazar—díd.*
*To come in* Sight, *dikháí dená, nazar áná.*
Sign, (mark) *nishán*; (hint) *ishára*; (to sign) *sahíh karná.*
Signs (traces), *nishán, khoj.*
Signal, *ishára, sankár.*
Signature, *dastkhatt.*
Silence, *chupkí—khámoshí.*
Silent, *chup* or *chupká—khámosh*, 644; (keep silent about a thing) *dam na márná.*
Silently, *chupke.*
Silk, *resham*; (of silk) *reshmí.*
Silver, *chándí—nuqra*; (of silver) *chándí ká—nuqraí.*
Similar, *eksán—mushábih.*
Similarity, *yaksání*; (likeness) *mushábahat.*
Simple, (artless) *bholá, sáda*; (easy) *ásán.*
Simpleton, *ullú ádmí, ahmaq* (pron. *aihmaq*).
Simply, *nirá, sirf.*
Sin, *gunah, páp.*
Sinful, *gunahgár, pápí.*
Since, *jab se, tab se*; (since I left) *mere jáne ke bád*, 4 to 7.
Sincere, *dil ká sachchá, ek rang.*
Sine quâ non, *shart*, 277, 317.
Sinew, *paṭṭhá, rag.*
Sing, *gáná*; (as a bird) *chahchaháná*, 505.
Singer, *gawaiyá.*
Singe, *jhulsáná.*
Singed, *jhulas gayá.*
Single, (not double) *ikahrá*; (one) *ek, ek to*; (unmarried) *mujarrad.*
Singly (one by one), *ek ek karke.*
Sink, *v.n.* (in water) *ḍúbná*; (in mud) *dhas jáná*, 70.
Sinner, *gunahgár.*
Sister, *bahin*, (sister-in-law, husband's sister) *nand.*
Sit, *baiṭhná.*
Site, *maqám, ṭhikáná.*
Situate, Situated, *wáqi.*
Sixth, *chhaṭṭá* or *chhaṭwán.*
Size, *miqdár, lambáí-chauṛáí*; (of a book, &c., where bulk is implied) *moṭáí.*
Skein (of thread, &c.) *lachchhá*

Sketch, (picture) *taswír*; (plan) *naqsha*.
Skilful, (as a workman) *kárígar*; (generally) *hunarmand*, *ustád*.
Skill, *chálákdastí*, *hunar-mandí*.
Skim (as milk), *káchhná*, *maláí utárná*.
Skin, *chamṛá*; (of an animal) *khál*; (*v.a.*) *khál khainchná*.
Skip (*v.a.*), *chhalángen bharná*.
Skirt, *dáman*.
Skull, *khoprí*.
Sky, *ásmán*.
Skylight, *tábdán*.
Slab (of stone), *paṭiyá*.
Slack, *ḍhílá*.
Slackness, *ḍhíláí*.
Slander, (*n.*) *buhtán*; (*v.a.*) *buhtán lagáná*.
Slanderer, *muftarí*.
Slant, (*n.*) *tirchháí*.
Slanting, *tirchhá*. See "Slope," &c.
Slap (*v.a.*), *thappaṛ* or *tamáncha márná*.
Slate, *takhtí*.
Slaughter, (animals for food) *zibh*; (pron. *zibeh*) *karná*.
Slaughter (carnage), *khúnrezí*.
Slave, *ghulám*.
Slavery, *ghulámí*, 623.
Slay, *már ḍálná*, *khapáná*.
Sleek, *chikná*.
Sleekiness, *chiknáí*.
Sleep, (*n.*) *nínd*—*khwáb*; (to sleep) *soná*.
Sleepiness, *únghái*—*ghunúdagí*.
Sleeplessness, *be-khwábí*.
Sleepy, *nindásá*; (to feel) *únghne lagná*; (*khwáb-álúda* is also "sleepy").
Sleeve, *ástín*.
Slender, *patlá*.
Slice (*n.*), *phánk* (sometimes *khanḍlá*).
Slide (slip), *phisal jáná*, *rapaṭ jáná*, 63.
Slight, (slender) *patlá*; (trivial) *halká*, *khafíf*; (thin) *ikahrá badan*.
Slime, *lu'áb*, *lasá*.
Slimy, *lu'áb-dár*, *laslasá*.
Sling (for stones), *gophan*—*falákhun*.
Slip (*v.n.*), *phisal jáná*, *rapaṭ jáná*, 63.
Slip (*n.*), *phisal* or *phislahan*—*laghzish*.
Slippery, *phislahá* or *phisalná*.
Slit, (*n.*) *chír*—*chák*; (*v.a.*) *chírná*.
Slope, *ḍhál*.
Sloping, *ḍhálú* or *ḍháldár*, *salámí*.
Slovenly, *phúhaṛ*, *mailá-kuchailá*.
*In a* Slovenly way (anyhow), *jon-ton*.
Slow, *ḍhílá*, *sust*.
Slowly, (lazily) *sustí se*; (in pace, &c.) *áhiste*; (to go slowly) *áhiste chalná*.
Slowness, *áhistagí*; (in work) *sustí*, *ḍhíláí*.
Smack on the back, *píṭh ṭhokná*.
Small, (in size) *chhoṭá*; (in quantity) *thoṛá*.
Small change, *kherjá*, 108.
Small coin, *rezgárí*, 107.
Smallness, (of size) *chhoṭáí*; (of numbers) *qillat*.
Small-pox, *chechak*, *sítalá*; (marked with) *chechak-rú*.
Smart (*v.n.*), *charparáná*, *dard karná*.

Smart, (active) *chálák, phurtílá;* (at repartee) *házir-jawáb.*
Smarting (*n.*), *charparáhat, dard.*
Smartness, (activity) *phurtí;* (at repartee) *házir-jawábí;* (of the reply itself) *barjastagí.*
Smear, (plaster) *lípná, thopná;* (with ointment, &c.) *chuparná.*
Smeared (plastered), *lipá húá.*
Smell, (*n.*) *bú, bás;* (*v.a.*) *súnghná.*
Smelt, (*v.a.*) *táo dená;* (to be smelted) *táo kháná.*
Smile, (*v.n.*) *muskuráná;* (*n.*) *muskurái—tabassum.*
Smiling, *muskuráte húe—mutabassim.*
Smilingly (cheerfully), *hansmukhí se—khandapeshání se.*
Smoke (*n.*), *dhúán.*
Smoke (*v.n.*), (as a chimney) *dhúán nikalná;* (as a man) *tamákú píná.*
Smooth, *chikná;* (level) *barábar.*
Smoothness (absence of roughness), *chiknáí.*
Smother ... *ke níche dabáke dam rokná.*
Smut (mildew), *lendhá.*
Snaffle, *dahána* (same word for "bit").
Snail, *ghongá.*
Snake, *sámp.*
Snap, (*n.*) *chat;* (*v.n.*) *chat se túţná.*
Snare (*n.*), *phandá, jál.*
Snarl, *dánt dikhláná.*
Snatch, *chhín lená.*
Sneer, *nák charháná.*
Sneeze, *chhínkná, chhínk márná.*
Snore, *kharráta márná,* 24, 25.
Snow, *barf.*
Snuff, *nás, súnghní.*
So, (therefore) *pas;* (accordingly) *gharaz;* (in like manner) *yúnhín, isítarah;* (so that, in order that) *táki;* (so that we see, &c.) *chunánchi;* (so long as) *jab talak;* (so much) *itná.*
Soak, (*v.n.*) *bhíngná;* (*v.a.*) *bhigo dená.*
Soap, *sábún.*
*To* Sob, *siskiyán bharná.*
Socks, *moza.*
Soft, *narm, muláim.*
Soft sawder, *charb-zabání.*
Softly, (gently) *haule haule;* (to tread softly) *dabe páon chalná.*
Softness, *narmí, muláyamat.*
Soil, (*n.*) *mitţí, zamín;* (*v.a.*) *mailá karná.*
Soiled, *mailá;* (soiled with) the affix *álúda* to the thing indicated.
Sold, *bik gayá;* (to be sold) *bikná.*
Solder, *jorná.*
Soldier, (European) *gorá;* (native) *sipáhí.*
Sole, (of foot) *talwá;* (only) *sirf yihí,* 272.
Solely, *faqat.*
Solid (not hollow), *ţhos,* 68.
Solidity (of a fortress, &c.), *matánat.*
Some, (money, &c.) *kuchh;* (books, &c.) *koí, kisí;* (some one) *koí* or *kisí ne,* as the case may be; (someone else) *aur koi, aur kisí ne.*
Somehow or other, *kisí na kisí tarah se;* (at all costs) *ba-har hál, ba-har súrat.*

Something (else), *aur kuchh*; (something or other) *kuchh na kuchh.*
Some time or other, *kisí na kisí waqt.*
Sometimes, *kabhí kabhí—bạzí auqát.*
Somewhere, *kahíṉ*; (somewhere or other) *kahíṉ na kahíṉ.*
Somewhere else, *aur kahíṉ.*
Song, *gít, gán—sarod, naghma.*
Soon, *thoṛí der meṉ, jaldí.*
Soothe, *ṭhanḍá karná—dilásá dená.*
Sore, (*n.*) *zakhm, gháo*; (sore at heart) *ranjída.*
Sorrow, *gham, afsos.*
Sorrowful, *dilgír.*
Sorry (to be), *afsos karná.*
Sort. See "Kind."
*A* Sort *of* (i.e. not a proper), *kuchh yúṉhí sá, ek tarah ká.*
Soul, *rúh, ján.*
Sound, (*n.*) *áwáz*; (of footsteps) *áhaṭ*; (indefinite, as of something moving in the house) *biṛak*, 240.
Sound, (healthy) *tandurust*; (generally) *sahíh*; (without blemish) *be-ạib.*
Soup, *shurwá.*
Sour, *khaṭṭá.*
Source, (of a river) *nikás—sar-i-chashma*; (generally) *masdar*; (origin) *jaṛ, múl.*
South, *dakhin—janúb.*
Southern, *dakhiní—janúbí.*
Southwards, *dakhin kí taraf.*
Space, (room) *jagah*; (open space) *fizá*, 176.
Spacious (roomy), *lambá-chauṛá—kusháda.*
Spade, *bel* or *belcha.*
Span (*n.*), *bálisht.*
Spare (*v.a.*), *bacháná, chhoṛná—amán dená.* (This last is much used by educated natives.)
Spark, *chingárí, patangá*; (a spark of humanity) *insániyat kí bú* (lit. "smell").
Sparkle, *jhamjhamáná, chamakná.*
Sparrow, *gauraiyá.*
Sparrow-hawk, *chippak—múshgír.*
Spasm, *ainṭh, maroṛ.*
Speak, *bolná*; (speak with) *bát* or *báteṉ karná.*
Speak out (don't mutter), *áwáz se bolo.*
Spear, *bhálá, barchhí.*
Special, *kháss.*
Species, *jins, qism*; (of the same species) *hamjins.*
Specific (particular), *sáf, saríh.*
Specification, *tasríh.*
Specify, *sáf batláná, tafsíl se batláná.*
Specimen, *namúna.*
Specious (plausible), *záhirdár.*
Speckled, *chitlá*; (on a grey ground) *chitkabrá.*
Spectacle, *tamáshá.*
Spectacles, *chashmak, ạinak*, 472.
Spectator, *dekhnewálá—tamáshái.*
Speech (way of speaking), *bolí, zabán.*
Speech (words spoken), *báteṉ, kalám.*
Speech (address), *taqrír.*
Speed, (fleetness) *chustí, tezí*; (expedition) *phurtí—shitábí.*
Speedy, *chálák, jald.*
Spell (*v.a.*), *hije karná.*

Spell-bound, *díwár ká naqsha.*
Spend, *kharch karná, sarf karná;* (one's time) *káṭná, ba-sar karná.*
Spendthrift, *uṛáú—musrif.*
Spices, *masálah.*
Spicy, *masálah-dár.*
Spider, *makṛí;* (large) *makṛá.*
Spider's web, *makṛí ká jál.*
Spike, *khúnṭí, kíl.*
Spill (*v.a.*), *girá dená, ḍhalkáná.*
Spin (as flax, &c.), *kátná, katáí karná.*
Spine (backbone), *ríṛh.*
Spiral, *pechdár.*
Spirit, *jí, rúh, ján;* (courage) *himmat, kaleja.*
Spirit (liquor), *do-átasha sharáb.*
Spiritual, *rúhání.*
Spit, (for cooking) *síkh;* (expectorate) *thúkná.*
Spite, *ḍáh—kína.*
Spiteful, *ḍáhí—kínawar.*
Splash, (*n.*) *chhiṭká;* (*v.a.*) *chhiṭká ḍálná.*
Splashed (to be), *chhiṭká lagná.*
Spleen, *tillí,* 519.
Splendour (brilliance), *tajallí.*
Splendour (magnificence), *ṭháṭh—hashmat.*
Splinter (*n.*), *khapách.*
Split, *chírná, phaṭná;* (as tight clothes) *masakná;* (as a horse's hoof, &c.) *chaṭakná.*
Split (*v.a.*), *chírná.*
Split (among friends), *phúṭ—tafriqa.* The verb to use with these is *paṛ jáná.*
Spoil (*v.a.*), *bigáṛná.*
Spoil, *n.* (plunder) *lúṭ—ghanímat.*
Spoilt, *bigṛá, bigaṛ gayá,* 410, 411.

Spoke (of a wheel), *aṛá.*
Sponge, *isfanj.*
Spoon, *chammach.*
Spoonful, *chammach-bhar.*
Sport, (pastime) *khel;* (shooting, &c.) *shikár.*
Sportsman, *shikárí.*
Spot, (mark) *dágh;* (place) *jagah, mauqa.*
Spotted, *dághí—guldár.*
Spotted deer, *chítal.*
Spout, (of a teapot, &c.) *ṭonṭí;* (semicircular) *jíbhá* (i.e. "tongue-shaped").
Sprain (*n.*), *moch,* 517.
Sprain (*v.a.*), *múchkáná.*
Spread, (*v.n.*) *phail jáná;* (*v.a.*) *phailáná.*
Spread (diffusion), *phailáo.*
Spring, (season) *bahár;* (of water) *sot—chashma.*
Spring (to leap), *kúdná—jast karná.* See "Jump" and "Leap."
Spring (of a watch, &c.) *kamání.*
Sprinkle, *chhiṛakná.*
Sprout (*n.*), *phungí, konpal.*
Sprout (*v.n.*), *konpal nikalná* (pron. *kompal*).
Spur (*n.*), *kánṭá.*
Spurious, *jhúṭhá, jálí;* (coin) *khoṭá—talbísí.*
Spurn, *lát márná.*
Spy, (*n.*) *jásús;* (his work) *jásúsí.*
Squander, *uṛáná, ganwáná,* 215.
Square, *chaukor, chaukhúnṭá;* (market square) *chauk.*
Squeak, *chichiyáná.*
Squeeze, *bhínchná, bhínch lená.*

*N.B.—Muhn bhínch lená,* means "pressing the hand on the mouth to prevent calling out."

Squeeze (water out of a sponge, &c.) *nichorná.*
Squint (*v.n.*), *tirchhá dekhná.*
Squinter, (a man) *bhingá;* (a woman) *bhingí,* 549, 618.
Squirrel, *gilahrí.*
Squirt, *pichkárí.*
Stab, *bhonkná;* (with a dagger) *khanjar márná.*
Stable, *istabal;* (firm) *mazbút, qáim.*
Stack (of straw, &c.), *kúb;* (of wood) *ṭál.*
Staff, *ḍanḍí—asá.*
Stage (on a journey), *manzil.*
Stagger, *laṛkhaṛáná.*
Stain, (*n.*) *dágh;* (on cloth) *dhabbá,* 31, 639.
Stained, *dághí.*
Stairs, *síṛhí—zína.*
Stale, *básí.*
Stalk, *ḍánṭhí; bonṭ,* 652.
Stall (in a stable, &c.), *thán.*
Stamen (of a flower), *tár,* 628.
Stammer, *hakláná.*
Stamp, (*n.*) *muhar;* (die) *ṭhappá;* (postage) *ṭikaṭ.*
*A man of the same* Stamp, *ekhí qabíl ká ádmí.*
Stamp (*v.a.*), *muhar márná, chhápná.*
Stand, *khaṛá honá;* (stand up) *khaṛá hojáná;* (on one side) *ek taraf hojáná.*
Standing up, *khaṛá.*
Star, *sitárá.*
Starch, *kalap, kánjí.*
Stare at, *tákná, ghúrná.*
Start, (set out) *rawána honá;* (wince) *chaunkná;* (an animal) *bhaṛakná;* (set going) *jári karná.*
Starve, (*v.n.*) *bhúkhon marná;* (oneself, &c.) *peṭ káṭná.*
State, (condition) *hálat;* (display) *ṭháṭh—hashmat;* (government) *sarkár.*
State (*v.a.*), *bayán karná.*
Statement, *bayán, kaifiyat.*
Station, (place of residence) *maqám;* (rank) *darja.*
Stationary (fixed), *qáim.*
*Like a* Statue, *but kí tarah.*
Stature, *qadd;* (of short stature) *náṭá;* (of middling) *ausat qadd.*
Stay, *rahná, ṭhairná* or *ṭhaharná.*
Steady, (not flinching) *sábitqadam;* (in conduct) *nek-chalan.*
Steal, *churáná, chorí karná.*
Stealthily (by stealth), *chorí chhipe.*
Steam, *bháph.*
Steamer, *dukhání jaház.*
Steel, *ispát, faulád.*
Steep (*adj.*), *únchá, bahut ḍháldár,* 33.
Stem (of a tree), *tana.*
Step (*n.*), *qadam.*
Steps (flight of), *paiṛí—zína.*
Step out, *qadam uṭháná.*
Sterile (land), *kallar, úsar.*
Stern, *kaṛá mizáj.*
Stick, (*n.*) *lakṛí;* (walking-stick) *chhaṛí.*
Stick (to adhere), *chipak jáná, jam jáná.*
Stick up for, *himáyat lená.*
Sticky, *chipchipá, laslasá.*
Stiff, *kaṛá, sakht.*
Stiffen (*v.n.*), *akaṛ jáná.*
Stiffness, (of the body) *akṛáṭ,* 507; (of anything else) *kaṛápan.*

Still, (motionless) *be-harakat*; (silent) *chup-cháp*; (as a lonely place) *sunsán*.
Still, (as yet) *abhí, abtak—hanoz*; (all the same) *taubhí*.
Stimulus, *tahrík*.
Sting, (*v.a.*) *ḍank márná*; (*n.*) *ḍank*.
Stingy, *tangdast, bakhíl*.
Stink (*n.*), *badbú—ta'affun*.
Stink (*v.n.*), *badbú karná* (or *honá* or *áná* with *se* prefixed).
Stinking, *ganda, bisáhindá*.
Stipulate, *shart lagáná*.
Stipulation, *shart*.
Stir, (move) *hilná*; (with a spoon) *págná*.
Stir (commotion), *dauṛá dauṛí, halchal*.
Stirrup, *rikáb*; (the leather) *tasma* or *doálí*.
Stitch, (*n.*) *ṭánká*; (*v.a.*) *ṭánke lagáná*.
Stock, (in trade) *bisát, sarmáya*; (of a gun) *kunda*; (take stock of) ... *ká ihtisáb karná*.
Stockings, *moza*.
Stolid (phlegmatic), *balghamí*.
Stomach, *peṭ—meda*; (stomach-ache) *pechish*.
Stone, *patthar*; (of fruit) *guṭhlí*; (precious stone) *nagína, thewá*.
Stony (or rocky) ground, *pat-thrílí zamín*.
Stool, *moṛhá*.
Stoop, *jhukná*; (bend over or downwards) *nihúṛná*.
Stop, (as rain) *tham jáná, band honá*; (generally) *mauqúf honá*; (stay at) *ṭikná, ṭhairná*.
Stop, (put a stop to) *bas karná, mauqúf karná*; (restrain) *rokná, báz rakhná*.
Stoppage, *rok-ṭok, aṭak*.
Stopped (checked), *ruk gayá*.
Stopper (of bottle), *ṭhekí*.
Store (a hoard), *zakhíra*; (store up) *zakhíra karná, jama kar rakhná*.
Store-room, *godám*.
Storehouse, *tosha-kháná*.
Storey (of a house), *manzila*; (two-storeyed) *do-manzila*.
Storm, *ándhí, túfán*.
Story, (tale) *qissa, kahání*; (long-winded) *rám-kahání*.
Stout, (portly) *moṭá*; (very stout) *dohrá badan*, 427.
Stove, *angeṭhí*.
Straight, *sídhá* (same word for "straightforward").
Strain (bodily injury), *lachak, maroṛ*.
Strain, (sift) *chhánná*; (be strained) *chhanná*.
Strait (sea-passage), *áb-náe*.
Straitened circumstances, *tang-hálí*; (to be in) *tang-hál*.
Strand (of a rope), *ḍas*.
Strange, (wonderful) *ajíb, ajab*; (very strange) *ta'ajjub kí bát*; (unfamiliar) *ná-mánús*; (foreign) *begána*.
Stranger, *ajnabí, ghair ádmí*.
Strangle, *galá ghonṭná*.
Strap (*n.*), *tasma*.
Stratagem, *híla-o-makar, chhal-bal*.
Straw, *puál*; (a single one) *tinká*, 611; (for bedding) *bichálí*.
Stray, *ral jáná, áwára honá, bhaṭakná*, 267.
Streak, *lakír, dhárí*.

Streaked (striped), *dhárídár.*
Stream, *dhárá*; (river) *naddí.*
*In two* Streams (a river), *do-gang, do-ṭukṛe.*
Street, *galí.*
Strength, *zor — táqat, qúwat*; (firmness, solidity) *mazbútí*; (of a current) *toṛ*, 69.
Strengthen, *mazbút karná.*
Stretch, (*v.a.*) *tánná, khínchná*; (when sleepy) *angṛáí lená*, 202.
Stretch out (extend), *baṛháná, phailáná.*
Strew about, *khinḍáná, chhitráná.*
Strewn about, *khinḍe húe, bikhare húe*, 121.
Strict, Strictly, *sakht.*
Strife, *khaṭpaṭ, jhagṛá-jhagṛí, qaziya.*
Strike, *márná*; (a nail, &c.) *ṭhokná*; (as a clock) *bajná.*
String, (twine) *rassí, jeoṛí*; (of a violin, &c.) *tánt, tár*; (of camels) *qatár.*
Strip (undress), *kapṛe utárná.*
Strip (of cloth, &c.), *dhajjí, lattá.*
Stripe, (as on a squirrel's back) *ḍanḍír, lakír*; (on cloth) *dhárí.*
Striped (as a tiger), *sínkiyá*; (as a dress) *dhárídár.*
Strive, *koshish karná.*
Stroke (caress), *háth pherná.*
Stroll (*n.*), *chihal-qadamí* (*i.e.* forty steps).
Strong, (as a man) *zoráwar*; (as a post) *mazbút*; (as tea) *gáṛhá*; (in good health) *mazbút.*
Struggle (*v.a.*), *kushtí karná, háthá páí karná.*
Struggle (*n.*), *lapṭá-lapṭí, háthá páí.*
Strut (walk affectedly), *ainṭhná, akaṛná.*
Stubble, *báḍh, ṭhenṭh.*
Stubborn, *magrá, gaṛiyár.*
Student, *tálib-ịlm.*
Study, *ịlm kí tahsíl.*
Stuff (or cram) in, *ṭhos dená.*
Stumble (*v.n.*), *ṭhokar kháná, ṭhes lagná.*
Stump, *ṭhúnṭh.*
Stupid, *be-wuqúf, ghámaṛ—kaudan.*
Stupidity, *kam-ạqlí—kaudaní.*
Stutter, *hakláná.*
Style (of writing or speaking), *tarz.*
Subdue, *dabá lená.*
Subdued, to be, *dab jáná.*
Subject (of discussion, &c.), *bát, amr* (pron. *amar*); (of a letter, &c.) *mazmún*; (of a king) *rạiyat.*
Subject to, (under the influence of) ... *ká dabel.*
Sub-lessee, *kiṭkinádár.*
Submission, *farmánbardárí.*
Subordinate (*adj.* and *n.*), *má-taht, mahkúm*, 583.
Suborn (tutor), *sikhláná—tạlím dená.*
Subpœna, *safína.*
Subscription (collection), *chandá, úgahní.*
Subsequent, *píchhe ká—má-bạd.*
Subsequently, *píchhe, bạd uske.*
Subside (a flood), *ghaṭ jáná*; (cool down) *ṭhanḍá ho jáná, faro hojáná.*
Substance, (material) *mádda*; (gist) *khulása.*

Substitute (*n.*), *badlí—ịwazí.*
Substitution, *badlái.*
Subterfuge, *híla-bahána* (or either word separately).
Subterranean passage, *surang, naqab.*
Subtle (as a distinction, &c.), *bárík, mihín.*
Subtract, *minhá karná, wazạ karná.*
Subtraction (deduction), *minhái.*
Suburbs, *sawád.*
Succeed, *kámyáb honá;* (as a project) *peshraft honá,* 117, 397.
Success, *kámyábí;* (of an undertaking) *peshraftí.*
Successive (in succession), *lagátár, mutawátir.*
Successor, *já-nishín, qáim-maqám.*
Such, *aisá, waisá;* (to such an extent) *yahán̲ tak;* (such a one as I) *mujh sá ádmí.*
Suck, *chúsná.*
Sudden, *nágahán, achának.*
Suddenly, *ek-á-ek, nágahání, achának.*
Sue (in court), ... *ke úpar dạ́wá karná.*
Suffer, (pain) *sahná, uṭháná;* (punishment) *uṭháná.*
*On* Sufferance, *ijázat se, parwánagí se.*
Suffice, *bas honá, kifáyat karná,* 502.
Sufficient, *bas—káfí.*
Suffocate, *sán̲s rokná, dam rokná.*
Suffocated (to be), *rukáo-sán̲s se marná;* (murdered) *gale-dabáo se marná.*
Sugar, (brown) *chíní;* (white) *misrí;* (coarsest kind) *guṛ.*
Sugar-cane, *íkh, ganná, paunḍá;* (a joint of it) *ganḍerí.*
Sugar-mill, *kolhú;* (process of extraction) *íkh ká peṛná.*
Suggest, ... *ká nám-lená,* ... *ká ishára dená.*
Suggestion, *zikr* (pron. *zikar*)—*ímá,* 640.
Suicide, *k̲h̲ud-kushi.*
Suit, (of clothes) *joṛá;* (in court) *dạ́wá.*
Suit, (as a climate) *muwáfiq áná;* (be in keeping with) *muwáfiq-hál honá;* (one's arrangements) *bandobast se miljáná.*
Suitable, *durust, munásib;* (fit) *láiq.*
Suitability, (fitness) *liyáqat;* (propriety) *munásabat.*
Sulky, } *magrá.*
Sullen, }
Sulphur, *gandhak.*
Sum, (of money) *mublag̲h̲;* (sum total) *kull-jamạ;* (a large sum of money) *bahut sá rúpiya.*
Summary, (as a judicial proceeding) *sarsarí;* (in a summary manner) *sarsarí taur par.*
Summary (*n.*), *mújaz.*
Summer, *garmí ká mausim,* or *garmiyán̲.*
Summit, (of a mountain) *choṭí;* (top of a tree) *phunang.*
Summon (*v.a.*), *talab karná.*
Summons (judicial process), *saman.*
Sun, *súraj—áftáb;* (sunbeams) *partau.*
Sunshine, *dhúp;* (to put in the sun) *dhúp dikhláná, dhúp men̲ rakhná.*
Sunday, *itwár.*

Superficial, *úparí—satahí*; (not real) *majází*, 239.
Superfluous, *fazúl*.
Superintend, (direct) *chaláná*; (an office, &c.) *ihtimám karná*.
Superintendence, *ihtimám*.
Superintendent, (of police, etc.) *mohtamim*; (head of an office) *sarrishtadár*.
Superior, (in station) *bará*; (in attainments, &c.) *ghálib*.
Superior (as master to servant), *bálá-dast*.
Supernatural, *kharq-i-ádat*.
Superstition, *khiyál-i-khám*.
Supervise, *nazar rakhná*.
Supple, *narm*.
Supplement (as a postscript, &c.), *tatimma*.
Suppliant, *faryádí*.
Supplication, *minnat*, *samájat*; (prayer) *munáját*.
Supplies, *rasad*.
Support, (as a family) *sambhálná*, *parwarish karná*; (back up) *pushtí karná*.
Support (prop, *n.*), *tek* or *tekan*.
Supporter (partisan), *jánibdár*.
Suppose, *jánná*, *samajhná*, *khiyál karná*.
Suppose it be as you say, *máná ki aisá hai*, *farz karo ki aisá hai*.
Supposition, *gumán*, *khiyál*, *qaiyás*.
Supposititious (imaginary), *qaiyási*, *khiyáli*.
Suppress, (put down) *dabáná*; (conceal) *dabá rakhná*.
Supreme, *sab se bará—álá*.
Sure (certain), *yaqín*.
Sure-footed, *páyal* or *pá'il*.
Surely (certainly), *yaqínan*.
Surety, *zámin*.
Surface, *sath* (pron. *sateh*); (of the earth) *rúe-zamín*.
Surgeon, *jarráh*.
Surpass (outstrip), *sabqat lejáná*, *píchhe dálná*, 337, 338.
Surplus, *fáltú rúpiya*, *fázil rúpiya*.
Surprise (*n.*), *ta'ajjub—hairat*.
*To be taken by* Surprise, *auchat men parná*.
*To be* Surprised, *ko ta'ajjub honá*.
Surrender (*v.a.*), *taslím karná*.
Surreptitiously, *chhipá chhipí—bálá bálá*.
Surround, *gherná* or *gher lená*.
Surveillance, *nigráni*.
Survey (of land), *jaríb-kashí*.
Survive (live after), *jánbar honá*.
Survivor, *pas-mánda*.
Suspect, *shubha karná*, *gumán karná*.
Suspended, (as a suspension bridge) *mu'allaq*, 498; (for misconduct) *mu'attal*.
Suspense, (anxiety) *khauf-o-rijá*, 378; (uncertainty) *dubdhá*.
Suspicion (bad impression), *bad-gumání*, 164.
Suspicious (distrustful), *bad-etiqád*.
Suspicious (as an entry in a book), *mushtabih*.
Swallow (bird), *abábíl*.
Swallow (*v.a.*), *nigalná*, *líl jáná*.
Swamp (*n.*), *daldal*, *jhíl*.
Swarm (*n.*), *jhund*.
Sway (rule, *n.*), *hukúmat*, *amal-dárí*, 625.
Swear, *qasam kháná*; (judicially) *halaf lená*.

Sweat, (*n.*) *pasíná; (v.n.) pasíná nikalná.*
Sweep, *jhárná, jhárú dená.*
Sweeper, *mihtar, bhangí.*
Sweepings, *kúrá-kurkuṭ.*
Sweet, *míṭhá.*
Sweetmeats, *miṭháí, halwá.*
Sweetheart, (man) *piyárá—máshúq;* (woman) *piyárí—máshúqa.*
Swell, (*v.n.*) *sújná;* (be puffed out) *phúl jáná.*
Swelling (*n.*), *sújan, waram,* 81.
Swift, *jald, tez.*
Swiftly, *tezí se.*
Swiftness, *tezí;* (of flight) *tez-parí;* (of a current) *tez-raví.*
Swim, *pairná.*
Swimmer, *pairák.*
Swindle (*v.a.*), *ṭhagáná.*
Swindler, *farebí.*
Swindling, *ṭhagáí, ṭhagámí.*
Swing (*v.n.*), *jhúlná, ḍolná.*
Swing (*n.*), *hanḍolá, jhúlá.*
Switch (*n.*), *qamchí.*
Swivel, *kazlak.*
Swoon (*n.*), *múrchhá, ghashí.*
Swoon (*v.n.*), *murchhá áná, ghash áná.*
Swoop, *jhapaṭná.*
Sword, *talwár;* (European) *kirich.*
Symbol, *nishán—alámat.*
Symmetrical, *motadil.*
Symmetry, *itidál.*
Sympathize, *hamdard honá.*
Sympathy, *hamdardí — riqqat,* 316, 317.
Symptom, *kaifiyat.*
Syringe, *pichkárí.*
System, *bandobast, tadbíren.*
Systematic (methodical), *qáida ke mutábiq.*

Table, *mez;* (table-cloth) *mez kí chádar* (or *chaddar.*)
Tablet (writing-board), *takhtí, páṭí.*
Tack, *gulmekh;* (of brass) *biranjí.*
Tact, *salíqa;* (having tact) *salíqa-mand.*
Tail, *dum, púnchh.*
Tailor, *darzí.*
Take, *lená;* (take, lead, or carry along) *liye jáná;* (take away) *lejáná,* 1; (take off with one) *le-chalná;* (take care, beware) *khabardár honá;* (take care of) ... *kí khabardárí karná;* (take off) *utárná;* (take out) *nikálná;* (take in good part) *bhalá mánná;* (take offence at) *burá mánná;* (take place) *honá, wáqi honá;* (take to pieces) *kholná;* (take up) *uṭháná.*
Take law into one's own hands, *khud-hákimí karná,* 445.
Taking advantage of my being a boy, *mujhko laṛká samajhkar* (lit. "acting on the knowledge of my being," 111, 113).
Take to task, *ṭokná,* 115.
Tale, *qissa, kahání.*
Talebearer, *lutrá, chughul-khor.*
Talebearing, *chughul-khorí, ghíbat.*
Talent, *hunar.*
Talented, *hunarmand.*
Talk, *bolná;* (talk with or to) ... *se báten karná,* or *bátchít karná.*

Talk of ... *ká zikr karná.*
Talking (conversation), *bátchít, guft-u-gú.*
Talk of the town or place, *charchá.*
Tall, *lambá—daráz-qadd;* (lofty) *únchá.*
Tally, ... *milná* or *miljáná.*
Talon, *changul.*
Tamarind—*imlí;* (the tree) *imlí ká darakht.*
Tame (domestic), *pálá húá.*
Tame (*v.a.*), *hiláná—rám karná,* 179, 181.
*To become* Tame, *hiljáná, pos mánná.*
Tamed, *hilá húá—rám.*
Tamper with (corrupt), *tor lená.*
Tangle (mess), *uljherá, hadrá.*
Tank, *táláo, táláb.*
Tanner, *chamár.*
Tantalize, *dil ko lahráná.*
Tap (to pat, as a plasterer does), *thapthapáná.*
Tap (pat), *n. tháp, thapak.*
Tape, *fíta;* (wide, used for beds) *.niwár.*
Tapering, *gáo-dum* (*i.e.* "like a cow's tail").
Tar, *koltár.*
Target, *chánd;* (target practice) *chánd-márí.*
Tariff, *nirkh.*
Task, *kám.*
Tassel, *jhabbá, phudná, latkan.*
Taste, *maza, swád,* 598.
Taunt (*v.a.*), *thatthá márná.*
Tax (*n.*), *mahsúl.*
Tax-gatherer, *mahsúl-lenewálá.*
Tea, *chá.*
Teapot, *chá-pochí* or *chádán.*
Teach, *sikhláná, parháná.*
Teacher, *ustád;* (woman) *ustání;* (of languages) *munshí.*
Teak, *ságún.*
Tear (of the eye), *ánsú.*
Tear, (*v.a.*) *phárná;* (tear up) *phár dálná.*
Tease, *chhërná, satáná, diqq karná.*
Teat, *chúnchí;* (of a cow) *bákh.*
Technical phraseology, *istiláh,* 508.
Technicality, *istiláhí bát.*
Tedious, *thakáú, bhárí.*
Telegram, *tár* (lit. "wire").
Telegraph office, *tár ghar.*
Telegraphic news, *tár kí khabar.*
Telescope, *dúrbín.*
Tell, *kahná, bol dená.*
Temper, Temperament, } *mizáj,* 273.
Temperate, (a person) *parhezgár;* (a climate) *motadil.*
Temple (Hindu), *mandir, shiwálá.*
Temple (of the head), *kanpatí,* 516.
Temporary, *chandroza.*
Temporizer, *zamána-sáz.*
Temporizing, *zamána-sází.*
Tempt, *targhíb dená, tamu dikhláná;* (as the devil) *warghalánná.*
Temptation, *imtihán.*
Ten, *das;* (tenfold) *dasguná.*
Tenacious, *sakht-gír.*
Tenant, (of a house) *kiráyadár;* (of land) *asámí.*
Tendency, *mail, mailán.*
Tender, *narm—muláim;* (delicate) *názuk.*
Tender-hearted, *narmdil, rahmdil.*
Tendril, *bel, belí.*

Tenet, *aqída.*
Tension, *khicháo—kashish.*
Tent, *derá, tambú*; (small) *shúldárí.*
Tent-peg, *mekh, khúnṭí*; (tent-walls) *qanát.*
Tent-pole, *chob.*
Tenth, *daswán.*
Tenure, *qabziyat.*
Tepid, *gunguná—shír-garm.*
Term, (phrase) *bát, lafz*; (period) *miád, muddat.*
*Friendly* Terms, *mel-jol.*
Termination, *ákhir, tamámí, intihá.*
Terrible, *daráoná—haulnák, haibatnák.*
Territory, *sarzamín.*
Terror, *bhai—dahshat, haibat.*
Test, (*v.a.*) *jánchná, ázmáná*; (*n.*) *jánch, ázmáish.*
Testator, *músí.*
Testify, *gawáhí dená.*
Testimony, *gawáhí—shahádat.*
Text (of scripture), *áyat.*
Texture, *qumásh.*
Than, the ablative with *se.*
Thank (*v.a.*), ... *ká dhan mánná, shukr karná.*
Thankful, *shukr-guzár.*
Thankless, ... *ná-shukr.*
Thanks, *shukr-guzárí.*
That, (demonstrative) *wuh*; (conjunction) *ki.*
That is to say (in other words), *yání.*
Thatch, (*n.*) *chhappar*; (the material) *phús*, 606.
Thatch (*v.a.*), *chháná.*
Thatching (*n.*), *chháoní.*
Thatcher, *gharámí.*
Theatre, *tamáshagáh.*
Theft, *chorí.*
Then, *tab, uswaqt*, (in that case) *to*; (this being so) *pas.*
Thence, *wahán se.*
Theoretical, *qaiyásí, farzí.*
Theorize, *qaiyás dauṛáná.*
Theory (hypothesis), *farz, qaiyás.*
There, *wahán*; (emphatic) *wuhín.*
Thereabouts, *kahín udhar.*
Therefore, *iswáste, isliye*; (emphatic) *isíwáste.*
Thick, (as a stick) *moṭá*; (as soup) *gáṛhá.*
Thicket, *jháṛ-jhankhár.*
Thickness, *moṭáí.*
Thief, *chor, choṭṭá.*
Thigh, *rán, jángh.*
Thimble, *angushtána.*
Thin, (lean) *dublá—lághar*; (as cloth) *patlá, mihín*; (as liquid) *patlá.*
Thing, *chíz—shai.*
Think, (consider) *sochná, ghaur karná*; (suppose) *jánná, samajhná, khiyál karná.*
Thinness, (leanness) *dubláí*; (of liquid, &c.) *patláí.*
Third, *tísrá.*
Thirst, *piyás—tishnagí.*
Thirsty, *piyásá—tishna-kám.*
Thirteen, *terah.*
Thirteenth, *terahwán.*
Thirtieth, *tíswán.*
Thirty, *tís.*
Thistle, *únṭ-kaṭárá.*
Thither, *udhar.*
Thong, *tasma.*
Thorn, *káṇṭá—khár.*
Thorny, *kaṭílá—khár-dár.*
Thorough, *pakká, púrá.*
Thoroughfare, *sháṛ-ámm.*

Thoroughly (effectually), *pakke taur se—qarár-wáqạí.*
Though, *agarchi—go, goki.*
Thought, *soch, khiyál;* (reflection) *ghaur, fikr.*
Thoughtful, *fikrmand.*
Thoughtfulness, *fikrmandí.*
Thoughtless, *be-fikr, be-parwá.*
Thousand, *hazár.*
Thousands, *hazárhá;* 100,000, *ek lákh.*
Thrash (corn), *dáoná, pítná.*
Thread, (*n.*) *sút, tágá;* (*v.a.*) *pironá.*
Threat, *dhamkí.*
Threaten, *dhamkáná, dhamkí dená.*
Threshing-floor, *khalihán, pair.*
Threshold, *ḍeoṛhí, dahlíz.*
Thrift, *kifáyat.*
Thrifty, *kifáyatí.*
Thrive, *baṛhtá jáná — taraqqí karná.*
Throat, *galá;* (Hindi) *kanṭh.*
Throb, *ṭís márná;* (as a headache) *dhamakná.*
Throne, *takht, masnad, gaddí.*
Throng, *bhíṛ—hujúm.*
Thronged (a market), *garm.*
Throttle, *galá ghonṭná.*
Through, (a window, &c.) ... *kí ráh se;* (a town, &c.) ... *hoke;* (from end to end) *is sire se us sire tak;* (by means of) ... *kí márifat;* (as an arrow) *ár pár,* 38, 435, 436.
Through (by reason of) ... *ke máre.*
Through the fields, *kheton khet.*
Throughout, *shurú · se ákhir tak.*
Throw, *phenkná;* (throw away) *phenk dená;* (throw down) *ḍál dená;* (throw into) *ḍálná;* (throw up, toss) *uchhálná;* (throw backwards) *pachháṛ dená.*
Thrum (seeds out of cotton), *oṭná,* 557.
Thrust in, *ghuseṛná, mel dená.*
Thrust (a prod), *khod, húl.*
Thumb, *angúṭhá.*
Thump, (*v.a.*) *mukká márná;* (pommel) *dhaul jaṛná.*
Thumping (pommelling), *dhaul-chhakkaṛ.*
Thunder, *bádal ká garaj.*
Thunder (*v.n.*), *bádal garajná,* 629, 630.
Thunderstruck, to be, *díwár ká naqsha ban jáná.*
Thursday, *jumerát, brihaspatí.*
Thus, *aisá, yún, istarah, isítarah.*
*N.B.*—*Tarah* is always pronounced *tareh.*
Tick, *kilní.*
Ticket, *ṭikaṭ.*
Tickle, *gudgudáná,* 272.
Tide (ebb and flow), *jawár-bháṭá —madd-o-jazr.*
Tidings, *khabar.*
Tidy, (as a room) *ṭhík-ṭhák, durust;* (in one's habits) *bahut-ṭhík.*
Tie (fasten), *bándhná.*
Tier, *darja.*
Tiger, *sher, bágh.*
Tigress, *sherní.*
Tight, *tang;* (as a girth, &c.) *kasá, kasá húá,* 453.
Tighten, *tang karná, kasná.*
Tile, *khaprá, khaprí.*
Tiled, *khaprail.*

Till, *tak, talak;* (until) *jabtak,* or *jabtak ki.*

Example.—Wait here till I return, *jabtak main na lauṭún tum yahín raho.* Note the negative. The meaning is "so long as I do not return."

Timber, *lakṛí, káṭh.*
Time, *waqt;* (occasion) *bár, dafa, martaba;* (delay) *muhlat;* (age) *zamána;* (leisure) *fursat;* (at all times) *har waqt,* 253.
Time-server, *zamána-sáz.*
Time-serving (*n.*), *zamána-sází.*
Timid, *ḍarpok, dil ká bodá.*
Timidity, *buzdilí;* (*lit.* "goat-heartedness.")
Tin, *qalạí, rángá,* (*v.a.*) *qalạí karná.*
Tinge (*n.*), *damak.*
Tingle, *sansanána.*
Tingling, *sansaní.*
Tinker, *ṭhaṭherá, kaserá.*
Tinkle, *jhanjhanáná.*
Tinsmith, *qalạí-gar.*
Tint, *rang, rangat.*
Tiny, *zarrá sá—adná sá;* (child) *nannhá.*
Tip (*n.*), *nok, sirá.*
Tipsy, *matwálá;* (to be) *nashe men honá.*
Tiptoe, *panjon ke bal,* 249.
Tire, (*v.n.*) *thak jáná,* (*v.a.*) *thakáná.*
Tired, *thak gayá, thaká húá.*
Tissue of lies, *sarásar jhúṭh.*
Title, (of distinction) *laqab, khitáb;* (right) *haqq, haqqiyat.*
To and fro, *idhar udhar;* (both ways) *áne jáne men.*
Toad, *beng.*
Toast (*v.a.*), *senkná.*
Tobacco, *tamákú, tambákú.*
To-day, *áj, áj ká din.*
Toe, *pair kí unglí;* (big-toe) *angúṭhá.*
Together, *ápas men—báham;* (all at once) *ek sáth;* (in one place) *ikaṭṭhe;* (along with) *sang—hamráh.*
Toil (*n.*), *mihnat—mashaqqat.*
Token, *nishání;* (signal) *ishára.*
Tolerable (bearable), *saháú—qábil-i-bardásht.*
Tolerate, *gawárá karná.*
Toll, *chúngí, mahsúl.*
Tomb, *qabar.*
To-morrow, *kal, kal ká roz.*
Tongs, *chimṭá, dast-panáh.*
Tongue, *jíbh;* (language) *zabán, boli.*
To-night, *rát ko,* or *áj rát ko.*
Too, *bahut, ziyáda;* (also) *bhí.*
Tool (workman's) *hathyár, auzár;* (housebreaker's, &c.) *ála.*
Tooth, *dánt;* (of a saw, &c.) *dántí.*
Toothpick, *khilál.*
Tooth-powder, *manjan.*
Top, (of a hill) *choṭi;* (of a tree) *phunang;* (upper part) *úpar kí taraf;* (on the top of) *ke úpar.*
Top (child's toy), *laṭṭo.*
Topaz, *pukhráj, sunelá.*
Topic of conversation (general), *charchá,* 118.
Topsy-turvy, *ulṭá pulṭá.*
Torch, *mashạl.*
Torch-bearer, *mashạlchí.*
Torment, *ạzáb, bhárí dukh.*

Torment (to worry), *satáná, dukh dená.*
Torpid, *sust.*
Torpor, *behoshí.*
Torrent, *báṛh, sailáb.*
Tortoise, *kachhúá.*
Torture, *azáb, aziyat, bhárí dukh*, 645.
Torture (*v.a.*), *dukh dená—aziyat dená.*
Toss, (as a bull) *uchhál de phenkná*; (as a coin) *uchhálná.*
Total, (of an account) *mízán*; (sum-total) *kull-jamạ.*
Totally, *bilkull.*
Totter, (as a building) *ḍagmagáná*; (as a man) *laṛkhaṛáná.*
Touch (*v.a.*), *chhúná.*
Touch (touching), *chhuáwaṭ, chheṛá.*
Touchiness, *tunuk-mizájí.*
Touching (affecting, *adj.*), *dilsoz*; (in contact with) *se lagá.*
Touchstone, *kasauṭí.*
Touchy, *tunuk-mizáj*, 222.
Tough, *sakht*; (leathery) *chimṛá.*
Tour, *safar*; (for pleasure) *sair.*
Tow (boats along a bank), *gun se khínch lejáná.*
Tow (hemp), *san.*
Tow-rope (for boats), *gun.*
Towards, *kí taraf.*
Towel, *ṭauliyá.*
Tower, *burj.*
Town, *shahr, nagar—qasba.*
Toy, *khilauná.*
Trace, (mark, clue) *patá, surágh*; (harness) *jot.*
Trade (*n.*), *len-den, saudágarí—tijárat.*
Trader, Tradesman, *saudágar.*
Tradition, *riwáyat.*
Traduce, *badnám karná.*
Traducer, *muftarí.*
Traffic. *See* Trade.
Train (railway), *relgáṛí.*
Train (animals), *sadháná*; (dogs, &c.) *báolí dená.*
Training (of athletes), *warzish.*
Traitor, *namak-harám.*
Tramp (vagrant), *áwára-gard.*
Trample (down), *páemál karná.*
Trance, *sakta, bekhudí.*
Tranquillity, *chain—ráhat.*
Transact, *byohár karná, muạmala karná.*
Transaction, *len-den, muạmala.*
Transfer, (*n.*) *intiqál*; (*v.a.*) *intiqál karná.*
Transferred, *muntaqil.*
Transform, *súrat tabdíl karná*, 260.
Transformation, *tabdíl-i-súrat.*
Transgress (deviate from), *se tajáwuz karná.*
Transient, *raftaní.*
Translate, *tarjuma karná.*
Translation, *tarjuma.*
Transparent, *shaffáf.*
Transport (for troops), *bárbardárí.*
Trap, *phandá—dám.*
Trash, *wáhiyát, agaṛ bagaṛ.*
Travel, *safar karná*; (traverse) *tai karná.*
Traveller, *musáfir.*
Tray, *khwáncha, kishtí.*
Treacherous, *daghábáz, be-wafá.*
Treachery, *khiyánat, be-wáfáí.*
Tread, (or trample on) *raundná*; (walk on) *qadam márná.*
Tread softly (*v.n.*), *dabe páoṉ chalná*, 251.
Tread down, *páemál karná.*

Treason, *ghadr* (pron.; *ghadar*), *khiyánat*.
Treasure, *khazána;* (treasure-trove) *dafína*.
Treasurer, *khazánchí*.
Treasury, *mál-khána, khazána*.
Treat (well), *kí khush-sulúkí karná*.
Treat (badly), *kí bad-sulúkí karná*.
Treat with great rudeness ... *ke sáth bahut be-adabí se peshána*, 114, 116.
Treatment, *sulúk;* (medical) *muálaja*.
Treaty (covenant), *ahd-o-paimán*.
Tree, *per, darakht;* (boot-last) *kálbud*.
Trellis-work, *jáfarí*.
Tremble, *kámpná;* (violently) *tharthar kámpná*.
Trembling (*n.*), *thartharáhat*.
Trench, *khandaq, khái*.
Trespass (*v.a.*), *mudákhalat karná*.
Trial, (test) *imtihán;* (of a case) *tajwíz;* (under trial) *zer-tajwíz*.
Triangle, (for flogging) *tiktikí;* (three angles) *tikoná*.
Triangular, *tikoniyá*.
Tribe, *firqa, qaum*.
Tribunal, *adálat*.
Tribute, *khiráj*.
Trick, (dodge) *chend;* (to be up to one) *chend karná*.
Trickery (fraud), *fann-fareb*.
Trickiness (dodginess), *chendbází*.
Tricky (dodgy), *chendbáz*, 199.
*To be* Tried (as a case), *kí tajwíz honá*.
Tried (of proved efficacy, &c.) *mujarrab*.
Trifle, (*n.*) *chhotí bát;* (to waste time) *waqt záya karná*.
Trigger, *lablabí*.
Trinket, *gahná, zewar*.
Trip (*v.n.*), *thokar khána, thes lagná*.
Trip, (excursion) *sair;* (to take one) *sair karná*.
Triumph, (*n.*) *fathyábí* (pron. *fatehyábí*); (success) *surkh-rúí*.
Triumph (crow) over ... *ke úpar shádiyána bajáná*.
Trivial, *halká—khafíf*.
Troop (of horse), *risála*.
Trooper, *sawár*.
Trot, *dulkí chalná*, 303.
Trouble, (difficulty) *diqqat;* (a scrape) *mushkil;* (distress) *taklíf*.
Troublesome, *diqqdár;* (a child) *natkhat*.
Trough, *kathrá, dongá*.
Trousers, *patlún*.
Trowel, *karní*.
Truck (for goods), *thelá*.
True, *sachchá;* (genuine, real) *asl, haqíqí*.
Truly, *sach-much—wáqaí*.
Trumpet, *turhí;* (animal's horn) *narsingá*.
Truncheon, *sontá, lath*.
Trunk, (proboscis) *súnd;* (box) *sandúq*.
Trust, (*n.*) *bharosá — etimád;* (credit) *etibár*, 302.
Trustworthiness, *motabarí*.
Trustworthy, *motabar*.
Trusty (faithful), *besh-qarár, ímándár*.
Truth, *sach;* (veracity) *sachái;* (the real facts) *haqíqat*.
Truthful, *sachchá—rástgo*, 548.

Truthfulness, *sachái—rástgoí.*
Try, *koshish karná;* (by way of experiment) *dekhná;* (a case in court) *tajwíz karná.*
Tub, *báltí.*
Tube, *nalí.*
Tuesday, *Mangal* or *Mangalbár.*
Tuft (of hair on top of head), *chondí.*
Tumble down, *gir parná, gir jáná.*
Tumbling about, *girtá partá.*
Tumour, *gúmrá, giltí.*
Tune, *rág—sarod, tarána.*
Turban, *pagrí, sáfa.*
Turbulent, *fasádí—shor-pusht.*
Turkey, *perú.*
Turmeric, *haldí.*
Turn, (*v.n.*) *phirná;* (*v.a.*) *pherná;* (turn round, *v.n.*) *ghúmná;* (*v.a.*) *ghumáná;* (turn back, *v.n.*) *phirjáná;* (*v.a.*) *phirá dená;* (turn out, *v.a.*) *nikál-dená;* (turn up, be found) *nikalná, mil-jáná.*
Turn (time), *bárí, naubat.*
Turn, (aptitude) *salíqa;* (to possess it) ... *ká salíqa rakhná.*
Turning the tables, the word "*ultá*" before the action described, 255.
Turnip, *shalgham.*
Turquoise, *fíroza.*
Turret, *kangura.*
Turtle, *kachhúá.*
Turtledove, *fákhta.*
Tusk, *dánt.*
Tutor, *ustád—muallim.*
Twang, (of a bowstring, &c.) *tankár;* (to twang) *tankorná.*
Twelfth, *bárahwán.*
Twelve, *bárah.*
Twentieth, *bíswán.*
Twenty, *bís.*
Twice, *dobára, do dafe;* (twice as much) *doguná.*
Twine (*n.*), *sútlí.*
Twinkle (as stars), *chhitakná.*
Twinkling of an eye, in the, *palak márne men—turfat-ul-ain men,* 631.
Twins (or twin), *tau'am.*
Twin (*adj.*), *hamzád.*
Twirl the moustache, *múchh ko táo dená.*
Twist, (as in rope-making) *batná;* (generally) *marorná.*
Twist, (*n.*) *bal;* (to get twisted) *bal kháná,* 609.
Two, *do.*
Two and a half, *dháí, arháí.*
Type (sample), *namúna, naqsha.*
Tyrannical, *zálim, zabardast.*
Tyranny, *zulm, zabardastí.*
Tyrant, *zálim.*
Tyro, *mubtadí.*

Udder, *than.*
Ugliness, *badsúratí;* (of a building, &c.) *badnumáí.*
Ugly, *badsúrat;* (a building, &c.) *badnumá.*
Ulcer, *násúr.*
Umbrage, *ranj;* (to take) *burá mánná.*
Umbrella, *chhátá.*
Umpire, *sális.*
Unable, to be, *nahin sakná.*
Unacceptable, *ná-pasand.*
Unaccountable, *samajh se báhar.*
Unaccustomed (to), ... *se ná wáqif;* (unfamiliar) *ná-mánús*
Unacquainted with, ... *se ná wáqif.*

Unadvisable, *ná-munásib.*
Unaffected (simple), *bholá—be-sákhta.*
Unaided, *akelá, be-madad.*
Unalterable, *ṭalne ká nahiṉ—qaṭaí.*
Unanimity, *ittifáq—yagánagí.*
Unanimous, *ek dil, ek ráe.*
Unanimously, *bil-ittifáq.*
Unanswerable, *lá-jawáb.*
Unarmed, *be-hathyár, kháli háth.*
Unassisted, *akelá, be-madad.*
Unattainable, *ná-muyassar.*
Unauthorized, *be-ḥukm.*
Unavailing, *be-fáida—lá-ḥásil.*
Unavoidable, *lá-tadáruk, ná-guzír.*
Unawares, *achának, nágahán.*
Unbearable, *bardásht ke báhar, asahajj.*
Unbecoming, *ná-munásib*; (looking bad) *badnumá.*
Unbelief, *be-eṭiqádí*; (religious) *be-ímání.*
Unbeliever, *be-ímán*; (infidel) *káfir.*
Unbend, (a bow, &c.) *ḍhílá karná*; (*v.n.* a person) *muláim honá.*
Unbidden, *be-talab.*
Unblemished, *be-dágh.*
Unbridled, *be-qaid.*
Unbroken, (intact) *sábit*; (consecutive) *lagátár, mutawátir.*
Unbrotherly, *ná-birádarána.*
Unceasing, unceasingly, *be-chhúṭne se, lagátár.*
Unceremonious, *be-takalluf.*
Uncertain, *be-ṭhikáná.*
Unchangeable, *be-tabdíl.*
Uncharitable, *badgumán.*
Uncharitableness, *badgumání.*
Unchaste, *bad-chalan.*
Uncivil, *rúkhá—kaj-khulq.*
Uncivilized, *ṭaksál-báhar, jáhil.*
Uncle, (paternal) *chachá*; (maternal) *mámú.*
Unclaimed, *lá-wárisí.*
Unclean, *ná pák.*
Uncoloured, *be-rangá, sáda.*
Uncomfortable, *be-árám.*
Uncommon, *nirálá—nádir.*
Unconcern, *be-parwáí, be-fikrí.*
Unconcerned, *be-parwá, be-fikr.*
Unconditional, *be-shartiya.*
Unconfirmed, *ná-sábit.*
Unconscious, *behosh, be sudh*; (unaware) *anján.*
Unconsciousness, *behoshí.*
Uncontrollable, *ikhtiyár se báhar, zabardast.*
Unconvinced, *ná-qáil.*
Uncouth, *bhadesalá.*
Uncover, *kholná.*
Uncultivated, *ghair-ábád, janglí.*
Undeniable, *lá-kalám.*
Under, *níche, taḷe*; (less than) *kam.*
Underdone, *kachchá, ádh-pakká.*
Underfoot, *páoṉ tale.*
Undergo, (as a punishment, &c.) *uṭháná, bhugatná,* 216; (as hardship, &c.) *khainchná*; (go through, experience) *jhelná.*
Underhand (a person), *ná-rást*; *sídhá nahiṉ.*
*In an* Underhand way, *chhipá chhipí—bálá bálá.*
Underneath, *níche, tale.*
Underrate, *halká samajhná, kam-qadar jánná.*
Understand, *samajhná*; (thoroughly) *samajh jáná*; *málúm karná.*

Understanding, *samajh, aql.*
Undertake, (a business) *ká bírá uṭháná*, 331, 333; (generally) *uṭháná.*
Undertaking, *bírá, kám.*
Undeserved / Undeservedly } *náhaqq.*
Undetermined, (irresolute), *mutaraddid;* (to be so) *ágá píchhá karná.*
Undiscerning, *be-tamíz.*
Undistinguishable, *ná-mumtáz.*
Undo, (as a knot, &c.) *kholná;* (nullify) *akárat karná*, 248.
Undoubtedly, *be-shakk.*
Undress, *kapṛe utárná.*
Undulate, *lahráná.*
Undutiful, *náfarmán — ná-khalaf.*
Uneasiness, *be-árámí, be-qarárí.*
Uneasy, *be-árám, be-qarár.*
Uneducated, *anpaṛhá — ná-khwánda*, 200, 510.
Unemployed, *be-kár.*
Unequal, *barábar nahin, mukhtalif.*
Unequalled, *lá-sání.*
Uneven (ground), *úncá-nícha, bíhaṛ.*
Unexpected, *ghair-mutaraqqib* (fem. *mutaraqqiba*).
Unexplored, *andekhá.*
Unfair, *náhaqq, be-insáf.*
Unfairness, *be-insáfí—ná-rástí.*
Unfaithful, *be-wafá, be-ímán.*
Unfaithfulness, *be-wafái, be-ímání.*
Unfamiliar, *ná áshná, ná-mánús*, 635.
Unfashionable, *be-dastúr.*
Unfasten, *kholná;* (let loose) *chhoṛná.*
Unfavourable, *mukhálif, khiláf-murád.*
Unfeeling, *be-dard.*
Unfettered, *ázád.*
Unfit, *ná-láiq—ná-qábil.*
Unfold, *kholná.*
Unforeseen, *ghair-mutaraqqib.* (*fem.*) *mutaraqqiba.*
Unforgiving, *be-rahm, be-shafaqat.*
Unfortunate, *bad-nasíb.*
Unfounded, *be-bunyád, jhúṭhá.*
Unfriendliness, *ná-áshnái.*
Unfriendly, *ná-áshná.*
Unfurnished, *baghair asbáb.*
Ungovernable (temper, &c.) *be-qaid, ammára.*
Ungracious, *be-mihr, be-murúwat.*
Ungrateful, *ná-shukr.*
Ungrudgingly, *be-daregh.*
*In an* Unguarded moment, *ghaflat ke waqt men.*
Unhappy, *dilgír—maghmúm.*
Unhealthy, *bímár;* (a place) *ná-muwáfiq tabíat ke.*
Unhesitatingly, *be-ta'ammul, turant.*
Uniform (dress), *wardí.*
Uniformity, *bárábarí, yaksání.*
Unimportant, *halká—be-qadar.*
Uninhabited, *ghair-ábád.*
Uninjured, *be-zarar.*
Unintelligent, *be-samajh, nádán.*
Unintelligible, *samajh se báhar.*
Unintentional, *anján—be-qasd.*
Unintentionally, *anjáne — ná-dánista.*
Uninteresting, *phíká—be-lutf.*
Union (unity), *mel—yagánagí.*
Unique, *ikká—táq.*
Unite, (*v.a.*) *joṛná;* (*v.n.*) *ek sáth honá.*
Universal, *amúm* or *amím.*

Universality, *ạmúmiyat.*
Universally, *ạmúman.*
Universe, *ạ́lam.*
Unjust, *náhaqq, be-insáf.*
Unjustifiable, *g͟hair-wájibí, ná-munásib.*
Unkind, *be-mihr, be-murúwat.*
Unkindness, *be-mihrí, be-murú-watí.*
Unlawful, *ná-jáiz.*
Unlearned, *anpaṛhá — ná-k͟hwánda.*
Unless, *magar us hál meṉ ki, magar jab ki.*
Unlicensed, *be-paṭṭá.*
Unlike, *eksáṉ nahiṉ, ná-mushá-bih.*
*To be* Unlikely, *qaiyás nahiṉ cháhná;* (if future referred to) *ummed nahiṉ honá* (see Note to "Likelihood.")
Unlimited, *be-hadd—be-g͟háyat.*
Unload, *bojh utárná.*
Unlock, *tálá kholná—qufl kholná.*
Unlucky, *bad-nasíb.*
Unmanageable, *bát nahiṉ suntá—be-zabt.*
Unmanliness, *ná-mardí.*
Unmanly, *ná-mard.*
Unmannerly, *be-ḍhang;* (rude) *be-adab.*
Unmerciful, *be-rahm, sak͟ht-dil.*
Unmistakable, *sáf, záhir.*
Unnatural, *k͟hiláf-i-ạ́dat.*
Unnecessary, *ná-zarúr.*
Unnoticed, *nazar bacháke, nazar se bachkar, bag͟hair mạlúm húe kisíke,* 38.
Unnumbered, *anginat, be-shumár.*
Unobjectionable, *kuchh burá to nahiṉ.*
Unoccupied, *k͟hálí.*
Unofficial (private), *k͟hángí.*
Unpaid (not made good), *anpaṭá, be-adá.*
Unpardonable, *qábil ạfú ke nahiṉ.*
Unpleasant, *ná-gawár;* (to be) *burá lagná—ná-gawár mạlúm honá.*
Unpolished (a person), *gaṉwár—ṭaksál-báhar.*
Unpractical, *ná-kardakár.*
Unprecedented, *be-nazír.*
Unpremeditated, (an act) *be-qasd pahle ke;* (a speech) *be-taiyárí pahle kí.*
Unprepared, *ná-taiyár.*
Unprincipled, *bad-diyánat, be-ímán.*
Unprofitable, *be-fáida—lá-hásil.*
Unpropitious, *ná-muwáfiq.*
Unprotected, *be-hifázat.*
Unproved, *ná-sábit,* or *g͟hair-sábit.*
Unprovoked, *be-sabab—bilá-wajh* (pron. *wajeh*).
Unpunctual, *der lagánewálá.*
Unpunished, *be-sazá.*
Unquestionable } *lá-kalám.*
Unquestionably }
Unravel, *udheṛná.*
Unreal, *majází.*
Unreasonable, *ná-mạqúl;* (it is unreasonable to suppose that) *qaiyás nahiṉ cháhtá ki,* 230.
Unrecorded, *be-tahrírí.*
Unregistered, *bilá-rijisṭarí.*
Unrelenting, *ná-muláim, be-sha-faqat.*
Unrewarded, *be-ajr* (pron. *ajar*).
Unrighteous, (person) *ná-rást;* (sentence) *be-insáf.*
Unripe, *kachchá.*
Unrivalled, *be-nazír.*

Unroof, *chhat utárná.*
Unruly, *ná-hamwár, be-lagám.*
Unsafe, *khatarnák.*
Unsatisfactory, *láiq itmínán ke nahin.*
Unscrew, *pench kholná.*
Unseasonable (an act or speech), *be-mauqa.*
Unseemly, *ná-sháista,* 633.
Unselfish, *be-gharaz.*
Unsettled, (restless) *be-qarár;* (not fixed) *be-ta'aiyun, muqarrar nahin.*
Unsightly, *badnumá, burá málúm detá.*
Unskilful, *anárí—be-hunar.*
Unstable / Unsteady — *be-qiyám—be-sabát;* (unsteady as a horse, &c.) *khará nahin rahtá.*
Unsuccessful, *ná-kámyáb—ná-kám.*
Unsuitable, *ná-láiq;* (to be) ... *se kám nahin áná.*
Unsullied, *be-dágh—be-laus.*
Unsuspecting, *be-gumán;* (fearing nothing) *be-fikr, be-khatká.*
Untenable, *be-bunyád.*
Untidy, *be-dhab, be-salíqa.*
Until, *jabtak, tak* or *talak.*

Examples.—Wait here until I return, *jabtak main na lautún tum yahín raho—tum yahín raho mere áne talak.* The negative is used with the first form, because *jabtak* has the meaning of "so long as"—"so long as I do not return."

Untimely, *be-waqt—be-hangám.*
Untrue, *sach nahin, jhúth.*

*N.B. jhúth* is "false" as well as *jhúthá,* just as *sach* is "true" as well as *sachchá.*

Unusual, *be-dastúr.*
Unwary, *be-khabar, gháfil.*
Unwelcome, *ná-mubárak-bád.*
Unwholesome, *ná-gawár.*
Unwilling, *ná-ráz.*
Unwillingness, *ná-rází.*
Unworthiness, *be-liyáqat—ná-sazáwárí.*
Unworthy, *ná-láiq.*
Up, *úpar;* (up and down) *únchá níchá;* (up to) *tak, talak.*
Uphill (*adv.*) *charháí men,* 329.
Upon, *par, ke úpar.*
Uppermost, (*adj.*) *úparwár;* (on the top) *sab ke úpar.*
Upright, *khará, diyánatdár,* 363.
Uproar, *shor-ghul, rúká-raulá.*
Upset (*v.a.*), *ulat dená.*
Upside down, *tale-úpar, pat, ultá.*
Upstart, *kal ká ádmí.*
Upwards, *úpar kí taraf.*
Urge (press), *isrár karná, hat karná, bajidd honá,* 318, 319.
Urgency, *zarúrat.*
Urgent, *zarúrí.*
Usage, *riwáj, dastúr.*
Use (*v.a.*) *baratná, istemál karná,* 52, 53.
Use (*n.*), *bartáo, istemál,* 144, 154.
Useful, *kám ká;* (beneficial) *mufíd;* (to be useful) *kám áná—kár-ámad honá,* 374.
Useless, *nikammá, kuchh kám ká nahin—ná kára.*
Usual, *mámúlí;* (the same as usual) *ba-dastúr.*
Usually, *beshtar, aksar, aksar auqát.*
Utility, *fáida.*

Utmost (to the utmost of one's power), *tá-maqdúr — hatt-al-maqdúr.*
Utter (sheer), *mahz.*

Vacancy, *jagah khálí.*
Vacant, *khálí.*
Vacate, *khálí karná.*
Vacation, *tátíl.*
Vaccinate, *ṭíká lagáná.*
Vaccination, *ṭíká.*
Vacillating, *ágá-píchhá kartá — mutaraddid.*
Vacillation, *ágá-píchhá—taraddud.*
Vagrancy, *áwáragardí.*
Vagrant, *áwáragard.*
Vague, *muhmil.*
Vain, (conceited) *khudpasand;* (futile) *bátil;* (as an excuse) *behúda—lá-táil;* (all in vain) *be-fáida, lá-hásil.*
Valid, *káfí.*
Valiant, *bahádur—shahzor.*
Valley, *dún, wádí.*
Valour, *baháduri—shahzori.*
Valuable, *qímatí—máliyatí.*
Value, *mol—máliyat,* 141.
Value (appraise), *ánkná, mol ṭhairáná.*
Vanish, (decamp) *champat honá, káfúr hojáná;* (disappear) *gháib hojáná.*
Vanity, (conceit) *khudpasandí;* (emptiness) *butlán.*
Vapour, *bháph—bukhárát.*
Variable, *be-ṭhikáná—mutalawwin.*
Variance, *ikhtiláf, farq.*
Variety, *farq;* (kind) *qism.*
Various, *tarah tarah ká, mukhtalif.*

Varnish, *luk, roghan;* (to varnish) *luk charháná, roghan dená.*
Vase, *phúldún.*
Vault (arch), *gumbaz.*
Vaulted, *gumbazdár.*
Vegetable, *tarkárí, sabzí—*(vegetables in general), *nabátát,* 647.
Vegetation, *roídagí.*
Veil, *ghúnghaṭ—niqáb;* (to draw it) *ghúnghaṭ kaṛhná, niqáb dálná.*
Vein, *rag, nas.*
Velocity (of a current), *tezraví.*
Velvet, *makhmal.*
Venerable, *buzurg.*
Venerate, *kí tázím karná.*
Veneration, *tázím, takrím.*
Vengeance, *intiqám;* (to take) *intiqám lená.*
Venomous, *zahrílá, zahrdár.*
Vent (outlet), *nikás, súrákh.*
Ventilate, *hawá dená.*
Venture (v.n.), *jokhim uṭháná.*
Verandah, *barámada, barandá.*
Verb, *fel, masdar.*
Verbal, *zabání.*
Verbatim, *lafz ba lafz, lafzan.*
Verdant, *hará—sarsabz.*
Verdict, *ráe, tajwíz.*
Verdigris, *zangár.*
Verdure, *harái—sarsabzí.*
Verge, *kinára—lab.*
Verification, *tasdíq.*
Verify, *kí tasdíq karná.*
Vermin, *múzí jánwar, múziyát.*
Vernacular, *des kí bolí.*
Verse, (of poetry) *bait—masnaví;* (of scripture) *áyat.*
Version (account), *riwáyat,* 478.
Very, *bahut, baṛá.*
Vessel, (ship) *jaház;* (utensil) *bartan.*

Vest (under vest), *banyain.*
Vested with (judicial powers, &c.) *mujawwaz.*
Vestige, not a vestige (remaining), *na nám na nishán*, 314.
Vex, (tease) *satáná, diqq karná;* (offend) *ranjída karná.*
Vexation, *ranjish, ranjídagí.*
Vexed, *ranjída* or *ranjída-khátir.*
Vial, *shíshí.*
Vibrate, *tirmiráná.*
Vibration, *tirmiráhat.*
Vice, *sharárat, luchpan.*
Vicinity, *pás-paros — qurb-o-jawár.*
Vicious, (as a horse) *tarrá;* (elephant, &c.) *be-pír.*
Victorious, *ghálib, fathyáb* (pron. *fatehyáb*).
Victory, *fath, fathyábí;* (to gain) *fath páná* (pron. *fateh*).
Victuals, *rasoí, khurák.*
View, (*n.*) *nazar;* (view in front) *pesh-nazar;* (to come in view) *nazar áná;* (with a view to) *ba-nazar ... ke.*
Vigilant, *jágtá, chaukas, hoshyár.*
Vigour, *zor, qúwat.*
Vigorous (in robust health), *hattá-kattá, mazbút.*
Vile (contemptible), *liháṛá, zalíl.*
Vileness, *zillat—khwárí.*
Vilify (run down) ... *kí mazammat karná.*
Village, *gáon.*
Villager, *gáonwálá, gáon ká ádmí.*
Villain, *sharír, púrá badzát.*
Villany, *sharárat—sharr.*
Vindicate (justify), ... *kí rástí záhir karná, ... kí safái karná.*
Vindictive, *kínawar;* (very vindictive) *shutur-kína.*
Vinegar—*sirká.*
Violence, *zabardastí, jabar;* (of a storm, &c.) *shiddat.*
Violent, *zabardast—sína-zor.*
Virgin, *kunwárí.*
Virginity, *kunwár-patá.*
Virtue, *nekí;* (chastity) *pársáí, pákízagí.*
Virtuous, *nekchalan—sálih* (fem. *sáliha*); (chaste, a woman) *pák-dáman.*
Visible, to be, *dikhái dená, nazar áná.*
Visit (*n.*), *muláqát, bhent.*
Visit (*v.a.*), ... *se muláqát karná,* ... *se milná.*
Visitor, *mulaqátí.*
Vital (important), *zarúrí.*
Vivacious, *zinda-dil.*
Vivacity, *zinda-dilí.*
Viz., *yání.*
Voice, *áwáz;* (loud) *buland áwáz;* (weak) *mihín áwáz.*
Volley, *báṛ;* (to fire) *báṛ uṛáná.*
Volume (book), *jild.*
Voluntary, *ikhtiyárí;* (act) *khushí kí bát.*
Voluntarily, *apní khushí se.*
Vomit, *chhántná, qai karná;* (vomit up) *ugal dená.*
Voracious, *baṛá kháú, chatorá.*
Vote (*n.*), *ráe, tajwíz.*
Vouch for ... *par khud gawáhí dená,* ... *ká khud zimmedár honá.*
Vow, *mannat, mántá;* (to vow) *mannat mánná.*
Voyage, *safar.*
Vulgar, (common) *ámm;* (as language) *ná-láiq, ná-máqúl.*
Vulture, *giddh—kargas*, 630.
Wadding (for a gun), *tiklí.*

Wade, (as in shooting) *pání pání chalá jáná;* (wade across) *pání men bar ke uspár chalá jáná.*

Wag (jester), *maskhara, thathe báz,* 637.

Wager, *shart, bází;* (to lay one) *shart* or *bází lagáná.*

Wages, *talab, tankhwáh;* (common labourer's) *mazdúrí.*

Waist, *kamar;* (waist-cloth) *kamarband.*

Wait, *thairná, sabr karná;* (wait for expectantly) *kí ráh dekhná* or *takná;* (wait for before doing something) ... *ká intizár karná,* 533.

Waiting for, (n.) *intizár;* (expecting) *muntazir.*

Wake, (v.n.) *jágná;* (wake up suddenly) *chaunk parna.*

Wake up (arouse), *jagáná.*

Wakeful, *jágtá—bedár.*

Wakefulness (want of sleep), *bekhwábí.*

Walk (v.n.) *chalná;* (up and down as a sentry) *tahalná;* (for exercise, inspection, &c.) *phirná.*

Walk (a horse up and down), *tahláná.*

To go for a Walk, *hawá kháne jáná.*

Short Walk (stroll), *chihal-qadamí.*

Wall, *díwár;* (of a tent) *qanát;* (round a city) *shahr-panáh.*

Mud-Wall, *pakhá.*

Wallet, *khurjí, jholí.*

Wallow, *lot-pot karná.*

Walnut, *akhrot.*

Wander, *áwára phirná, hándná.*

Wanderer, wandering, *áwára;*

(homeless wanderer) *dánwándol.*

Wandering (n.), *áwáragí.*

Wane (v.n.), *ghatná.*

Waning (declining, adj.), *ghatiyá.*

Want, (to desire) *mángná, cháhná;* (to need) ... *ko cháhiye, ko darkár honá.*

To be in Want of, *ká muhtáj honá, kí hájat honá.* See "Need."

Want (necessity), *zarúrat, hájat.*

Wanting in (lacking) ... *se khálí,* ... *se be-bahra,* 384, 385.

Wanton, *athkhel, chanchal.*

Wantonness, *athkhelí, chanchaláhat.*

War, *larái—jang.*

Warble (a bird), *chahchahaná.*

Warbling (n.), *chahchahá.*

Wardrobe, *almárí.*

Wares, *jins.*

Warfare, *larái-bhirái — jang-áwarí.*

Warlike (a soldier, &c.), *laráká.*

Warm, (adj.) *garm;* (nice and hot) *garmá garm.*

Warm (v.a.), *garm karná.*

Warmth, *garmí—harárat.*

Warn, (apprise) *jatá dená—ágáh karná,* 417; (caution) *samjháná, daráná.*

Warned (put on one's guard), *ágáh,* or *ágáh húá.*

Warning (caution), *chitáoní, ágáhí.*

Warp (v.n.), *ainth jáná.*

Warrant (judicial), *wárant.*

Wart, *masa.*

Wary, *jágtá, hoshyár, chaukanná.*

Wash, *dhoní;* (wash up as plates) *dho dálná.*

Washed, (*adj.*) *dhulá húá*; (has been washed) *dhoyá gayá*.
*To be* Washed, *dhulná*, *dhoyá jáná*.
Washer (in a wheel, &c.), *chakel*.
Washerman, *dhobí*; (his wife) *dhobin*.
Washing (*n.*), *dhuláí*.
Wasp, *birní*, *barr*.
Waste (*v.a.*), *nuqsán karná—záyą karná*.
Waste (*n.*), *nuqsán—barbádí*.
Waste (uncultivated), *partí—uftáda*.
Wasteful, *uṛáú—fazúl-kharch*.
Watch, (timekeeper) *ghaṛí*; (guard) *pahra*.
Watch, (look on at) *dekhá karná*, *dekh rahná*; (keep one's eye on) *kí nigrání karná*, *dekhtá rahná*.
Watch for. See "Wait for."
Watchful, *jágtá—bedár*.
Watchmaker, *ghaṛí-sáz*.
Watchman, *chaukíkár*.
Water, *pání*; (for drinking) *píne ká pání*.
Water, *v.a.* (flowers) *pání dená*; (a horse) *pání piláná*.
Water-carrier, *bhishtí—saqqá*.
Waterfall, *jhál*, *jharná*.
Water-fowl, *murghábí*.
Water-lily, *kanwal—nílofar*, 630.
Water-mill, *panchakkí*.
Water-pot, *ghaṛá*; (of brass) *ṭhiliyá*.
Watering-pot (for flowers), *panhárí*.
Wave (*n.*), *lahar—mauj*.
Wave, (as a flag in the wind) *phahráná*; (as herbage in the wind) *lahakná*.
Wave (as a signaller does his flag), *hiláná*.
Wavy (as hair), *lahriyá*.
Wax, (*n.*) *mom*; (wax-candle) *mom-battí*; (wax-cloth) *mom-jáma*.
Waxen (made of wax), *momí* or *mom ká*.
Way, (road) *rasta*, *ráh*; (of doing things) *tarah*, *taur*, *ḍhab*, 275.
*In any* Way you (I, he, or they) can, *jis tarah bane*.
*Stop the* Way, *báṭ rokná*, *saṛak rokná*.
*Get out of the* Way! *bach jáo! haṭ jáo! baghal hojáo!*
Waylay ... *kí ráh márná*.
Weak, *kamzor*, *ná-táqat*; (infirm) *zạíf*; (as tea) *patlá*.
Weakness, *kamzorí*, *ná-táqatí*.
Weal (mark of a blow), *ḍaulí* 64.
Wealth, *dhan-daulat*.
Wealthy, *daulatmand*, *máldár*.
Wean, *dúdh chhuṛáná*.
Weapon, *hathyár*, 479.
Wear, (put on) *pahinná*, *oṛhná*; (have on) *pahne honá*, *oṛhe honá*; (wear away) *ghisná*, *khiyá jáná*, 2, 268.
Weary, (*adj.*) *thaká húá*, *mánda*; (*v.a.*) *thakáná*.
Wearisome, *thakáú*.
Weather (*n.*), (fine) *pharchhá*, *ásmán sáf*; (wet) *jhaṛiyán*.
*To* Weather (as a storm, &c.), *bach nikalná*, *salámat nikalná*.
Weave, *bunná*.
Weaver, *tántí*, *juláha*; (his shop) *kargah*.
Web (of a spider), *jál*.

Wedding, *shádí, biyáh.*
Wedge, *phaní, pachchar.*
Wednesday, *budh, budh ká roz.*
Weed (pull up weeds), *sohná.*
Weeds, *jangal;* (widow's) *rand-sála.*
Week, *hafta;* (weekly) *hafta-wár;* (every week) *hafta hafta.*
Weep, *roná;* (bitterly) *zár zár roná.*
Weeping (*n.*), *rohat—girya*
Weevil, *ghun.*
Weigh, *taulná, wazn karná.*
Weight, *taul, wazn;* (importance) *waqát.*
Weighty (heavy or important), *bhárí—girán.*
Welcome (*v.a.*), *kí mubárakbádí karná, marhabá kahná.*
Welcome, (*n.*) *mubárakbádí;* (the greeting itself) *mubárak-bád! marhabá!*
Welfare, *bhaláí, bihtarí, khair áfiyat.*
Well, (of water) *kúán* or *kúá;* (dry well) *andhá kúá.*
Well, (*adj.*) *achchhá, bhalá;* (well-born) *asíl,* 633.

*N.B.*—"Well" as a prefix is represented variously by the prefixes *khúb, khush,* and *nek.*

Well (*interj.*), *khair, achchhá.*
Well-done! *shábásh!*
Well-off, well-to-do, *ásúda,* 483.
Wen, *sújan, waram, gúmṛá.*
West, *pachchhim—maghrab.*
Westerly, *pachchwá—maghribí.*
Wet, *bhíngá, gílá;* (to get so) *bhíng jáná;* (dripping wet) *tar ba tar, shor-bor.*
Wet (*v.a.*), *bhigoná* or *bhigo dená.*
What (*interrog.*) *kyá?* with what? *káhe se?* of what? *káhe ká,* in what? *káhe men?* 9, 8, 11.
What (which of several), *kaun? kaun sá?* (what then?) *phir to?*
Whatever, (at all) *bhí; e.g.* (none whatever) *kuchh bhí nahin.*
Whatever, (thing) *jo kuchh; e.g.* (whatever you can get) *jo kuchh háth áwe.*
Whatever, Whatsoever (of whatever country he be), *go wuh kisí mulk ká kyún na ho.*

*N.B.*—The *kyún na ho* in this sentence exactly answers to our "no matter what."

Whatever may happen (come what may), *jo kuchh ho.*
Wheat, *gehún.*
Wheedle, *phusláná, dam dená,* 111, 308.
Wheel (*n.*), *pahiyá;* (the box) *awan;* (nave) *náh;* (felloe) *puṭhí;* (spoke) *ará;* (axletree) *dhurá;* (tire) *hál.*
When? *kab?* (at what time) *kiswaqt?*
When (relative) *jab;* (as, as I was going, *e.g.*) *jiswaqt,* 1.
Whence? *kahán se? kidhar se?*
Whence (relative) *jahán se.*
Whenever, *jab kabhi, jiswaqt.*
Where? *kahán? kis jagah?* (relative) *jahán, jis jagah.*
Whereabouts? *kis taraf? kidhar?*
Whereas, *chúnki;* (whereas really) *hálánki,* 334, 404.
Wherever, *jahán jahán, jahán kahín.*
Whether (to go or not, &c.), "*ki áyá*" followed by "*yá.*"

Whether (it be good or bad, &c.) "*cháhe*" followed by "*cháhe*," or "*khwáh*" followed by "*khwáh.*"
Whether (he has come or not.) Here the word would be altogether dispensed with: *e.g.* (I don't know whether he has come or not) *nahin málúm áyá ki nahin áyá.*
Whetstone, *sán.*
Which? *kaun? kaun sá?* (relative) *jo, ki jo, jo ki*; (inflected, *jis*) *jisne, jiská, jismen,* &c.; (plural) *jin, jinne, jinká, jinko,* &c.; (inflected interrogative) *kisne? kiská?* &c.; (plural) *kinne? kinko?* &c.
Whichever, *jis, jon*; *e.g.* (whichever way you look) *jistaraf dekho*; (whichever you like) *jonsá* (*jonsí*) *cháho.*
Whichever (of them all), *jo jo, jis jis, jin jin,* &c.
Whiff (*n.*), *mahak—ríh.*
While, (when) *jiswaqt*; (so long as) *jab tak,* or *jab tak ki*; (a little while) *thori der, thorá arsa*; (a long while ago) *kabkáke-* or *kí* according to the gender and number of the governing noun.
Whim, *lahar—wahm.*
Whimsical, *lahrí—khiyál-parast.*
Whip, (*n.*) *chábuk*; (*v.a.*) *chábuk márná.*
Whirl (round and round, *v.n.*), *ghúmná, chakkar márná.*
Whirlwind, *bagúlá*; (small) *bawandar.*
Whiskers, *gal-múchh.*
Whisper (*v.a.*), *phusphusáná,* 251.
Whispering, *phusarphusar, kánáphúsí.*
Whistle, (*v.a.*) *siṭí bajáná*; (railway or other) *siṭí.*
White, *sufed, dhaulá.*
Whiteness, *sufedí, dhaulái.*
Whitewash (*v.a.*), *sufedi dená, puchárá dená.*
Whither, *kidhar*; (which way), *kistaraf.*
Whiz (as a bullet), *pinpináná.*
Who? *kaun? kisne?* (relative) *jo, jisne.*
Whoever, *jo koí.*
Whole, (full amount) *kull, tamám*; (entire) *samúchá, sábit*; (the whole fifteen, &c.) *pandrah ká pandrah.*
Wholesale to sell by, *thok bechná.*
Wholesale dealer, *thokdár.*
Wholesome, *khush-gawár,* 224; *muwáfiq-tabíat.*
Whom? *kisko?* (relative) *jisko*; (pl.) *kinko* and *jinko.*
Whose, *kiská, kinká*; (relative) *jiská, jinká.*
Why? *kyún? kiswáste? kyá sábab?*
Wick, *battí.*
Wicked, *sharír.*
Wickedness, *sharárat.*
Wide, *chauṛá, chauṛá-chaklá.*
Widen, *chauṛáná.*
Widow, *bewá, bidhwá.*
Widowhood, *bewagí.*
Width, *chauṛái, chauṛán*; (of a river) *páṭ*; (of cloth) *páṭ, arz,* 631.
Wife, *jorú, bibí, aurat*; (village term) *logái.*
Wild, *janglí*; (dissolute) *be-lagám,* 620.

Wild-fowl (*duck, teal*, &c.), *murgháhí.*
Wilful, *khudsar, gariyár.*
Will (pleasure), *marzí, khushí;* (testament) *wasiyat*, 253.
Willing, *rází;* (ready) *taiyár.*
Willingly, *khushí se.*
Willingness, *razámandí;* (readiness) *taiyárí.*
Win, *jítná, jít lená;* (at play) *bází lejáná.*
Wince, *chaunk uṭhná.*
Wind, (*n.*) *hawá;* (hot wind) *lúh;* (to get wind of) *kí ágáhí páná*, 353.
Wind (as a river), *pher khháná.*
Wind (a clock, &c.), *kúkná.*
Windings (in a river), *bánk.*
Window, *khiṛkí—daricha.*
Windpipe, *nareṭí, narkhaṛá.*
Wine, *sharáb—mai.*
Wing) *par, bázú;* (both wings) *ḍain.*
Wink (*v n.*) *palak márná, ánkhen maṭkáná.*
Winner in a race, *mírí*, 649.
Winnow, *bhus usáná*, 462.
Winnowing (basket), *chháj, súp.*
Winter, *jáṛá, jáṛe ká mausim.*
Wipe, *ponchhná.*
Wiper (rag, &c.), *ponchhan.*
Wire, *tár.*
Wisdom, *dánáí, aqlmandí.*
Wise, *dáná, aqlmand.*
Wiseacre, *lál-bujhakkaṛ*, 600.
Wisely, *aqlmandí se.*
Wish, *árzú, sád—tamanná*, 194, 195; (*v.a.*) *cháhná—ká árzúmand honá.*
Wisp (of straw), *ánṭí.*
Wit (humour), *zaráfat.*
Witch *ḍáen* or *ḍáyin.*
Witchcraft, *jádú, jádúgarí.*
With, (by) *se;* (together with) *ke sáth, ke sang;* (along with) *sáth, sang, hamráh, mae.*
Withdraw (from), *se alag hojáná, ... se kináre hojáná.*
Withdraw (to cancel), *mansúkh karná, fiskh karná.*
Wither, *kumhláná, súkhjáná.*
Withered, *kumhlá gayá, súkh gayá—pazhmurda.*
Withhold, *báz rakhná—daregh karná.*
Within, (*adv.*) *bhítar men, andar men;* (*prep.*) *ke bhítar, ke andar.*
Without (not having), *be, baghair—bidún.*
Without fail, (for certain) *zarúr;* (without break or intermission), *bilá nágha*, 21.
Without being told, *be-kahe.*
Without feeding the horse, *be dána diye ghoṛe ko.*
Withstand, *ká sámhná karná, ká muqábala karná.*
Witness, *gawáh;* (to witness) *apní ánkhon se dekhná.*
Witticism, *latífa.*
Wittingly, *ján bújhke—dída-o-dánista.*
Witty, *zaríf, latífa-go.*
Wolf, *bheṛiyá.*
Woman, *aurat, ranḍí;* (village term) *logáí.*
Women (in general), *aurat log, ranḍí log.*
*Pertaining to* Women (feminine), *zanána.*
Womb, *peṭ.*
Wonder, *ta'ajjub;* (cause for wonder), *ta'ajjub kí bát.*

*To* Wonder, *ta'ajjub karna, ... ko ta'ajjub honá.*
Wonderful, *ajíb, ajab, achambhá.*
Wonderfully, *ajab tarah se, ajíb taur par.*
*As was his* Wont, *apne mámúlí taur par.*
Wonted, *mámúlí.*
Woo, ... *kí diljoí karná.*
Wood, *lakṛí, káṭh;* (forest) *ban, jangal.*
Wooden, *lakṛí ká—chobí.*
Wool, *ún;* (woollen) *úní.*
Word, *bát, lafz;* (to keep one's word) *qaul nibáhná.*
*True to one's* Word, *sádiq-ul-qaul.*
*To send* Word, *kahlá bhejná.*
*To put* Words in another's mouth, *se kahwáná.*
Work, *kám;* (to work), *kám karná.*
Working man, *mazdúr;* (artisan) *kárígar.*
Workmanship, *kárígarí, sákht, gaṛhat.*
Workshop, *kár-khána.*
World, *dunyá, jahán.*
Worldliness, *dunyádárí.*
Worldly, *dunyádár;* (secular) *dunyawí.*
Worm, *kíṛá;* (earth-worm), *kenchwá.*
*To* Worm out secrets, *rázjoí karná.*
Worn (as a horse's shoe), *khiyá gayá,* 268.
Worry, *bakheṛa, diqqdárí.*
*To* Worry, *diqq karná, satáná;* (as a dog) *bhambhoṛná.*
Worship (*n.*), *pújá, parastish, ibádat.*
*To* Worship, *pújá karná, kí parastish karná.*
Worshipper (of God), *khudá-parast.*
Worsted (beaten), *hárgayá.*
Worth, *qadar;* (money value), *qímat, máliyat.*
Worthless, *nikammá, kuchh kám ká nahin—nákára.*
Worthy, *láiq—sazáwár.*
Wound, (*n.*) *zakhm, ghác;* (*v.a.*) *zakhmí karná, gháil karná,* 479.
*To* Wound (another's feelings), *ko ranj dená.*
Wrangling (*n.*), *qaziya, jhagṛá-jhagṛí.*
Wrap, (*v.a.*) *lapeṭná;* (fold up) *tai karná.*
Wrapper, (common native) *kammal, loí;* (better class) *labáda;* (washerman's, &c.) *beṭhan.*
Wrath, *ghazab—qahr.*
Wrathful, *ghazabnák;* (to become so) *jhunjhláná.*
Wreath, *hár, sihrá, málá.*
Wreck (n.), *tabáhí.*
Wrench (away), *zor se chhín lená.*
Wrestle, *kushtí laṛná;* (wrestling) *kushtí.*
Wretch, *kambakht, nigoṛá.*
Wretched (miserable), *kharáb-ahwál.*
Wretchedness (misery), *kharáb-hálí.*
Wriggle, *pech-o-táb karná.*
Wring, (squeeze out) *nichoṛná;* (the hands with vexation) *háth malná.*
Wrinkle, (permanent) *jhurrí;* (temporary) *chín.*
Wrinkled, *jhurriyán paṛ gaín,* 344.
Wrist, *pahunchá, kaláí.*
Write, *likhná—tahrír karná.*

Writer, (clerk) *muharrir;* (writing), *likháwat, tahrír.*
Written (*adj.*), *tahrírí;* (past part.), *likhá gayá.*
Wrong, (incorrect) *ná-durust;* (improper) *ná-munásib.*
*What is there* Wrong (improper) in this? *is men kyá qabáhat?*
*Nothing* Wrong, I hope? *khair to hai?*
Wrong (injustice), *andher, be-insáfí.*
Wry faces (to make), *munh terhá karná.*

Yard (measure), *gaz;* (courtyard) *ángan, sahn.*
Yarn, *sút.*
Yawn, *jamháí lená;* (yawning) *jamháí.*
Year, *baras, sál;* (year by year) *sál ba sál.*
*The* Year 1890, *san athárah sai nawwe, íswí;* (*íswí*, Christian era.)
*Last* Year (*adv.*), *pár sál, parke sál.*
*This* Year (*adv.*), *abke sál—san-hál men.*
*He is ten* Years of Age, *umr das baras kí hai.*
Yearly, (*adj.*) *sálána;* (yearly return) *sál-tamámí;* (every *year*), *har sál.*
Yearn for, *ká bahut mushtáq honá, ke liye turasná.*
Yeast, *khamír.*
Yell, *chillúná.*
Yellow, *pílá, zard;* (the colour) *píláí, zardí.*
Yellowish, *zardí-máil,* or *máil ba zardí.*
Yesterday, *kal, gayá kal.*
Yet, *abtak;* (still, as yet) *hanoz, abhí;* (nevertheless) *taubhí—táham.*
Yield, (in argument) *qáil honá, mán jáná;* (consent) *rází honá, mánná;* (produce) ... *se hásil honá.*
Yield (of a field, &c.), *paidá-wárí.*
Yoke, (*n.*) *júá;* (yoke together) *jotná.*
Yolk (of an egg), *zardí.*
You, (to an inferior) *tum, tum ne,* &c.; (an equal or superior) *áp, áp ne,* &c.)
Young, *chhotá, bachcha, kam-umr,* 407.
Younger, *chhotá;* (younger than) *se chhotá.*
Youngest, *sab se chhotá.*
Your, (to an inferior) *tumhárá;* (an equal or superior) *ápká.*
Yourself, *tumhí;* (to yourself) *tumhí ko.*
*You* Yourself said so, *khud tumhí ne kahá thá.*
*He told you* Yourself, *khud tumhí ko kahá thá.*
Youth, *nau-jawání.*
Youthful, *kam-umr, nau-jawán.*

Zeal, *sargarmí.*
Zealous, *sargarm.*
Zenith, *samtu-r-rás.*
Zest, *maza, mazáq;* (with zest), *raghbat se, shauq se.*
Zigzag, (*adj.*) *terhá bánká.*
Zinc, *dastá.*
Zodiac, *rás-chakr, mintaqat-ul-burúj.*
Zoology, *ilm-i-haiwánát.*

# ADDENDA ET CORRIGENDA.

All at once, *ek-á-ek—dafátan.*
Apathy, add *be-parwáí,* and for *sahlangárí,* read *sahl-angárí.*
At last (at length), *báre.*
Bear (endure), add *sahárná.*
Blame (condemn), *ilzám dená.*
Business (what business of yours ?), add *tumhárá kyá kám ?*
Captain, *kaptán.*
Cess-pool, *chah-bachcha.*
Charitable (in thought), *nek-gumán.*
Clever, add *hunarmand.*
Coincidence, *ittifáq;* (happy coincidence), *husn-ittifáq.*
Comfort (*n.*), add *ásáish.*
Common cause with (to make), ... *ká sáth dená.*
Constantly, for *hamesha,* read *har dam.*
Cost (expense), add *kharch.*
Creek, *kol, khárí, khál.*
Dense (as jungle), add *gajhin.*
Devoted to, ... *se girawída.*
Disclosure, add *isrár.*
Disease, add *rog* (the Hindi word.)
Dissolute, *chhutkhelá, aubásh.*
Divulge, add *kholná.*
Doctor, *dáktar.*
Embankment, for *pushta-bandí,* read *bándh—pushta;* (making one), *pushta-bandí.*
Enumerate, *ginwáná* (not *ginná.*)
Escape from (get clear of), *bach nikalná.*
Fever, *tap, bukhár;* (to be attacked with), *tap charhná, bukhár áná.*
Finished (to be), *ho chukná, tamám honá.*
Flap, for *jhatás márná,* read *jhatak marná;* (as the wings), *phatphatáná.*
*To* Forfeit (a sum of money), *ba taur táwán ke dená.*
Generosity, add *karámat.*
Gentleness, add *muláyamat.*
Get on with any one, ... *ke sáth nibáhná.*
Grandeur (state, dignity), *shaukat.*
Gristle, *kurrí, murmurí haddí.*
Hindrance, add *rukáwat.*
Intoxication, *badmastí.*
Invitation, add *buláwá.*
Likelihood, add *ehtimál* to *ummed.*

Revised note.—Though *ummed* really means 'hope,' it is occasionally used with a negative for 'no likelihood,' even in regard to things of an unwelcome nature.

Manage (a business), *chaláná.*
*If it can be* Managed, *agar bane to,* or simply *bane to.*

Means (procuring cause), *wajh, zaría.*

Meanwhile, put *itne men* first and *is darmiyán men* second.

Mention (*n.*), add *nám.*

Mention (*v. a.*), add *nám lená.*

Moisture, add *taráwat.*

Mountain of mole-hill, to make, *bát ká bataggar banáná.*

Not fit to be seen, *ná-dídaní.*

Not fit to live, *ná-shudaní.*

Nowadays, add *in dinon.*

Only (simply), add *akele, nirá.*

Pre-eminent, *sab se barhá charhá.*

Prowl, *para phirna.*

*Raison d'être, gharaz-aslí,* preceded by *se,* not by *ki.*

Reception (civilities, &c.), *mudárát, tawázu.*

Retrace one's steps, *ulte páon phirná.*

Roll, (as a ball) *luraknä;* (cause to roll) *lurkáná.*

Ruined, *gayá guzrá húá—tabáh-hálat.*

Self-respect, *ghairat.*

Shout, (*v. n.*) add *lalkárná;* (*n.*) *lalkár.*

So much as (even), *tak* after the thing signified.

Some day or other, *ek roz.*

Sooner or later, *ákhir.*

Sordid, (mean) *khasís;* (sordidness), *khissat.*

*Quite* Sufficient (ample), *bahut.*

Supremacy, &c., *fauqiyat.*

There and then (right away), *khare khare.*

Very reluctantly (there being no help for it), *ná-chár.*

Whole 24 hours, *áthon pahar.*

N.B. At p. 157, for Isrue and *nikalná* read Issue and *nikalná.*

www.ingramcontent.com/pod-product-compliance
Lightning Source LLC
Chambersburg PA
CBHW031750230426
43669CB00007B/569
* 9 7 8 3 3 3 7 1 5 7 1 7 3 *